Suicide Creek
and the Battle for
Cape Gloucester

Contents

Introduction

David Thurman Miller   4

Foreword

Gy. Sgt. Thurman I. Miller   8

Suicide Creek

Asa Bordages   20

Cape Gloucester: The Green Inferno
88

First Marine Division Special Action Report: Cape Gloucester 210

Revised edition

Compiled and adapted by David T. Miller

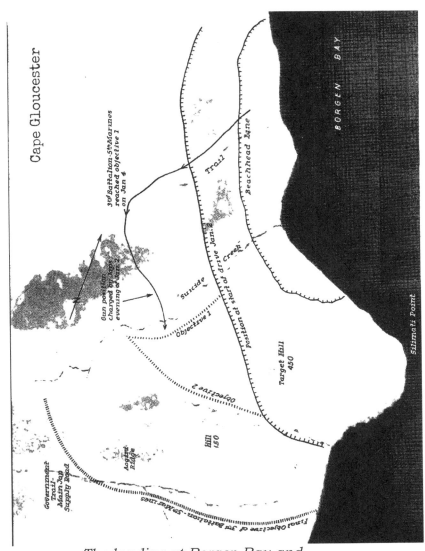

The landing at Borgen Bay and advance to Suicide Creek

Introduction –

David Thurman Miller

As a young man I had only a fragmented understanding of what my father had seen and done as a member of the storied First Marine Division in World War II. From our many conversations, and then by helping him write his life story, I came to learn he was one of the first men off the boat on Guadalcanal and barely survived that hellish island. He recovered in the wilds of Australia, fought on an obscure island called New Britain, and returned stateside to train future officers as a drill instructor at Camp Lejeuene. But although I came to be very familiar with the details of his life from his Appalachian boyhood through his time on Guadalcanal and long post-war coal mining career, I heard relatively little about New Britain.

Guadalcanal was a turning point in the war, the first American counter-offensive against the Japanese, the first break in their stranglehold over the South Pacific. Plenty of movies and novels have been set on that island, with varying degrees of accuracy. By contrast, taking back the island of New Britain had been deemed essential when the plans were laid for it, but turned out to be much less important to the outcome of the war. Perhaps because of this neither the battle nor the men who fought it have gotten the recognition they deserve.

Over the years I had the privilege of interviewing and meeting many of the men with whom my father served, and discovered that his natural modesty had prevented his telling me about his leadership and courage in the South Pacific; his friends had no such reticence, and I came to view him with even more admiration, for he had retained a deep sense of humanity and good humor despite the unbelievably difficult circumstances in which the marines fought.

As I attended First Division reunions with him and talked with these men, I noticed they passed around battered many-generation copies of an obscure 1945 magazine article. I found a better copy in my father's archives and for the first time read the full story of Suicide Creek. I wouldn't have believed any battles could be worse than the worst of Guadalcanal, and yet the men who fought in both--my father included--agreed that Suicide Creek and the battle for New Britain had been even more ruthless and ravaging.

Understandably, considering its middle-American audience at the time, the 1945 article clearly understates the bitterness and inhumanity of the fighting there. But it was the best contemporary account of New Britain and deserves to still be read, and I became determined to see it back in print.

Combined here with that article are my father's firsthand recollection of the battle, the declassified battle plan for New Britain, and a detailed after-action analysis. This book therefore hopes to present a broad look at the battle from the point of view of an individual marine, a respected journalist, the war planners, and the historians.

It is our hope that together these will help the reader understand the significance of the battle for New Britain and Suicide Creek, and the bravery of the men who fought to take and hold it.

David Thurman Miller

Foreword –

Gunny Sgt. Thurman I. Miller, K/3/5

We staged in Milne, New Guinea. Plans for the landing on the Cape were finally complete. We were informed that our Third Battalion, Fifth Marine Regiment would be held in reserve for one week. Our initial landing was Christmas Eve, 1943. We knew by sheer instinct that we would be committed wherever the greatest need would be. A reporter was beating his gums at not being where the action was; a lieutenant informed him that in a few days he would have plenty to write about.

As far as we knew the landing had gone as planned, so for that remaining week of 1943 we waited. It was a given that we would plug the hottest hole they had encountered in the first few days. Upon landing we assumed our positions and began the trek into the thick jungle. We could hear the fighting not far off but at first we encountered no resistance. Eventually we spotted a small island, about 100 feet long and 10 feet wide. One side of the little island the water was very warm and the other side it was cold. This was from a volcano atop the huge mountain which dominated the whole area. The jungle was so dense it was difficult to keep in touch with the man to the right or left.

We came upon a stream and our orders were to cross it. In the words of typical Marine lingo, the "shit hit the fan" and thus began the fight toward a ridge we had no inkling was even there.

Considering our experience on Guadalcanal, the resistance we met told us that something important must be up ahead. As Technical Sergeant Bordages describes it, the distance from the beach to the summit was only an hour's trek were we just walking. But it was slow going. Our regimental command had determined that a prominent hill, if taken, would give us more firepower. They were waging a battle on another part of the line and it became apparent that the hill in question was elsewhere. At the same time, the hill on which we were advancing became the center of action. The Japanese began pouring everything they could spare into its defense. We ran into numerous firefights on our way up through the jungle and as we attempted to cross the creek we began taking heavy fire from the other side. Lieutenant Dykstra was our 2d platoon leader and he and I happened to wind up behind the same log. Suddenly he yelled, "TI, I'm shot!" Sure enough a round had blown his entire elbow off. I used the last of my bandages from my belt and tied it around his elbow. I cut two sticks and used my helmet mosquito net to make a splint and crawled on back to a corpsman.

The fighting seemed to come in small bursts. A sudden banzai charge that was over in a matter of minutes. At times during this twelve-day ordeal we got ahead of our supplies. While on the move one day they brought some gallon cans of fruit cocktail up and told us to open them and eat while on the march. The first man opened the can with his service knife, stuck his dirty hand in, and got a hand full. The rest of us did the same, on down the line. The last hand full was rather dirty. At one point we ran out of anything to eat and we sent a couple of men back along our lines to pick up the hard tack we had thrown away, already green with fungus. We cut the green off and ate it anyway.

We were three days the taking the hill. The first day we gained ten feet. That night, we did not pull back to our former positions but rather dug in and held on to the ten feet. Next day we took ten more. We dug in again and began what turned out to be a major battle of the whole campaign. We were in a very hard fight where progress is measured in feet rather than miles or even yards. Our platoon had received an order to encounter and destroy a pocket of the enemy. I gave the order to one of my squad leaders to attack. He told me it was a suicide mission. I told him it was an order. Without another word he turned, gathered his squad, and left. That was the last I ever saw him. I heard him engage the enemy. I heard him cry out when he got hit. I heard him dying, and in the din of battle, the rattle of his breathing was sharp and unnatural.

He had been shot in the throat and the air sucked into the hole made the sound of snoring. He was about fifteen minutes dying. Sergeant Thompson was twenty-three years old, clean cut and a good man. His death became a personal thing with me and for many years the sound of his dying would awaken me from sleep. Even now it's as if it happened yesterday.

We had been given a new platoon leader. His name was Toelle but we called him "Tully" and we all liked him. He was an easy-going guy and I always felt he had missed his calling. He hadn't been married long, and I guess his mind was on other matters.

During that day, we made preparations to hold onto the lines at all costs. I saw Lieutenant Tully raise a rock and put something under it. "My wedding band, T.I. I don't want these yellow bastards with it."

That night, all hell broke loose again. We could see the summit and also watch the enemy's movement. All night he came, one attack after another. All the firepower at our disposal was put into the task. When dawn

came and heads were counted Lieutenant
Tully was listed killed in action. His instinct
had been true.

We left our holes again and started toward
the summit. Again, the enemy resisted.
Again, we tried everything we had. Finally our
battalion commander came up. He had a
.37mm cannon which a truck had brought
part of the way. The jungle was so thick it
had to be brought by hand the rest of the
way. We hewed a trail out literally by hand
until the cannon reached our lines. Then it
was loaded with antipersonnel shells, which
would spray out in a wide path. The cannon
was loaded and fired and while it was being
reloaded everyone would fire as many rounds
as possible in order to keep the enemy pinned
down. Foot by painful foot, we pushed
the cannon up the hill. Firing, reloading,
firing, reloading. Finally, we reached the
summit.

Ahead of us, many of the enemy lay still.
Behind us, the cry, "Corpsman!" The summit,
the valley. Mount Everest and Death Valley at
the same level. Walt's Ridge.

With the taking of Walt's Ridge, our company
had been reduced in number to such an
extent it was no longer regarded as a battle
unit and was therefore relieved from front-
line duty. By platoons, we were changed out.
The replacement platoon leader, a lieutenant,
asked who was the leader in my platoon. On

a head count, I was the senior noncommissioned officer (NCO) in charge. Counting myself, I had exactly thirteen men left. The Lieutenant paled.

After some brief R & R on the beach, our next mission on New Britain was laid out as follows: One reinforced platoon would march a day's journey up the coast and move out to the beach and establish a perimeter of defense.

Another platoon would land by boat and the next day do the same thing, and so on until we controlled the entire area. We encountered many Japanese patrols whose duty it was to delay our march, for we also learned that the commanding general of the Japanese forces of New Britain was on the run up the coast on his way to Rabaul. Now, we couldn't very well take a man prisoner if he was shooting at us, could we? The First Marine Division had been hardened by our experiences on Guadalcanal: Like the Japanese, our policy was not to take prisoners. Day after day, we chased the enemy up the coast, destroying his supplies but keeping his rice and sake. I had been introduced to one young lieutenant before starting to Talesea and was informed he was our new platoon leader. I could tell by looking he was fresh out of stateside and green in the ways of combat. After the initial landing at Talesea we set up nightlines at dark. It had always been our practice for two men to share their ponchos and make a small tent. I invited the Lieutenant to share mine but he informed me he was perfectly capable of caring for himself. So be it, I thought.

Next morning after the hard rains there wasn't a dry thread on him. I wasn't altogether dry but then I wasn't altogether wet either. He just glared at me. That same day I noticed he still had on the little gold bars that indicated his rank. I begged his pardon, but told him it would be better if he would remove his bars. Again, he gave assurance he was capable of making such decisions himself. I never said much after that, but before long I noticed that he had removed the bars and rid himself of any semblance of authority. He had frequently given orders that were unwise for this type of warfare. The men, some of whom I had served with since boot camp, would look to me first. I would either nod or shake my head as to whether to follow his orders. Once we came upon a clear mountain stream coming down into a waterfall on the trail.

It looked good for drinking and he yelled for the platoon to gather around and fill canteens. They all stood still where they were. I held up two fingers and said, "two at a time." I explained that one grenade would wipe out the whole outfit and my way only two would have been killed. After this, he began to trust and confide in me more.

We billeted in the rain many nights. One evening we came up on about ten grass huts in a small village. They were built on stilts about ten feet high to protect the natives from wild animals. A ladder hung down from each hut. The huts were about twelve feet square and seven or eight feet high at the sides. In the center of the floor was a box about two feet square filled with six inches of sand and we could see evidence of recent fires. In the center of the cone-shaped roof was a six-inch hole for the smoke to go out, although we built no fires that night. What a find, we thought, as we got out of our field packs and laid out our gear. Laying our ponchos down was a great relief and just to lie down on something dry was pure luxury. This lasted only a few hours, until the natives returned. "Fall out!" came the order. One night, with the help of our canine scouts, we surprised a large squad of Japanese soldiers. They had a look of shock and disbelief on their faces, for they had been led to believe they were winning the war. Certainly, they thought they had won the island of New Britain. They prepared to die. They began by going to their knees. They touched their foreheads to the ground and lay there waiting for the doom that was sure to come. They had been taught that capture meant certain death. Ordinarily, this would have been their last living position. I touched the one directly in front of me on the head with my boot. He glanced up and I told them all to stand. I had the power in my trigger finger. I had them here in the palm of my hand. I controlled their destinies. I looked at my men and saw nothing but hatred. I looked at myself and saw nothing but contempt. I looked intently at the Japanese soldier directly in front of me. Scarcely two feet separated us. I had come face to face with one of the enemy. Our eyes met. Two aliens stood facing each other, both far removed from their homes, separated from their families. They did not understand each other's language. Their cultures very different, each alone in a hostile land, each seeking to survive. I had been filled with the desire to kill. As I looked into his eyes, I suddenly thought of the fact that he too had been indoctrinated with hatred and the desire to kill. He was supposed to kill me without hesitation or regret. To him, he was the oppressed and I was the oppressor. I looked long and thoughtfully at him. I felt a slight change come over me. I looked again and a little sadness crept into my heart, a little feeling for this man whose destiny I held. But suddenly I returned to reality and realized I must be about the business of war. There may have been those of my platoon who did not share my thoughts. The Lieutenant ordered me to take full charge of the prisoners. "Aye aye, Sir." I turned the prisoners over to the Army men.

I set watches through the night and told them they were responsible for the prisoners' safekeeping. I lay down on the beach after setting out our defensive lines and the night was clear now. From my position, just in from the beach, I would see anyone who chose to walk around. As the night wore on I could look out to sea and watch the light from the upcoming moon cast a dim glow on the water. The sea was an unholy calm. The waves were very small and made only a slight rustling on the sand. I lay still and listened for the jungle to speak. It too seemed unholy because there was no sound. Its very silence bespoke the presence of intruders. The natural residents were gone; the thunder of the human animal had caused them to depart. The light of the moon increased and the sound of the incoming waves grew louder. Their thunder brought my mind back to the business at hand. I rolled over and began thinking about tomorrow.

By now it was evident that capture of the Japanese general we were chasing was no longer possible. We were returned to our original positions and stayed there our remaining time on New Britain. Our mission once again complete, we stood by for relief, and again we boarded ship. Another mission? The First Marine Division would be used to its fullest. It was like pouring water into a leaking bucket. Pour it into the top and it runs out the bottom.

As we sailed away I looked back at the skyline with the live volcano in the background.

The rugged coastline and the rainforest fell away as I looked long and hard at this place I was never to see again. Its memories are embedded in my soul: The sound of Sergeant

Thompson dying. Lieutenant Tully hiding his wedding band. The sickness. The rain. The spiders. My skin had wrinkled up. My fingernails and toenails had dried up and I had picked them off and thrown them away. My skin hung like drapes. I felt old and worn out. Talk now began of the rotation system. You needed a total of points in order to be sent home. Points were given based on time in the Corps, overseas duty, and the number of campaigns you fought in.

When they gave us the details I started counting. I had been given credit for three separate battles, Guadalcanal, Cape Gloucester, and Talesea. I had 138 points.

The day came that we were told to pack up and prepare for embarking at 0800 the next day. No big deal for me. I had had my bag packed for a long time. That night, long after dark, there came a knock on my tent door. It was the young lieutenant. I saw no malice as I gazed into his eyes for the last time. I saw the honest look of a man who had found himself. He was now tempered with battle, hardened by life in the jungle and wiser in his ways. He held out his hand and thanked me for the help I'd been. I told him I was only doing my job and it had been a pleasure knowing him.

Years later, I saw Lieutenant Dykstra at a reunion at Camp LeJeune. I noted his elbow was permanently bent at a 45- degree angle. But his arm was intact, and he was alive.

Only those of us who were there really know
the hard task that led to the recording the
name of that hill so far away now in memory
and miles: *Walt's Ridge.*

Thurman I. Miller

*Gy. Sgt. Miller volunteered for the U.S. Marine
Corps in 1940 and fought on Guadalcanal and
New Britain. He has written four books about his
life, including his experiences with the First Marine
Division and as an instructor for the Officer
Candidate Applicant school at Camp Lejeuene.*

Suicide Creek

Originally presented in Collier's Magazine, May 26-June 2, 1945

Part I

The battle lasted nine days. It took the Marines that long to fight their way through the jungle a distance a man might stroll in an hour. It was on Cape Gloucester, New Britain Island. It may not have been as bad as the later battle of Iwo Jima but it was worse than the worst of Guadalcanal.

The Marines who won them both say so. They say, "This time we bought a corner lot in hell."

"Pop" Haney says it was worse than that. He is a sun-dried little man: Platoon Sergeant St. Elmo Murray Haney, as hard as hobnails, with more battles under his belt than most Marines have years of service. He fought in this same regiment in World War I. He remembers that Belleau Wood was vastly bigger and lasted longer. He remembers titanic artillery duels in Belleau Wood and many, many times more casualties. But, Pop Haney says, "I never saw anything worse than this."

It was only part of a battle, really; only one battalion's part in the Marines' general offensive against Hill 660. But if this battalion had not pushed the right flank of our line as far as they did, if they had not captured a concealed enemy stronghold on a ridge that did not show on our maps, then the American lives paid for Hill 660 might have been spent in vain. For the ridge controls the jeep-wide Government Trail that runs through the jungle below it. And that trail was the supply artery for Japanese defense or counterattack on Hill 660. The chances are we could not have held 660, with that fortified ridge in enemy hands so close on our flank.

That is what the strategists say. They call Hill 660 the lock that secures our grip on Borgen Bay; on Cape Gloucester and the airdrome. They call that ridge the key to the lock. The Japanese called it Aogiri Ridge in orders that said it must be held at all costs.

The enemy was a veteran battalion of Japan's 141st Infantry Regiment, battle-seasoned troops who had been cited by General Masaharu Homma for valor at Bataan. They were well fed, well supplied, sure of victory, still carrying the loot of Manila in their packs. They were on the defensive, dug in— which in the jungle means they had all the aces.

Concealed Enemy Stronghold

The enemy could pick the spots where the Marines had to fight. All the Japs had to do was wait in hidden pillboxes so well camouflaged you might walk over them without knowing they were there. All they had to do was wait, with plenty of food, plenty of ammunition, in comparative comfort, until the Marines came groping through the jungle into the enemy line of fire. Then the Japs could cut them up without the Marines ever seeing a target to shoot at. That happened repeatedly.

The Third Battalion of the 5th Marines landed a week after the invasion began. They were detached from their regiment; brigaded with another outfit. As they lay in their first night's bivouac, the folks back home were celebrating New Year's Eve. The Marines couldn't have lights. They didn't have music. They couldn't smoke. Some of them sat around chewing the fat, arguing the same old questions: Whether Georgia is better than Pennsylvania. Whether blondes are better than redheads. Whether liberty is better in New York than L.A. Questions Marines can argue for hours.

Our left flank for the offensive against Hill 660 rested on the shores of Borgen Bay. The line ran crookedly inland into the jungle. The Third Battalion was moved to the right end of the line. It was commanded by Lieutenant Colonel David S. McDougal, of Coronado, California. He led it into battle January 2d.

The battalion was spread over a front of 500 yards. It moved slowly through the jungle, groping for the enemy through the forest of trees 100 feet high and higher, some of them twenty feet or more around; giant trees that shut out the day. The jungle was dense with undergrowth, with tangles of brush and vine so tough, so thick in places, that a man would have had trouble cutting through with a machete. The Marines could not see the snipers shooting at them as they advanced. A man could see only the trees and brush. A man could only walk on slowly through the jungle, waiting for the next shot; trying not to think that he might be dead before he could take another step. Fingers of living men pushed into the jungle as you might spread your own fingers and push them into a tub of dough.

Pfc. Jim Moore of Lucedale, Mississippi, was one of them. He was 26, older than most of them, a married man with three children. He'd never seen his youngest child. Now he was in his first battle. Jim didn't have to be there. He could have stayed safe at home. All he ever said was, "Some things a man's got to do."

He was a funny guy. A kind of religious guy. Not that he ever bothered anybody with it. He never cracked at the men for bawdy talk, for carousing on liberty or anything like that. He just didn't do those things himself. All he seemed to care about was his wife Nancy and the kids and getting the job done so he could go home to Mississippi.

He was the first man of his company hit. A sniper got him in the head. He had time for only four words. Even then Jim Moore didn't swear.
"Gosh," he said, "they got me."

The others went on. One man wondered if you ever heard the shot that killed you. He couldn't remember how fast sound traveled. It bothered him all day.

They went on. The invisible snipers kept pecking at them. A man here, a man there. Not much of a toll in the casually lists, but the end of the world for the boy with a hole between his eyes. He didn't have time even to be surprised.

Corporal Charles F. Somerville, 22, of Clarksburg, West Virginia, happened to glance up and see a rifleman aiming at him. The West Virginian fired first. The rifleman fell.

An officer yelled, "Be careful! Marines are down here!"

Corporal Somerville spat. "If he was a Marine, he oughta known better than sight in on me."

It wasn't a Marine. It was the first Jap killed in the battle.

Vengeance with a Machete

Sometimes the sniper fire was heavy enough to hold up a squad or a platoon. One sniper shot eight Marines before they could spot him in a tree. Tommy guns blasted him out. They tell of a sniper who got twenty Marines, killed and wounded, and then tried to escape. He didn't make it. A Marine saw him. The Marine had a machete.

Sergeant Harrison E. Ludy, 22, of Binghamton, New York, walked into four Japs. They whipped up their rifles, but Ludy's tommy gun was blasting as he dived. He got two—and a wound in the foot. He was the maddest man in New Britain.

They went on. The Japs were pounding them with mortars. It took all a man had to stick; just to hug the deck and wait for the next shell to hit. You feel sometimes that dying wouldn't be as hard, really, as was waiting for that next shell.

They came to "Suicide Creek." It had no name and it was not on the map, but that is what the Marines called it after they had fought two days in vain to win a crossing.

The creek is swift, two or three feet deep, perhaps twenty feet across at the widest, twisting between steep banks. It flows over rocks that make footing difficult, and here and there a tree has fallen into the stream. The banks rise steeply from ten to twenty feet, up to little ridges in the jungle.

The Marines didn't know the creek was a moat before an enemy strong point. They couldn't see that the heavy growth across the creek was salted with pillboxes—machine-gun emplacements armored with dirt and logs, some of them dug several stories deep, all carefully spotted so they could sweep the slope and both banks of the stream with interlacing fire.

Only snipers shot at the Marine scouts who crossed the creek feeling their way through the thickets. More Marines followed, down into the creek, up the steep bank, on into the jungle. Then they got it. The jungle exploded in their faces. They hit the deck, trying to deploy in the bullet-lashed brush, trying to strike back. Marines died there, firing blindly, cursing because they couldn't see the men who were killing. Or not saying anything. Just dying. The others could only hug the ground as bullets cut the brush just above their heads like a sweeping blade of fire. They couldn't even help the wounded.

Snipers picked off some of them as they lay there. It's perfect for snipers when machine guns are firing. Then you can't hear the sound of their rifles. You can't hear the single pop above the heavier fire. You don't know you're a target until you're hit.

From the American side of Suicide Creek Marines gave the trapped platoon overhead fire. The idea is to fling such a volume of fire at the enemy's position that he must hunt cover and slacken his fire. The overhead fire spread an umbrella of bullets above the pinned-down platoon, enabling them to crawl out, crawl back across the creek, pulling out their wounded.

That's how it went all day as Marine detachments felt their way in the jungle; felt for a gap or a soft spot in the enemy's positions along the creek. They would be hit and pull back, and then detachments would push across the creek at other points, seeking a weak spot in the enemy's defenses. Then they'd be blasted by invisible machine guns, and leave a few more Marines dead in the brush as they fell back across the creek. Then they'd do it all over again.

There was nothing else they could do. There is no other way to fight a jungle battle;

not in such terrain; not when the enemy is dug in and your orders are to advance. You don't know where the enemy is. His pillboxes are so camouflaged, you can find them usually only when they fire on you. So you push out scouts and small patrols until they're fired on. Then you push patrols from different directions until they, too, draw fire. Thus you locate the enemy. Then you have to take the emplacements, the pillboxes, one by one in desperate little battles. A lot of men get hit. Men die without ever getting a chance to fire a shot. But it is the only way you can do the job.

A Day to Remember

Pfc. Calvin B. King, 20, of Pen Mar, Pennsylvania, remembers his platoon crossed the creek four times in a single day and four times had to stumble back under enemy fire. And not until the last time did they see it Jap.

"That time we got maybe a hundred and fifty feet into the brush and then we saw them coming at us," he said. "They had slipped around and were coming in from our flank to wipe us out. There were a lot of 'em. I don't know how many. It looked like they was everywhere.

"They didn't make a sound. They were just coming at us through the trees. We were firing, but they kept coming at us. There was too many of them to stop. We had to pull out. Machine guns were shooting at us from everywhere. And all them Japs coming. We'd pull back a little way and stop and fire, and then we'd fall back a little more.

"Somebody was saying, 'Steady. . . Steady there.. .' But I don't know who it was. I just kept firing. You don't think about nothing. You just shoot. Guys were getting hit. We had to pull them along with us. You can't leave a wounded guy for the Japs to get. The things they do to 'em..."

There was a private first class from Oakland, California. He was blinded by powder burns. He couldn't know it was only temporary. All he could know was that he was blind in the middle of a battle. He was saying, "I can't see." He was fumbling around, trying to feel his way in the brush. The bullets were cutting all around, and he was trying to crawl away. But he couldn't tell which way to crawl. He kept saying, "I can't see." He didn't ask anybody to stop fighting, to help him. He just hung on to his rifle, like they tell you to, and tried to crawl out, but he couldn't see where to crawl.

Corporal Lawrence E. Oliveira of Fall River, Massachusetts, grabbed the blind boy by the arm, pulling him along as they withdrew. He'd pause to fire, and the blind Marine would wait beside him as he got off a few shots, and then Corporal Oliveira would lead him back a little farther.

"The boy didn't moan or pray or nothing. He just kept saying, every now and then, 'I can't see.'" By the time they got back to the creek, the Japanese were close on them, charging now. But the Marines had machine guns at the creek. They piled the Jap dead in the brush. They broke the charge.

Another platoon tried crossing the creek at another point. Near the head of the line was The Swede, a private first class from some place out West. He was a big guy, built like a truck, the last man in the world you'd ever suspect of being sentimental. His big ambition was to send his kid sister through college. It took some doing, but he was doing it on his service pay. The Swede was just stepping into the creek when he got it.

"You could hear the bullet hit him in the stomach," said Platoon Sergeant John M. White. "He just stood there a minute. He said, 'Them dirty bastards!' Then he fell down. He was dead."

Brother's Dream to Be Realized

Later they said they thought The Swede had made out his insurance to his sister. So he'll be sending her through college, after all.

"When we got across the creek," said Sergeant White, "the fire was so hot we couldn't do a thing. You couldn't see a single Jap. All you could see was where the bullets were hitting around us. And men getting hit. But no matter how bad it got, I never saw one of the boys pass up a wounded man."

Pfc. Charles Conger, 21, of Ventura, California, was one of those hit. A machine gun cut his legs from under him. He couldn't get up. He had to crawl. Nobody saw him. Nobody could have heard him if he'd yelled. The firing was too heavy. He was as alone as a man can be.

It was slow, painful, dragging through the brush, crawling headfirst down the bank, dragging limp legs. He had to pull himself on by inches, then bellying down the bank sprayed with bullets as thickly as rice thrown at a bride. He tumbled into the creek. The rocks were sharp. He was gasping in the swift water, struggling across against the force of the stream. It was only blind luck that White saw him. White was too far away to help, but he stopped and waved his arms to attract attention, ignoring cover until two Marines who were nearer saw the wounded man in the creek.

Self-Preservation Not the Rule

Those Marines were almost across. Safety lay just ahead. They didn't have to stop. But they went sloshing through the water to the wounded man. They half-carried, half- dragged him with them.

The battalion tried all day to win a crossing at the creek. In the end, they could only withdraw to the ridge on the American side and dig in for the night.

It was getting dusk as one machine-gun platoon finished its gun emplacements. Then the men began digging their foxholes. Most of them were stripped to the waist and they laid aside their weapons as they dug.

That was the moment the enemy chose to charge. They must have slipped across the stream and up the slope and watched the digging men. They must have seen that if they could reach those emplacements, if they could get those machine guns, they could swing them and smash the infantry company holding the next section of the line with enfilading fire. That is why the Japanese, perhaps fifty of them, did not yell and did not fire a shot. They rushed with bayonets.

Down among his infantrymen, Captain Andrew A. Haldane, of Methuen, Massachusetts, was talking with First Lieutenant Andrew Chisick, of Newark, New

Jersey. They heard a Marine yell. They looked up and saw the Japs racing toward the emplacements. They saw weaponless Marines scattering out of the way. Some were trying to reach their rifles. Some had no chance of getting to their weapons. The Japs were hardly thirty yards from the nearest gun, and closing fast. Other Marines were firing.

It all happened quicker than the telling. More Marines were firing, but it wasn't enough to stop the charge. The nearest Japs were hardly ten feet from the guns.

Captain Haldane ran toward the guns, firing as he ran. Lieutenant Chisick ran with him. Others, too, joined the charge, some with bare hands, some with clubs or entrenching tools snatched from the ground. The Japs reached one gun. They swung it to enfilade the line. A Jap was in the gunner's seat. The Marines' charge hit the gun before he could fire a shot. He got a bayonet through the chest. The enemy broke, and the Marines cut them down. More than twenty dead Japs were scattered in the brush by the time it was quiet again.

The Marines were bombed that night. Dive bombers. The enemy set up a heavy fire of tracer bullets to show the bombers where their own lines were; to show them where they should drop their bombs in the dark. Some part of our lines was bombed almost every night. Nobody will ever be able to describe a bombing. You can't describe hell. You can only go through it.

The Marines had to take the bombing after a day of battle. They had to take it without any way of hitting back. The next morning, January 3d, they attacked again. The enemy threw mortar shells. Sergeant White saw a shell explode. He ducked down the line to see if anyone was hit.

"A kid was sitting there in his foxhole. He didn't have any head. He just had a neck with dog tags on it."

All through that second day, the Marines pushed small units across the creek at different points, still trying to find a soft spot in the Japanese defenses. Each time they were hit. They knocked out some of the machine guns, but each time, in the end, they had to fall back across the creek.

There was a boy firing from behind a log. His face was gray. He stopped firing and looked around. His eyes were dull, without hope.

"It don't do any good," he said. His voice was flat. He wasn't speaking to anybody. He was just saying it. "I got three of 'em, but it don't do any good."

Winning the Battle of Despair

Platoon Sergeant Casmir Polakowski—known as Ski—said, What the hell are you beefing about? You get paid for it, don't you?"

Polakowski of Wilkes-Barre, Pa. He beat black despair with grim humor

The kid managed a grin. As Ski crawled on down the line, the boy was fighting again, squeezing them off.

A platoon was pinned down in the jungle on their flank. The platoon could neither go forward nor withdraw. They could only lie in the brush, held there by a crisscross net of machine-gun fire, while snipers took pot shots at them. Ski's platoon was ordered to lend a hand. They were bone-tired, but Ski said, "Let's get going," and they got.

Three of them were Denham, Melville and O'Grady. Just three of the guys in the ranks. The guys who carried the ball.

Private Harry Denham, 21, of Nashville, Tennessee, was called "Pee Wee" because he was so small. They say he went to "some fancy military school." But he didn't ask favors of anybody and he wouldn't back down before the biggest man in the regiment. Just a bantam rooster of a kid who'd take on anything that walked.

Pfc. John O'Grady, 21, of Ogdensburg, N.Y., left the talking for the trio to Denham and Melville. He was a quiet guy who never had much to say to anybody, but he seemed to talk plenty when the three of them were off by themselves. Maybe he told them what he wanted to be after the war. The kids all think about that. It's something to look forward to—and a guy needs something to look forward to.

Pfc. John William Melville was called "Pete," but nobody seems to know why. His home was Lynn, Massachusetts. He was 26, almost an old man. He quit a white-collar job with the General Electric Company in Boston to join the Marines.

They hit the enemy on the flank—Denham, Melville and O'Grady, and Levy, Jones and Brown. They flung themselves at the enemy's flank so he'd have to break the fire that had the other platoon caught. Men dropped, but they kept going forward—fighting from tree to tree. They pushed the enemy back. They pushed him back long enough, held him long enough for the trapped platoon to pull out. That was long enough for the Marines to form a line so they couldn't be rolled up by counterattack.

Another lull then. The jungle was still. First Sergeant Selvitelle asked Ski how it was going. Ski was smoking a cigarette. His voice sounded tired.

"They got Denham, Melville and O'Grady," he said.. They were lying out there in the brush somewhere and he was smoking a cigarette.

The word came to move up. There was firing ahead. Maybe an hour later Ski was behind a tree when he saw a wounded Marine lying in the open. A sniper was shooting at the boy. Ski could see the dirt flung up when the bullets hit. The boy was trying to crawl away, but he couldn't.

Ski ran from cover and pulled him to a tree. The sniper saw him. All the sniper had to do was wait until Ski started to return to his post. Then he shot Ski in the back.

Others Attempt a Crossing

That was about the time Tommy Harvard's platoon crossed Suicide Creek, lugging their heavy machine guns. Tommy Harvard was the code name for First Lieutenant Elisha Atkins, who played football at Harvard, belonged to the Dekes and the Owls, and got his B.A. in 1942. "Very quiet and polite as hell" is the way a sergeant describes him.

OFFICIAL PHOTOGRAPH U. S. MARINE CORPS
1st Lt. Elisha Atkins (Tommy Harvard)—"very quiet and polite as hell"

The enemy let Lieutenant Atkins and about half of his men cross the creek before they opened up. Six automatic weapons blasted them at point-blank range. There were at least three machine guns with perfect fields of fire. It happened too quickly for anybody to duck.

Sergeant Wills says, "I saw a man ahead of us and just as I saw he wasn't a Marine, they all let fly."

Marines were hit. Somebody was screaming. Corporal John R. Hyland of Greenwich, Connecticut (21 Prospect Street), was frowning as he tried to knock out the nearest machine-gun next with rifle fire. The screaming man stopped.

Corporal Hyland said, "We ought to get the hell out of here." But he didn't move to go. He kept his place, still shooting at the spot of jungle where he guessed the gun port was, until the order was passed to withdraw.

The machine guns swept the brush just higher than a man lying flat. The trapped Marines rolled down the bank or pushed backward on their bellies until they could tumble into the creek. The screening bush was their only protection against the snipers perched in trees. As they rolled into the stream, they hunkered down as low as they could in the water. Some got down so only their faces showed above the water. All of them pressed against the Japanese bank as bullets slashed through the undergrowth above them, splattering the creek and the American bank beyond.

Death Trap in the Creek

Two of the Marines had fallen on a big log lying in the creek. One of them was hit in the leg and couldn't move, but he was near enough for Sergeant Wills to pull him into the creek. Other Marines dragged him up against the brush-choked bank; but they couldn't reach the other boy on the log. He lay too far out in the field of fire. He'd caught a full machine-gun burst. He must have had twenty holes in him, but he was still alive. He was hung over the log, partly in the water. He was calling weakly, "Here I am, Wills... Over here..."

They couldn't help him. They could only listen to him.

"Wills...I'm here...Wills ...

There were other wounded in the creek above them. They couldn't help them, either. Most of those crouching in the bushes against the bank were wounded, too. The kid on the log was getting weaker. Just listening was harder than anything Sergeant Wills ever had to take.

"He was calling me, and I couldn't help him. All of them were guys we knew, but we couldn't do a thing. We had to lay in the water and listen to them. It was the coldest damn' water I ever saw. Their blood kept flowing into our faces."

OFFICIAL PHOTOGRAPH U.S. MARINE CORPS

More than once the waters of Suicide Creek ran red. All the Japs had to do was wait, hidden in deep jungle undergrowth, till the Marines came groping through into their field of fire. (Map above shows development of the nine-day battle)

Their only chance was to creep downstream close against the bank and then make a dash, one by one, for the American shore. A little way down the twisting stream there was a spot where a man would have a chance to make it. Most places, a man would have to stop to climb the bank. Only a man who wanted to commit suicide would try that.

It was slow work for the men in the creek, crawling downstream in the racing water. They were hampered by the thick tangles of vines and brush. Men caught in the vines struggled helplessly.

Everybody had to cut everybody else loose as he went along, "says Pfc. Luther J. Raschke of Harvard, Illinois.

He found young Tommy Harvard, tangled in the vines. The lieutenant was wounded, struggling to free himself. Raschke cut the officer loose.

"I tried to help him along, but he wouldn't come. He'd been hit three times. A slug had smashed his shoulder. He was losing blood pretty fast. But he wouldn't leave. He was trying to see that everybody got out first. He told me, 'Go on, go on!' He wouldn't let anybody stop for him. He said, 'Keep the line moving!' He made us leave him there."

They made their dash; got safely out and safely to the line of foxholes to which the battalion had fallen back again after that second day of vain fighting to win the crossing of Suicide Creek.

But Raschke couldn't forget the wounded officer they'd left in the creek. He said, "I guess everybody else is out."

"Yeah," said Corporal Alexander Caldwell of Nashville, Tennessee. (1209 Cedar Lane.)

"Well...

"Yeah," said Corporal Caldwell.

So they got permission to go back into no man's land to hunt for their platoon leader. Corporal Caldwell took along two more volunteers. They might have to carry Lieutenant Atkins, if they found him, and they might have to fight their way out. That was why Caldwell took extra men. They were Louis 3. Sievers of Johnstown, Pennsylvania (311 Everhart Street) and Joseph V. Brown of Middletown, New York (14 William Street), both privates first class.

It was getting hard to see when they crawled down to the creek. Raschke stopped. They lay listening, but they could hear nothing except the rushing stream and, now and then, the sound of the Japanese talking. They had to make their choice then. They could go back without the lieutenant. Or they could risk calling. Nobody would blame them if they went back. Nobody would know they hadn't done everything they could to find him.

Raschke lay on the edge of the stream and he remembers clearer than anything else how close the water was under his nose. The others were in the bush, rifles ready to fire if the enemy discovered him. Not that it would do any good. He'd be dead. For that matter, if the machine guns opened up, they'd all be dead.

"I was scared stiff," Raschke says. "I called as softly as I could, 'Tommy Harvard...Tommy Harvard...'"

"A voice said, 'I'm down here.'

"It sounded weak, but we figured it might be a trap. So I said, 'What's your real name?'

"The voice said, 'Elisha Atkins.' So we knew it was him. We crawled down and pulled him out. He said, 'God! Am I glad to see you!'"

He was shaking from hours in the chill water, weak from loss of blood, but still calmly Harvard as they carried him to the rear.

During the two days the Third Battalion had been fighting vainly to win the crossing of Suicide Creek, the outfit on its left had been trying as stubbornly and as vainly, to get across its segment of the stream.

Road-Building for the Tanks

During those two days, Marine Pioneers were toiling to build a corduroy road through the dismal swamp in their rear so that tanks could be moved up to the line. The tanks finally reached the outfit on the Third Battalion's left, but they found the banks of the creek too steep for crossing. The gully formed a natural tank trap.

So a Marine bulldozer, the machine that can work miracles, was called to cut down the banks of the creek; to make a fill in the stream so that the tanks could cross against the enemy.

The Japanese saw their danger. They concentrated fire on the bulldozer. Man after man was shot from the driver's seat. Some killed, some wounded. But there was always a Marine to jump in the seat. He had no shield, no protection at all. He sat up in the open like a shooting-gallery target for all the enemy's fire. But all the fire the Japs could muster wasn't enough to stop the Marines' bulldozer. They kept on till the fill was made; till the tanks were rolling across the creek.

The advance of the tanks made the positions of the enemy opposing the Third Battalion untenable. If they tried to hold against the frontal attack of the Third Battalion, they would be hit by tanks and infantry from the flank. They'd be a nut in a nutcracker. They had to retreat or be crushed, and they retreated. The crossing of Suicide Creek had been won.

The Marines pushed through the Jap positions, mopping up the remnants of resistance. They pushed on toward the next objective. That day the rain began. From that day on, there was hardly an hour that it did not rain. Savage, slashing, torrential rain that struck hard enough to hurt. If you faced it, it made you gasp. It turned the jungle into a bog— a slough of despair. Exhausted men floundering through the mud sank often to their knees.

They fought at times in mud above their knees. Sometimes they sank too deep to move their legs and had to be pulled free.

Sometimes the rain pounded with such fury that you could not hear the man next to you unless he shouted. Sometimes it slackened to a cold drizzle. They were wet, chilled through, twenty-four hours a day... every day.

It was impossible to supply the battalion by truck or jeep. These couldn't get through the mud. The only way to get up supplies, the only way to get the wounded out, was by amphibian tractors, the lumbering Alligators. On them and them alone the supply line depended. That line was life to the battalion--as vital as the umbilical cord to an unborn child.

The enemy could hear the clattering, banging Alligators. Snipers stalked them. And when their clattering was heard, the enemy threw mortar shells, trying to blast the supply line. Even the Alligators couldn't go all the way. Some bogged down and had to be abandoned. But others kept rumbling, waddling up over a twisted road they smashed through the jungle.

They came as far as they could, and there Marines shouldered the heavy boxes of ammunition and canned rations for the rest of the trek to the lines. The wounded were carried that far on stretchers and there loaded on the Alligators for the jolting agony of the ride out.

The distance the carrying parties had to go was only a few hundred yards at first and never more than a mile or perhaps only three quarters. But through the jungle, through that rain and mud, it was endless miles.

Man's Endurance Knows No Limit

Sometimes they got lost in the dark. Sometimes they wandered for hours in blind circles in the jungles. One man was in a stretcher party that started from the line with wounded at 7:30 p.m. They had 300 yards to go. They got through at 4:30 a.m. Nine hours to go 300 yards.

There was no hot food in the line. Once or twice, hot coffee got up to some units of the battalion. But not once during those nine days of battle, those days of rain and exhaustion, did the chilled Marines in the line have a mouthful of hot food.

Sleep was something most of them forgot. Japanese slipped around the lines at night, trying to get close enough to lob a grenade on a gun; close enough to bayonet a dozing man and slip away.

Mosquitoes were torture--big, black, savage. Those are not just words. They bit men so badly their eyes swelled almost shut. The men couldn't wear head nets for protection. A man can't see as well through a head net. So he endures the mosquitoes and ants and bugs, a million things that sting and bite. A man has to be careful about slapping them off in the dark. The sound might give him away to a waiting Jap.

They kept on fighting. They forgot the days. Time ceased to mean anything. The craziest things seemed funny. They laughed at things that wouldn't have seemed funny at all back home.

After a while, it is sometimes hard to tell from the sound whether a man is laughing or crying.

Pfc. Frederick E. Yeiser, 18, of Akron, Ohio, is an example. Just as he reached the line with a stretcher party, a bullet hit him in the leg. He fell back on the stretcher he'd been carrying. He beamed at them.

"This time," he said, "I'm riding!"

The corpsmen were taking a beating. They always do, going in with the combat units, sometimes ahead of the line, going wherever a Marine is hit to give him aid. They can't wait for the fire to slacken. Minutes may mean life to a wounded man. The Marines say that there wasn't a corpsman who didn't stick his neck out to hell and gone, beyond what the book requires.

For example, Pharmacist's Mate Edward L. Rochester, 26, of Camden, New Jersey, was making his way in short dashes from tree to tree, trying to reach a wounded Marine lying beyond the line. A sniper got the corpsman in the back. He was standing against a tree when he was hit and he didn't fall. He just stood there.

E. L. Rochester of Camden, N. J.
His legs gave up but his heart kept on

The shot had paralyzed him--
temporarily, at least. He couldn't slide down
to the ground. He couldn't move. He just
stood there, pressed against the tree, with
bullets thudding into the bark beside him.

Supervising the Rescue

A Marine started crawling toward him,
but Rochester waved him away. He yelled for
the rescuer to get the wounded Marine
instead. "He's bad hit! Get him out of there!"

The men saw Rochester hit again. This
bullet jolted him so he fell. Then they could
pull him back through the bushes. He

couldn't move his legs, but he still kept telling them what to do for the wounded Marine.

The wounded were carried to the aid station near the CP. Usually, it was just a space beside some big tree that might give a little shelter from enemy fire. There weren't enough stretchers. They made stretchers with poles and ponchos. They laid wounded men on ponchos spread on the mud. It was pouring rain.

A couple of Marines lugged in a limp boy. If the boy was alive, his pulse was so weak you could hardly detect it.

'Plasma," said the battalion surgeon. "Two hundred and fifty cc's."

He wiped the back of his hand wearily across his eyes, clearing the rain out of his face, He was swaying from exhaustion before it was over. He got so he didn't even look up when a shot zinged by. He was fighting for so many lives and he was so tired. That is how it was for Lieutenant Ivor Hugh Morris, Jr., whose father is a doctor, too, in Aurora, Illinois.

Now he was giving plasma to the boy who seemed a corpse. Somebody back home had taken time to give blood to the Red Cross. So now you could see the color coming back in the boy's face. That's what plasma does. The Marines who'd brought the boy from the line were staring at him bug-eyed.

"Christ," the tall one said, and he wasn't cursing. "It brings the dead back to life."

Corpsman Stafford remembered that, but he couldn't remember the wounded boy's name. There were so many.

One thing the corpsman remembered was an Irishman from New York, Sergeant J. P. Murray.

They'd found Japanese canned heat in a bivouac area from which the enemy had been driven. They had some tiny boxes of coffee powder. So they made hot coffee with rain water caught in helmets. It was the only thing hot they had to give the wounded.

Sergeant Murray had been hit twice, but he drank two plasma cans of scalding coffee and said, "That's right on."

Then he took a small book from his pocket and began reading as he waited for his turn to be carried out. It was a volume of Kipling's verse.

"This is good dope," the sergeant said. "Listen to this one."

Corpsman Stafford doesn't remember what poem Sergeant Murray quoted. He was too busy trying to ease a boy who was dying, while the wounded sergeant lay quoting Kipling.

Part II

The rain kept on. The battle kept on. Each day the Marines fought deeper into the jungle. There'd be a pillbox, a nest of machine guns, and the Marines would have to blast them out to advance. The enemy had tricks, too. Good tricks, some of them. He'd draw his men back, abandoning a bivouac area or a nest of foxholes. A Marine patrol scouting through the jungle would report the way clear and pass on. The enemy would filter back into the position, and the larger body of Marines following the patrol would be hit from ambush.

On January 7th, the sixth day of battle, Lieutenant Colonel McDougal went ahead of the line with a small party and inspected an abandoned bivouac area. You wouldn't have thought there was a Jap in miles. The Marines even pawed over some abandoned gear and picked up a few souvenirs. A little later, as the advance continued, McDougal returned to this bivouac area to set up his forward CP.

The jungle was still. But the enemy had seeped back into the area. As the CP party came into a clearing, the Japs cut loose.

The Marines dived for the deck with bullets cutting around them. Some crouched behind a big log. Some were in the open, with only weeds and bush for protection. Some were wounded. Colonel McDougal was firing his pistol at a machine gun when he was hit in the right shoulder.

He rolled over on his other side and said, "I guess I can't use that hand anymore." He changed his pistol to his left hand. Then he lay there, firing at them with his left hand and hollering for a telephone.

Command of the battalion was assumed by Major Joseph Skoczylas, of Philadelphia, a varsity track and soccer man at the Naval Academy. He was shot in the face. It was a bad day for officers. Lieutenant Chisick was hit. So was Lieutenant Claus W. Larson of Meridian, Texas. So was Captain Thomas F. Guffin, Jr., of East Point, Georgia.

Then there was "Barney O'Goodman." The records list him as Captain Howard K. Goodman, a New York lawyer, but they called him "Barney O'Goodman" because he could sing more Irish songs than any man in the regiment. They called him "Bugle Boy," too, because he blew his company's calls in camp. It was the only company in the Marine Corps with a captain for a bugler. It was pretty much a company secret.

Captain Goodman's parents live in Long Beach, N. Y. They say there wasn't a lot of money in the family, and young Howard Goodman had to work his way through school. He was the pride of his parents. He would be a lawyer, maybe a judge even.

Capt. H. K. Goodman, whose parents live in Long Beach, N. Y., won the Silver Star and died a hero's death

Instead, he went to Guadalcanal, won the Silver Star for heroism and came to Cape Gloucester to die. He was 25. He was killed that afternoon because he exposed himself to spot the enemy rather than order one of his men to do it.

It was a bad day for enlisted men, too. They fought all day to push ahead, and the enemy was pounding harder with mortars. The Marines couldn't get at them. They could only duck, sprawl flat in the mud and hope the shrapnel would pass over them.

The Marines didn't know that this was the spot prepared by the enemy for the final showdown. They didn't know that just ahead of them was the stronghold of Aogiri Ridge. They knew that not far ahead was the Government Trail, their objective, but they thought the dense growth between hid only more jungle flats. The map didn't show any ridge, and the jungle screen concealed it.

Aogiri wasn't a big ridge. From the base of one nose, across the crest and down the slope to the base of the opposite nose, it was perhaps 200 yards long. The ground in front of the ridge begins rising slowly, the pitch gradually increasing until it starts sharply upward at an angle as great as 40 degrees. That last steep rise to the crest is only about 50 or 60 feet. Against this face of the ridge, hidden from them by the jungle, the Marines were advancing.

The enemy had prepared an elaborate network of camouflaged bunkers and machine-gun emplacements. They were all along the crest of the jungle-masked ridge, thick along its steep face, stretching down the noses of the ridge and off on either flank into the jungle flats. There was no spot on the approaches to the ridge that could not be covered by the defenders' machine-gun fire. And the area was thick with foxholes of supporting riflemen.

The enemy was dug in even on the reverse of the ridge, which sloped down into a little valley through which ran the Government Trail, the enemy's precious supply line for the Hill 660 sector. Across that little draw was another ridge. There the enemy had prepared positions from which his force on Aogiri Ridge received strong supporting fire.

The Japs Were Sitting Pretty

The Japanese stronghold was manned by a battalion of veteran troops. A large part of them had been resting in bivouac, well fed, as comfortable as men can be in the jungle, during all the time the Marines were bludgeoning their way through the jungle, the rain and the mud—fighting on their nerve, sick from exhaustion, from dysentery, from fungus infection. And now "the bug" was beginning to hit them again. Malaria.

Some of the sick had to be sent out with the wounded. But if a man could walk, if he could shoot, he stayed in the line.

When Major Skoczylas was wounded the afternoon of January 7th, the enemy was hitting them from the front, from the flank, and snipers were picking men off from the rear. When night came, the battalion had lost contact with the unit on its left and was forced to form a tight circular defense, a despondent circle in the dark. To make matters worse, a strong pocket of Japs separated one company from the rest of the battalion. This isolated company had to form its own defense circle in the rainy dark.

The men were out on their feet. A captain who has been recommended for the Navy Cross says, "They'd taken all men could. The will to fight was gone. I couldn't blame them."

A platoon sergeant, one of the noncom regulars who are the backbone of the Corps, put it this way: "They'd have kept on fighting. They'd have kept on as long as you told them to. But it wouldn't have been no use. This battalion was licked. They'd gave up hope."

That was the situation Lieutenant Colonel Lewis W. Walt, 30, of Vallejo, California, faced the next morning when he came slopping through the jungle to take command of the battalion. It was January 8th.

With him came his runner, Corporal Lawrence H. Larson, 21, a Guadalcanal veteran, an orphan from Muskegon, Michigan. The new commander's first act was to reconnoiter his lines, slipping out as much as fifty yards in front of the line to see how the land lay.

They told Lieutenant Colonel Walt of their losses from snipers each time they started forward, and he ordered them to "give those trees a good spraying before we move out." They did, with heavy machine guns. It cost the Japs a batch of snipers. They struck back with a furious fire of automatic weapons and machine guns from two sides. Walt remembers, "We were pinned down for ten minutes."

But he had to attack. He had to re-establish contact with the main line and between his own units. He had to turn those circular defense positions into a battle line and push forward this flank of the general Marine offensive. He had to keep advancing until he was astride the Government Trail.

Lieutenant Colonel Walt ordered the weary companies to push out their flanks; to extend their lines to make contact. The enemy opened up with automatic weapons as the Marines began to move. Men were lost, but contact was re-established between all units; the whole battalion was brought into line of battle. Walt's pitiful reserves were the carrying parties, the clerks and specialists of the Headquarters Company. Those who have fought with him in other battles could have told the battalion: "When Walt attacks, he attacks with everything he's got—including himself."

Our mortars opened up. All through the battle, lone Marines crawled out in front of the line to act as eyes for their mortars. They wormed their way through undergrowth, slashed and raked by enemy fire. They searched until they found a spot from which they could observe the targets and report the effect of our fire. It was a one-man job, a job for volunteers; it was a job only for a man who could make himself forget that in a few minutes he probably would be killed.

Sergeant Oliver Ermin Pitts, 22, of Guilford College, North Carolina. was one who crept out to observe for the mortars. Enemy snipers located him, firing at him, but Sergeant Pitts didn't go back to a foxhole. He stayed until he was killed.

When they got his body, when they buried him in a temporary grave, they wanted some mark besides a helmet on a stick. They used the oval top of a mess tin, nailing it on a stick with a nail from a broken supply box. The epitaph was scratched on the mess tin with a knife.

It wasn't much of an epitaph. You could call it corny. But it was the best this Marine could do, whoever he was. There was his dead friend's name, his serial number and the date. And there was this: A FRIEND TO ALL

That first attack of the battalion jumped off at 10:30 A.M., January 8th. Captain Haldane's company, on the right of the battalion line, was walking straight into the face of Aogiri Ridge. They had gone into battle with 174 effectives. They now had 90.

The enemy opened up with everything he had. A Marine said, "It was like all the seams of hell busted open at once."

They were held one hundred yards from the base of the ridge. The company was deployed in a ragged line through the brush. They still didn't know the ridge was there.

.

The order was advance. To stand up was suicide. Captain Haldane passed the word for the Marines to advance by crawling. They started crawling under the enemy fire, inching forward on their bellies, trying to get near enough to rush the machine guns. It seemed that nothing could live in that sleeting fire, but the Marines advanced seventy-five of those hundred yards before the Jap fire stopped them.
They lay behind whatever cover they could find, too dulled by battle and by weariness to feel—or even care. But they hung on.

It was some time during this day that they found they were attacking a ridge. Some of them discovered it when they started to climb it; some when they noticed the ground they were crawling over was beginning to rise. Some guessed it when they noticed that enemy fire was coming from above them. But they couldn't see it. They couldn't tell how long it was, how high it was, or how much the enemy had on it.

Lean and battle-weary after 19 days of front-line fighting, Marine Pfc. George C.
Miller of Jersey City carries a machine gun over a jungle trail on Cape Gloucester

One of the first who discovered the
ridge was "Dutch" Schantzenbach, of
Macungie, Pennsylvania. Dutch was 22, but
he was one of the veterans, a noncom
regular. Now he lay behind a log with bullets
drumming on it, lay there with another
Pennsylvanian, his platoon leader. First
Lieutenant William R. Reckus, of Wilkes-
Barre.

Major Dillard came crawling up. The
Marines couldn't push forward another foot.
But they had to push forward. They had to
straighten the line at this point or the whole
position was endangered. It was one of those
things. It couldn't be done, but it had to be
done. It was up to Lieutenant Reckus.

He could have ordered his middle squad forward, of course. He could have stayed behind the log and ordered them to attack; to go forward until the line was straight. But these men were exhausted, the hope drained out of them. It was up to him.

He heaved a grenade. He stood up. "Come on, Dutch," he said. "Let's show 'em how the boys from Pennsylvania do it."

Reckus was stepping out. He turned to see if the men were moving up. Dutch was at his heels. Maybe Bill Reckus saw the others starting up. Or maybe he was hit too quickly. He fell, and Dutch pulled him back behind the log.

"Well, Dutch . . . It don't look like the boys from Pennsylvania did so good."

But they'd done all right. The men had seen him fall. They'd seen proof, if they needed it, that no man could go forward against that fire. But they went. Bill Reckus' men went forward until the line was straight.

A corpsman was dressing the lieutenant's wound. Bill Reckus said, "Give me the straight dope. How bad am I hit?"

The corpsman tried to tell him he'd be okay. "Don't kid me," Bill Reckus said.

They dragged in a stretcher and put him on it. He said, "So long. Dutch." A sniper shot at them. Later, he died.

All that afternoon they hung on at the foot of the ridge. but, in the end, Walt had to order them to drop back to the position they'd held that morning. There the company was bent in an arc to give the battalion protection against attack on its open flank during the night. At that time, they were the extreme right flank of the Marine front line.

It was raining. They tried to sleep— those who were not keeping watch. They needed sleep as men need air to breathe. Tomorrow morning they would attack again.

Bringing Up the Big Gun

Meanwhile, Walt had called back for a 37-mm. fieldpiece. It was held up in the jungle somewhere behind the battalion until an artilleryman from the 11th Marines said he might get the gun through with a caterpillar tractor. There was only one way he could go. For fifty yards or more that way ran right along the front line. It was through heavy mud; slow going. And he would be completely exposed to the enemy's fire. They told him that, but Pfc. Ellery Everett Marvell said he'd give it a go.

The battle was at a furious pitch as he came clattering along the front, perched high on the driver's seat of the tractor, perched there like a hen on a roost, the plainest target a man could have, with the whole enemy line blazing at him. Bullets banged on the cat, on the gun, and bullets hit within inches of him, but by crazy luck "that marvel Marvell" wasn't hit. He swung in at last at battalion headquarters. He lighted a cigarette,

"Here she is," he said. "Where do you want her?"

They told him the spot in the line. He said "Okay" and trundled off to deliver the gun. Then he swung homeward. They fig-tired he was a dead man sure. He'd made it once, a million-to-one shot, and at those odds you don't repeat.

Again bullets banged and clattered against the ambling cat. Hundreds of bullets spitting past the driver's head. But the long shot came through again. It was plain impossible, but he didn't get a scratch.

A company of the 7th Marines was moved up as reinforcement that night, but it hardly brought Walt's force to a full battalion. This company was commanded by Captain John E Weber, of Rochester, New York. Captain Weber's company was moved up on the left of Captain Haldane's hard-hit company.

Lieutenant Colonel Walt's battle order for the next day, January 9th, was that the two companies forming the right half of his line should hold. Haldane's company would swing like a door until it was on a line and would then make a holding attack against the face of the ridge. On Haldane's left, Weber's company would swing inward in an enveloping movement against the far nose of the ridge, flanking the enemy's position, rolling him up so that Captain Haldane's men could press home the frontal attack.

The attack began at 10:30 A.M. Captain Weber's company swung wide, advancing up the nose of the ridge on a line roughly at right angles to the main Marine line. They pressed forward against increasing resistance, fighting their way up the jungle-choked nose of the ridge until they were "utterly pinned down." They had advanced perhaps fifty yards along the rising nose. That was about one fourth of the length of the ridge from nose to nose. On that advance up the nose, every foxhole was a battle to the death. Some of them nobody won. The Jap and the Marine killed each other.

On the face of the ridge, Captain Haldane's battered company was advancing against the machine guns that had stopped it the day before. They had been hammered all that morning, the seventh day of battle, and now they were charging, veterans and green kids together, flinging grenades, clawing, firing, tearing at the steep slope to reach the enemy, to get within bayonet thrust.

Stopped Just Short of Winning

The fury of that charge, the fury of desperation, almost carried them to the top. Against any ordinary defense, it might have won the crest. But they were stopped; pounded like a punch-drunk fighter who can only cover up and clinch, hanging on for no reason in the world except that he won't give up.

They did not know then that one Marine kept going on alone. They did not know the high tide of their charge until the battle was over. There will be no monument erected there; no stone and bronze to mark the place. The high tide of the Marines was marked only by the body of a boy.

He went forward ahead of the others, alone. He shot and stabbed his way past three machine-gun nests—shot and stabbed Japs in the foxholes in his path.

They found his body at the edge of a Japanese emplacement. There were two enemy dead beside a machine gun there. That was high tide of the charge. A dead boy with a dirty face marked it. His body lay almost thirty yards beyond the most advanced point the others had reached. The boy was Private Robert Lee Gray of Los Angeles, California. He was 20.

Now across the nose of the ridge, Captain Weber's company lay in an irregular line at an angle of about 60 degrees from Captain Haldane's line fronting the face of the ridge. There was a gap between the companies; a gap that was an invitation to the enemy.

That gap had to be closed. Lieutenant Colonel Walt ordered the nearest platoon to swing forward on a pivot and link the companies. Perhaps this was when a young officer protested that his men could not do any more; could not advance another foot.

Walt's voice was ice. "*Advance*," he said, "*or be relieved.*"

They advanced. Somewhere the men found the will, the strength to go forward one more time. They closed the gap under heavy fire. They bought contact with casualties. They had all they could do then just to hang on. There were long periods of quiet, of the waiting that saps men's will and strength, saps even faith. The enemy sat back. Whenever the Marines tried to move, he pounded them with fire, a storm of fire that stopped them; held them; left a few more dead crumpled in the brush. There were Marines, good men, who gave up hope that afternoon. They held on, hung on, because

Marines are taught that way, but they had no hope of winning the battle. They had no hope even of living.

"It was the lowest ebb of spirit," Lieutenant Colonel Walt remembers. It was about that time that Brigadier General Lemuel C. Shepherd, Jr., made one of his visits to the front. He and Walt lay behind a tree discussing the situation while machine-gun bullets clipped the trunks of the trees around them. General Shepherd remembers a sudden burst of machine-gun fire that made them flatten out beside the tree roots. Walt had only one comment to make.

"General," he said, "we are going to take that ridge and we are going to hold it."

Most of the battalion would have said he was talking through his hat. Weber's company lying across the nose of the ridge was pinned down. Haldane's company fronting the face of the ridge was pinned down. The other companies couldn't help. They had all could handle just to keep their part of the line unbroken. There was no reserve.

"So I played my last card," says Walt.

That was the fieldpiece. It was half a ton of gun, and the Marines had to move it into the line by hand. They had to haul and shove the fieldpiece through mud, dense jungle growth and enemy fire. It took them an hour and a half to move the gun 150 yards.

Walt proposed to blast his way with canister up the steep, jungle-thick face of the ridge. The gun would have to be manhandled up step by step in the face of murderous fire. There were fallen trees, over which the 1,000-pound gun would have to be lifted. And the last of the slope up which they had to take the gun had a pitch of forty degrees.

It was late afternoon, almost dusk, when Walt gave the order to advance. It took about a dozen Marines, besides the gun crew, to move the piece. A few Marines took hold to heave the gun forward, but there weren't enough of them. The rest, sprawled on the ground in the brush, only stared and made no move to help. They just didn't believe the hill could be taken.

It was a moment of defeat. In that moment the whole outcome of that battalion's fight teetered in the balance. Walt saw it.

"Come on, Larson," he said. "Let's lend a hand.'

He and Corporal Larson got a grip on the gun with the others. Bullets were banging against the shield; whipping the brush. The air was thick with the sound, the angry *ssspinggg!* a bullet makes. The Marines at the gun heaved, all together, privates, noncoms and the lieutenant colonel.

The gun began to move.

The men were getting up now—getting up, grabbing hold, fumbling, dull-eyed, stumbling maybe, but in the fight again. One of them tried to explain afterward how it was.

"You saw the colonel out there, straining a gut with the guys, and you figured, 'Oh, what the hell,' and got going again."

A Renewal of Fighting Spirit

Some explain by saying that the will to fight came back to them. Some merely note that dozens of men had cracked up in the battle before that moment. But after it, though they had to fight their way foot by foot up the ridge, though they had to hold what they took against night attack and five banzai charges, in all the battalion there were only two cases of combat fatigue. The others had gone beyond weariness. They could be killed, but they could not be stopped.

The gun was heaved three or four yards ahead of the riflemen's line. Sergeant Muzzey and his gun crew fired a few rounds of canister each time. They stopped, tearing a swath through the jungle, blasting a road for the gun. Then the infantry moved forward, moving up even with the gun, bringing their line a few feet farther up the hill, firing to cover the next slow step in the gun's advance. Then they did the whole thing all over again.

It cost men to get the gun up, but there was always a Marine to step into each empty place; always men to keep the gun moving up.

When they were part way up the face of the ridge, they flung a few high-explosive shells at the Jap bunkers on the crest. They knocked out three machine-gun nests in their path. The line of riflemen coming up on either side of the gun killed the enemy that were in their way. They had to go slowly, but they weren't stopping now. Not for anything. They inched on. The Marines were at close quarters now. They could use the bayonet. This was what they'd been waiting for. They hacked, stabbed and clubbed their way until they got a toehold on the crest.

All this time, Captain Weber's company lying across the nose of the ridge supported the advance by pouring machine-gun fire into the Jap position from the flank. His linking squads had gone forward, too. Now if the Marines advanced farther, they would come under their own fire. And it was almost dark. It was not a good defensive position, but if they withdrew down the hill, they would have it all to do all over again in the morning.

As darkness fell on Aogiri Ridge, Pfc. Rumbley was entrusted with the defense of the fieldpiece. He put three machine guns close around it. He told a couple of Marine to crawl into the foxholes in front of it with rifles and bayonets. He crawled off and brought back some extra ammunition. The he sat back with his tommy gun.

There was sporadic firing through the night. The Marines and the Japanese tossed hand grenades. A man couldn't see a grenade thrown in the dark. Hour after hour, a man could not know at what moment a grenade would explode in his face.

It was 11 P.M. The Marines heard wild screaming off on their left flank, down where the next outfit in the line had stopped for the night. They heard the screaming and a bedlam of gunfire. The enemy was hitting the next outfit. The Marines on the ridge couldn't know whether the line was holding or breaking. They could only wait for the enemy to come smashing through the darkness.

The moon came out, filtering down through the jungle, and for a little while they could see dimly. They could hear the babbling of Japanese off in the jungle now, beyond the crest of the ridge. The Nips were up to something. The Marines waited.

It was 3:30 A.M. Black clouds rolled over the moon, and the stinging rain began again. The foxholes were muddy tanks in which men crouched up to their shoulders in chilled water. There were strange bird calls off in the dark. Only they weren't birds. They were Japanese signaling to one another as they moved in the blackness.

It was 4 A.M. The Japanese began chanting in the dark. The whole night, the whole jungle seemed full of their voices:

"Marines, you die! Prepare to die!"

Walt knew what that meant. So did Tom Rumbley. And Dutch Schantzenbach. And all the rest who fought on Guadalcanal during those months the Marines hung on while the enemy bombed them at will; while the enemy pounded them with naval gunfire and they had no way of hitting back. They learned then what it means when the Japanese start chanting:

"Marines, you die! Prepare to die!"

It went on and on, and the Marines lay silent in the dark, in the driving rain, listening to the war chant of the Japanese. It sounded like a whole army out there chanting:

"Marines, you die! Prepare to die!"

They could see nothing. All they could do was wait. That is the hardest thing a man can do. Harder than fighting. Yet nobody got trigger-happy. Not even when the enemy screamed insults; not even when Japanese crept close to the line and yelled, daring them to shoot. Not a man revealed his position by firing. They just waited, dead-silent, ready.

The rain was sluicing down. The tempo of the chanting was wilder now and rising, rising. The Marines waited. Nobody said anything. This was the pay-off.

Then they came. They came shrieking. "*Banzai!*" The cry of death. "*Banzai!*"

It was 4:15 A.M.

The charge was preceded by a heavy machine-gun barrage from the supporting hill behind Aogiri Ridge. The Japanese on the ridge added their fire at close range and flung grenades into the Marine positions. The charge was made by a reserve unit, fresh troops, eager for the kill, rushing forward with the bayonet on a front of slightly more than 100 yards.

The Japanese wanted the fieldpiece that had enabled the Marines to gain a foothold on the ridge. If they could break through the thin line of Marines, if they could get that gun, they could sweep the Marines off that tiny part of the crest they'd won.

The shrieking charge came close to the gun. Men fought it out with bayonets close enough almost to touch the gun. But the gun didn't fire. If it fired once, if its position in the dark was revealed, the enemy's charge could converge on it.

Some of the Japs got to the line. Some tried to crawl in under the machine-gun fire; the Marines met them with rifles, with bayonets. The charge broke. The wave receded.

There was gabbling off in the darkness. The enemy was re-forming. They'd be coming again. The Marines waited. Some of the wounded were moaning. The rain poured down. Perhaps five minutes passed. Or maybe ten. The enemy came again. They came fast, bent low, screaming death. They got within a dozen feet of the gun. They got to the line, hacking, frenzied, screaming triumph. This time they'd go through! This time they'd sweep the ridge!

It was hand to hand in the dark, in the pelting rain. Man against man in the dark, in the darkness ripped by flame. Man against man. Smashing, clawing in the dark. Stabbing, clubbing. Slipping in the mud. Gasping, grunting, dying. Each man alone in the blackness, not knowing what was happening on his right or on his left, but holding until he died the ground where his feet were planted. And the wild charge broke, dwindling, ebbing into the dark, broken on the rock of Marines who died but would not step back.

No Thought of Retreat

The Marines could hear the enemy reforming again, gathering strength for another charge, fresh men filling the gaps in their ranks. The Marines waited. Ammunition was running low. Carrying parties were groping through the rain-drenched darkness to reach them.

But if the enemy charged before they got the ammunition up? What could they do? What could a man do when his last shot was fired?

"Fix bayonets and drive them back," Sergeant Louis Gargano said. His folks live in Bayonne, New Jersey. His Miriam was working in a plane factory waiting for him to get home. Then they were going to have a child. That's what he wanted most, Miriam and a kid. That was something a man could work for. Now there won't ever be any kid. Louis Gargano died to hold Aogiri Ridge.

Sergeant Schantzenbach—Dutch Schantzenbach—was talking with Tom Rumbley. You remember Dutch. He helped save the guns when the Japanese charged at Suicide Creek. He crawled up the enemy's fire lanes to spot pillboxes. He charged with Bill Reckus to show them how the boys from Pennsylvania did it. He pulled the dying lieutenant out of the line of fire to cover and then went on in the attack that took the ridge. He was in the line that broke the banzai charges in the rainy blackness.

On Guadalcanal, his whole squad was wiped out, killed or wounded, all except Dutch. On Cape Gloucester, his whole squad was wiped out again, all except Dutch. Now he told Tom Rumbley, "I wonder how much longer my luck's gonna hold."

It ran out on Aogiri Ridge. Dutch was 22. In less than an hour that morning of January 10th, in the pitch-blackness before the dripping jungle dawn, the enemy flung five furious charges against the weary line of Marines. The fourth charge broke the Marines' line. The Japanese spear stabbed through the line over dead Marines. But only three Japs got through—three officers. Their spear of troops was shattered by fire, by bayonets, as Marines closed the gap. The three Jap officers must have tried to find the fieldpiece in the darkness behind the line so they could blast it with grenades, but Marines hunted them down; killed each of them in the dark.

Walt had called for artillery fire. He ordered it brought close to the ridge. He took time to warn his men along the line that there'd be one hell of a lot of shells falling. "Get down in your holes," he told them. "We're going to bring it down pretty close."

The artillery started firing at 200 yards or better in front of the line. The range was pulled down little by little until the center of impact was only 50 or 75 yards in front of the Marines. There is always danger of a short round of artillery falling among your own men. The danger is greater when it is raining because a powder charge may not fully ignite; may hurl the shell only far enough to burst among your own men. But that chance had to be taken on Aogiri Ridge.

The Japanese were forming their fifth charge. It would be a supreme effort. A full company would lead the way, fresh troops who had been waiting in reserve. They were big men, some of them over six feet, shock troops. They were the last of the Japanese reserve. The Marines had no reserve. They had only the tired men who had been fighting for more than a week without relief.

A Marine machine-gun platoon was entirely out of ammunition. Others were almost out. It looked like the end of the road. Lieutenant Colonel Walt used the field telephone to call the CP for more ammunition.

"Get it up damn' fast," he said, "or start setting up a line. They'll be coming through."

Platoon Sergeant Haney was in charge of the ammunition party—"Pop" Haney, who'd been a Marine before most of them were born.

He was born in 1898. He fought in this regiment through World War I. He tried the outside world for six years, selling vacuum cleaners, but he didn't like it. He's been a Marine ever since. He's done duty in most of the places Marines have been. Now he is past 46, a leathery little man, a stickler for discipline, as rigid as a ramrod, a man who knows the book backward.

OFFICIAL PHOTOGRAPH U.S. MARINE CORPS

Platoon Sgt. "Pop" Haney, a Marine since Chateau Thierry. This fight was much the worst he had ever seen

His job was getting the ammunition up. He had to get that straggling line of Marines to the front before the enemy charged. They were out on their feet, staggering under their loads. They couldn't see one another to keep contact, but he had to keep them together, keep them going, get them to go faster, though already they were stumbling.

The firing grew heavier all the time. Great blasts of flame that shook the ground. Maniac chatter of machine guns. Explosion of grenades, of mortar shells. Both sides were throwing all the fire they had before the charge; everything they had before the last toss that would decide who should have Aogiri Ridge.

Pop Haney's caravan came crawling up. There were places in the line they couldn't reach because of the fire, and the ammunition had to be passed slowly from foxhole to foxhole. But it got there. Pop Haney got the ammunition to the line just four minutes before the enemy charged. That is by the lieutenant colonel's watch.

The last charge was stronger, more furious than any the enemy threw except the first. But it was only a fraction of the punch they had massed to throw. The artillery fire Walt had called for blunted the rest of it.

It was almost dawn when the last charge broke, when the conquerors of Bataan backed down before the victors of Guadalcanal.

As daylight came, the Marines pushed out their line to cover the whole ridge, mopping up pockets of enemy left on the hill. Another fieldpiece was in the line now, firing as the enemy was pushed out of the flats off the nose of the ridge. The Marines were doing the mauling now. They'd been taking it for eight days, but now, on the ninth, they were dishing it out. They liked it. They had their dead to settle for. An officer reported that he had to hold his men back to keep them from pushing beyond the ridge.

Rifles cracked sharply now and again. Snipers were still scattered through the jungle. A grenade exploded somewhere. Now and then there was a short burst of automatic fire. Walt, going over the ridge, found two boys in a foxhole.
"I thought they were dead," he said. "They were in water up to their armpits. They were sound asleep."

By the time night fell, the Marines held all of Aogiri Ridge, and Walt had reorganized his force to resume the attack. The attack began at 8:15 the next morning, January 11th. There ahead of them was the Government Trail, the enemy supply line. That was the Marines' final objective. A colonel who watched the attack said, "It was the prettiest thing you ever saw."

There was an artillery barrage. Then for ten minutes before the jump-off, the mortars fired smoke shells. They laid down a screen of smoke 300 yards deep over the entire battalion front to cover the infantry's advance.

The Marines moved forward with six companies in assault. The sixth company had been sent from another outfit as reinforcements after the ridge was taken. Lieutenant Colonel Walt was attacking again with all he had. But he didn't need reinforcements. The conquerors of Bataan had pulled out. The Marines walked through to their final objective.

They caught up with a few stragglers, killed them, and went on. In the mess of a shell- shattered Japanese bivouac area they found table-tennis sets, baseball equipment and even officers' uniforms. The Marines also captured several American machine guns and small arms from the enemy during the nine days battle. They must have been captured on Bataan or maybe Wake Island. Today those weapons are being used by Americans again, by Marines.

Lieutenant Colonel Walt pushed on past the Government Trail and began setting up a defense line to clinch their grip on the trail and on Aogiri Ridge. The Marines had learned the name of it by that time, and a draftsman was going to mark it on the map. But Brigadier General Shepherd came along the line, checking his positions for the next phase of the offensive, and the general ordered a different name put on the map.

"*We will call it Walt's Ridge*," he said.

That was 3 P.M., January 11, 1944. The battalion's part of the battle was over.

The end
T. Sgt. Asa Bordages

CAPE GLOUCESTER: THE GREEN INFERNO

Marines in World War II Commemorative Series
by Bernard C. Nalty for the
USMC History and Museums Division

On the early morning of 26 December 1943,
Marines poised off the coast of Japanese-held
New Britain could barely make out the mile-
high bulk of Mount Talawe against a sky
growing light with the approach of dawn.
Flame billowed from the guns of American
and Australian cruisers and destroyers,
shattering the early morning calm. The men
of the 1st Marine Division, commanded by
Major General William H. Rupertus, a veteran
of expeditionary duty in Haiti and China and
of the recently concluded Guadalcanal
campaign, steeled themselves as they waited
for daylight and the signal to assault the
Yellow Beaches near Cape Gloucester in the
northwestern part of the island. For 90
minutes, the fire support ships blazed away,
trying to neutralize whole areas rather than
destroy pinpoint targets, since dense jungle
concealed most of the individual fortifications
and supply dumps. After the day dawned and
H-Hour drew near, Army airmen joined the
preliminary bombardment. Four-engine
Consolidated Liberator B-24 bombers, flying

so high that the Marines offshore could barely see them, dropped 500-pound bombs inland of the beaches, scoring a hit on a fuel dump at the Cape Gloucester airfield complex and igniting a fiery geyser that leapt hundreds of feet into the air. Twin-engine North American Mitchell B-25 medium bombers and Douglas Havoc A-20 light bombers, attacking from lower altitude, pounced on the only Japanese antiaircraft gun rash enough to open fire.

On 26 December 1943, Marines wade ashore from beached LSTs passing through a heavy surf to a narrow beach of black sand. Inland, beyond a curtain of undergrowth, lie the swamp forest and the Japanese defenders. Department of Defense (USMC) photo 68998

The warships then shifted their attention to the assault beaches, and the landing craft carrying the two battalions of Colonel Julian N. Frisbie's 7th Marines started shoreward. An LCI [Landing Craft, Infantry] mounting multiple rocket launchers took position on the flank of the first wave bound for each of the two beaches and unleashed a barrage intended to keep the enemy pinned down after the cruisers and destroyers shifted their fire to avoid endangering the assault troops. At 0746, the LCVPs [Landing Craft, Vehicles and Personnel] of the first wave bound for Yellow Beach 1 grounded on a narrow strip of black sand that measured perhaps 500 yards from one flank to the other, and the leading elements of the 3d Battalion, commanded by Lieutenant Colonel William K. Williams, started inland. Two minutes later, Lieutenant Colonel John E. Weber's 1st Battalion, on the left of the other unit, emerged on Yellow Beach 2, separated from Yellow 1 by a thousand yards of jungle and embracing 700 yards of shoreline. Neither battalion encountered organized resistance. A smoke screen, which later drifted across the beaches and hampered the approach of later waves of landing craft, blinded the Japanese observers on Target Hill overlooking the beachhead, and no defenders manned the trenches and log-and-earth bunkers that might have raked the assault force with fire.

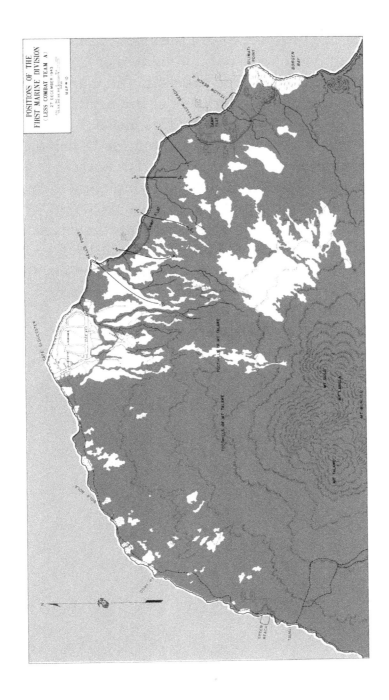

The Yellow Beaches, on the east coast of the broad peninsula that culminated at Cape Gloucester, provided access to the main objective, the two airfields at the northern tip of the cape. By capturing this airfield complex, the reinforced 1st Marine Division, designated the Backhander Task Force, would enable Allied airmen to intensify their attack on the Japanese fortress of Rabaul, roughly 300 miles away at the northeastern extremity of New Britain. Although the capture of the Yellow Beaches held the key to the New Britain campaign, two subsidiary landings also took place: the first on 15 December at Cape Merkus on Arawe Bay along the south coast; and the second on D Day, 26 December, at Green Beach on the northwest coast opposite the main landing sites.

MajGen William H. Rupertus, Commanding General, 1st Marine Division, reads a message of congratulation after the capture of Airfield No. 2 at Cape Gloucester, New Britain. Department of Defense (USMC) photo 69010

Major General William H. Rupertus, who commanded the 1st Marine Division on New Britain, was born at Washington, D.C., on 14 November 1889 and in June 1913 graduated from the U.S. Revenue Cutter Service School of Instruction. Instead of pursuing a career in this precursor of the U.S. Coast Guard, he accepted appointment as a second lieutenant in the Marine Corps. A vigorous advocate of rifle marksmanship throughout his career, he became a member of the Marine Corps Rifle Team in 1915, two years after entering the service, and won two major matches. During World War I, he commanded the Marine detachment on the USS Florida, assigned to the British Grand Fleet.

Between the World Wars, he served in a variety of assignments. In 1919, he joined the Provisional Marine Brigade at Port-au-Prince, Haiti, subsequently becoming inspector of constabulary with the Marine-trained gendarmerie and finally chief of the Port-au-Prince police force. Rupertus graduated in June 1926 from the Army Command and General Staff College at Fort Leavenworth, Kansas, and in January of the following year became Inspector of Target Practice for the Marine Corps. He had two tours of duty in China and commanded a battalion of the 4th Marines in Shanghai when the Japanese attacked the city's Chinese defenders in 1937.

During the Guadalcanal campaign, as a brigadier general, he was assistant division commander, 1st Marine Division, personally selected for the post by Major General Alexander A. Vandegrift, the division commander, whom he succeeded when Vandegrift left the division in July 1943. Major General Rupertus led the division on New Britain and at Peleliu. He died of a heart attack at Washington, D.C., on 25 March 1945, and did not see the surrender of Japan, which he had done so much to bring about.

Two Secondary Landings

The first subsidiary landing took place on 15
December 1943 at distant Cape Merkus,
across the Arawe channel from the islet of
Arawe. Although it had a limited purpose—
disrupting the movement of motorized barges
and other small craft that moved men and
supplies along the southern coast of New
Britain and diverting attention from Cape
Gloucester—it nevertheless encountered stiff
resistance. Marine amphibian tractor crews
used both the new, armored Buffalo and the
older, slower, and more vulnerable Alligator to
carry soldiers of the 112th Cavalry, who made
the main landings on Orange Beach at the
western edge of Cape Merkus. Fire from the
destroyer USS Conyngham, supplemented by
rocket-equipped DUKWs and a submarine
chaser that doubled as a control craft, and a
last-minute bombing by B-25s silenced the
beach defenses and enabled the Buffaloes to
crush the surviving Japanese machine guns
that survived the naval and aerial
bombardment. Less successful were two
diversionary landings by soldiers paddling
ashore in rubber boats. Savage fire forced one
group to turn back short of its objective east
of Orange Beach, but the other gained a
lodgment on Pilelo Island and killed the
handful of Japanese found there. An enemy

airman had reported that the assault force was approaching Cape Merkus, and fighters and bombers from Rabaul attacked within two hours of the landing. Sporadic air strikes continued throughout December, although with diminishing ferocity, and the Japanese shifted troops to meet the threat in the south.

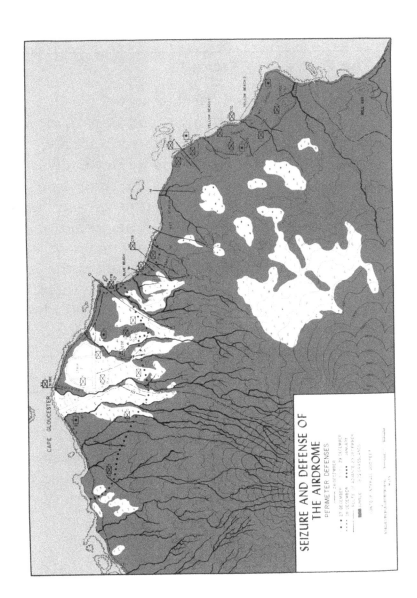

The Fortress of Rabaul

Located on Simpson Harbor at the northeastern tip of New Britain, Rabaul served as an air and naval base and troop staging area for Japanese conquests in New Guinea and the Solomon Islands. As the advancing Japanese approached New Britain, Australian authorities, who administered the former German colony under terms of a mandate from the League of Nations, evacuated the Australian women and children living there. These dependents had already departed when the enemy landed on 23 January 1942, capturing Rabaul by routing the defenders, some of whom escaped into the jungle to become coastwatchers providing intelligence for the Allies. The Australian coastwatchers, many of them former planters or prewar administrators, reported by radio on Japanese strength and movements before the invasion and afterward attached themselves to the Marines, sometimes recruiting guides and bearers from among the native populace.

Once the enemy had seized Rabaul, he set to work converting it into a major installation, improving harbor facilities, building airfields and barracks, and bringing in hundreds of thousands of soldiers, sailors, and airmen, who either passed through the base enroute to operations elsewhere or stayed there to defend it. Rabaul thus became the dominant objective of General Douglas MacArthur, who escaped from the Philippines in March 1942 and assumed command of the Southwest Pacific Area. MacArthur proposed a two-pronged advance on the fortress, bombing it from the air while amphibious forces closed in by way of eastern New Guinea and the Solomon Islands.

Even as the Allies began closing the pincers on Rabaul, the basic strategy changed. Despite MacArthur's opposition, the American Joint Chiefs of Staff decided to bypass the stronghold, a strategy confirmed by the Anglo-American Combined Chiefs of Staff during the Quadrant Conference at Quebec in August 1943. As a result, Rabaul itself would remain in Japanese hands for the remainder of the war, though the Allies controlled the rest of New Britain.

The other secondary landing took place on the morning of 26 December. The 1,500-man Stoneface Group—designated Battalion Landing Team 21 and built around the 2d Battalion, 1st Marines, under Lieutenant Colonel James M. Masters, Sr.—started toward Green Beach, supported by 5-inch gunfire from the American destroyers Reid and Smith. LCMs [Landing Craft, Medium] carried DUKW amphibian trucks, driven by soldiers and fitted with rocket launchers. The DUKWs opened fire from the landing craft as the assault force approached the beach, performing the same function as the rocket-firing LCIs at the Yellow Beaches on the opposite side of the peninsula. The first wave landed at 0748, with two others following it ashore. The Marines encountered no opposition as they carved out a beachhead 1,200 yards wide and extending 500 yards inland. The Stoneface Group had the mission of severing the coastal trail that passed just west of Mount Talawe, thus preventing the passage of reinforcements to the Cape Gloucester airfields.

The trail net proved difficult to find and follow. Villagers cleared garden plots, tilled them until the jungle reclaimed them, and then abandoned the land and moved on, leaving a maze of trails, some faint and others fresh, that led nowhere. The Japanese were slow, however, to take advantage of the confusion caused by the tangle of paths. Not until the early hours of 30 December, did the enemy attack the Green Beach force. Taking advantage of heavy rain that muffled sounds and reduced visibility, the Japanese closed with the Marines, who called down mortar fire within 15 yards of their defensive wire. A battery of the 11th Marines, reorganized as an infantry unit because the cannoneers could not find suitable positions for their 75mm howitzers, shored up the defenses.

Marines man a .75 MM gun

One Marine in particular, Gunnery Sergeant Guiseppe Guilano, Jr., seemed to materialize at critical moments, firing a light machine gun from the hip; his heroism earned him the Navy Cross. Some of the Japanese succeeded in penetrating the position, but a counterattack led by First Lieutenant Jim G. Paulos of Company G killed them or drove them off. The savage fighting cost Combat

Team 21 six Marines killed and 17 wounded; at least 89 Japanese perished, and five surrendered. On 11 January 1944, the reinforced battalion set out to rejoin the division, the troops moving overland, the heavy equipment and the wounded traveling in landing craft.

MacArthur's Marines

After the fierce battles at Guadalcanal in the South Pacific Area, the 1st Marine Division underwent rehabilitation in Australia, which lay within General MacArthur's Southwest Pacific Area. Once the division had recovered from the ordeal of the Solomon Islands fighting, it gave MacArthur a trained amphibious unit that he desperately needed to fulfill his ambitions for the capture of Rabaul. Theoretically, the 1st Marine Division was subordinate to General Sir Thomas Blamey, the Australian officer in command of the Allied Land Forces, and Blamey's nominal subordinate, Lieutenant General Walter Kreuger, commanding the Sixth U.S. Army. But in actual practice, MacArthur bypassed Blamey and dealt directly with Kreuger.

During the planning of the New Britain operation, Gen Douglas MacArthur, right, in command of the Southwest Pacific Area, confers with LtGen Walter Kreuger, left, Commanding General, Sixth U.S. Army, and MajGen Rupertus, whose Marines will assault the island. At such a meeting, Cal Edwin A. Pollock, operations officer of the 1st Marine Division,

advised MacArthur of the opposition of the Marine leaders to a complex scheme of maneuver involving Army airborne troops. Department of Defense (USMC) photo 75882

When the 1st Marine Division became available to MacArthur, he still intended to seize Rabaul and break the back of Japanese resistance in the region. Always concerned about air cover for his amphibious operations, MacArthur planned to use the Marines to capture the airfields at Cape Gloucester. Aircraft based there would then support the division when, after a brief period of recuperation, it attacked Rabaul. The decision to bypass Rabaul eliminated the landings there, but the Marines would nevertheless seize the Cape Gloucester airfields, which seemed essential for neutralizing the base.

The initial concept of operations, which called for the conquest of western New Britain preliminary to storming Rabaul, split the 1st Marine Division, sending Combat Team A (the 5th Marines, reinforced, less one battalion in reserve) against Gasmata on the southern coast of the island, while Combat Team C (the 7th Marines, reinforced) seized a beachhead near the principal objective, the airfields on Cape Gloucester. The Army's 503d Parachute Infantry would exploit the Cape Gloucester beachhead, while Combat Team B (the reinforced 1st Marines) provided a reserve for the operation.

Revisions came swiftly, and by late October 1943 the plan no longer mentioned capturing Rabaul, tacit acceptance of the modified Allied strategy, and also satisfied an objection raised by General Rupertus. The division commander had protested splitting Combat Team C, and Kreuger agreed to employ all three battalions for the main assault, substituting a battalion from Combat Team B, the 1st Marines, for the landing on the west coast. The air borne landing at Cape Gloucester remained in the plan, however, even though Rupertus had warned that bad weather could delay the drop and jeopardize the Marine battalions already fighting ashore. The altered version earmarked Army troops for the landing on the southern coast, which Kreuger's staff shifted from Gasmata to Arawe, a site closer to Allied airfields and farther from Rabaul with its troops and aircraft. Although Combat Team B would put one battalion ashore southwest of the airfields, the remaining two battalions of the 1st Marines were to follow up the assault on Cape Gloucester by Combat Team C. The division reserve, Combat Team A, might employ elements of the 5th Marines to reinforce the Cape Gloucester landings or conduct operations against the offshore islands west of New Britain.

During a routine briefing on 14 December, just one day before the landings at Arawe, MacArthur off handedly asked how the Marines felt about the scheme of maneuver at Cape Gloucester. Colonel Edwin A. Pollock, the division's operations officer, seized the opportunity and declared that the Marines objected to the plan because it depended on a rapid advance inland by a single reinforced regiment to prevent heavy losses among the lightly armed paratroops. Better, he believed, to strengthen the amphibious forces than to try for an aerial envelopment that might fail or be delayed by the weather. Although he made no comment at the time, MacArthur may well have heeded what Pollock said; whatever the reason, Kreuger's staff eliminated the airborne portion, directed the two battalions of the 1st Marines still with Combat Team B to land immediately after the assault waves, sustaining the momentum of their attack, and alerted the division reserve to provide further reinforcement.

The Japanese in Western New Britain

A mixture of combat and service troops operated in western New Britain. The 1st and

8th Shipping Regiments used motorized barges to shuttle troops and cargo along the coast from Rabaul to Cape Merkus, Cape Gloucester, and across Dampier Strait to Rooke Island. For longer movements, for example to New Guinea, the 5th Sea Transport Battalion manned a fleet of trawlers and schooners, supplemented by destroyers of the Imperial Japanese Navy when speed seemed essential. The troops actually defending western New Britain included the Matsuda Force, established in September 1943 under the command of Major General Iwao Matsuda, a specialist in military transportation, who nevertheless had commanded an infantry regiment in Manchuria. When he arrived on New Britain in February of that year, Matsuda took over the 4th Shipping Command, an administrative headquarters that provided staff officers for the Matsuda Force. His principal combat units were the under-strength 65th Infantry Brigade—consisting of the 141st Infantry, battle-tested in the conquest of the Philippines, plus artillery and antiaircraft units—and those components of the 51st Division not committed to the unsuccessful defense of New Guinea. Matsuda established the headquarters for his jury-rigged force near Kalingi, along the coastal trail northwest of Mount Talawe, within five miles of the Cape Gloucester airfields, but the location would change to reflect the tactical situation.

As the year 1943 wore on, the Allied threat to New Britain increased. Consequently, General Hitoshi Imamura, who commanded the Eighth Area Army from a headquarters at Rabaul, assigned the Matsuda Force to the 17th Division, under Lieutenant General Yasushi Sakai, recently arrived from Shanghai. Four convoys were to have carried Sakai's division, but the second and third lost one ship to submarine torpedoes and another to a mine, while air attack damaged a third. Because of these losses, which claimed some 1,200 lives, the last convoy did not sail, depriving the division of more than 3,000 replacements and service troops. Sakai deployed the best of his forces to western New Britain, entrusting them to Matsuda's tactical command.

Establishing the Beachhead

The landings at Cape Merkus in mid-December caused Matsuda to shift his troops to meet the threat, but this redeployment did not account for the lack of resistance at the Yellow Beaches. The Japanese general, familiar with the terrain of western New Britain, did not believe that the Americans would storm these strips of sand extending only a few yards inland and backed by swamp. Matsuda might have thought differently had he seen the American maps, which labeled the area beyond the beaches as "damp flat," even though aerial photographs taken after preliminary air strikes had revealed no shadow within the bomb craters, evidence of a water level high enough to fill these depressions to the brim. Since the airfields were the obvious prize, Matsuda did not believe that the Marines would plunge into the muck and risk becoming bogged down short of their goal.

Marines, almost invisible amid the undergrowth, advance through the swamp forest of New Britain, optimistically called damp flat on the maps they used. Department of Defense (USMC) photo 72833

Besides forfeiting the immediate advantage of opposing the assault force at the water's edge, Matsuda's troops suffered the long-term, indirect effects of the erosion of Japanese fortunes that began at Guadalcanal and on New Guinea and continued at New Georgia and Bougainville. The Allies, in addition, dominated the skies over New

Britain, blunting the air attacks on the Cape Merkus beachhead and bombing almost at will throughout the island. Although air strikes caused little measurable damage, save at Rabaul, they demoralized the defenders, who already suffered shortages of supplies and medicine because of air and submarine attacks on seagoing convoys and coastal shipping. An inadequate network of primitive trails, which tended to hug the coastline, increased Matsuda's dependence on barges, but this traffic, hampered by the American capture of Cape Merkus, proved vulnerable to aircraft and later to torpedo craft and improvised gunboats.

The two battalions that landed on the Yellow Beaches—Weber's on the left and Williams's on the right—crossed the sands in a few strides, and plunged through a wall of undergrowth into the damp flat, where a Marine might be slogging through knee-deep mud, step into a hole, and end up, as one on them said, "damp up to your neck." A counterattack delivered as the assault waves wallowed through the damp flat might have inflicted severe casualties, but Matsuda lacked the vehicles or roads to shift his troops in time to exploit the terrain. Although immobile on the ground, the Japanese retaliated by air. American radar detected a flight of enemy aircraft approaching from Rabaul; Army Air Forces P-38s intercepted, but a few Japanese bombers evaded the fighters, sank the destroyer Brownson with two direct hits, and damaged another.

The first enemy bombers arrived as a squadron of Army B-25s flew over the LSTs [Landing Ships, Tank] enroute to attack targets at Borgen Bay south of the Yellow Beaches. Gunners on board the ships opened fire at the aircraft milling overhead, mistaking friend for foe, downing two American bombers, and damaging two others. The survivors, shaken by the experience, dropped their bombs too soon, hitting the artillery positions of the 11th Marines at the left flank of Yellow Beach 1, killing one and wounding 14 others. A battalion commander in the artillery regiment recalled "trying to dig a hole with my nose, as the bombs exploded, "trying to get down into the ground just a little bit further."

The Jungle Battlefield

On New Britain, the 1st Marine Division fought weather and terrain, along with a determined Japanese enemy. Rains brought by seasonal monsoons seemed to fall with the velocity of a fire hose, soaking everyone, sending streams from their banks, and turning trails into quagmire. The terrain of the volcanic island varied from coastal plain to mountains that rose as high as 7,000 feet above sea level. A variety of forest covered the island, punctuated by patches of grassland, a few large coconut plantations, and garden plots near the scattered villages.

Much of the fighting, especially during the early days, raged in swamp forest, sometimes erroneously described as damp flat. The swamp forest consisted of scattered trees growing as high as a hundred feet from a plain that remained flooded throughout the rainy season, if not for the entire year. Tangled roots buttressed the towering trees, but could not anchor them against gale-force winds, while vines and undergrowth reduced visibility on the flooded surface to a few yards.

No less formidable was the second kind of vegetation, the mangrove forest, where massive trees grew from brackish water deposited at high tide. Mangrove trees varied in height from 20 to 60 feet, with a visible tangle of thick roots deploying as high as ten feet up the trunk and holding the tree solidly in place. Beneath the mangrove canopy, the maze of roots, wandering streams, and standing water impeded movement. Visibility did not exceed 15 yards.

Both swamp forest and mangrove forest grew at sea level. A third form of vegetation, the true tropical rain forest, flourished at higher altitude. Different varieties of trees formed an impenetrable double canopy overhead, but the surface itself remained generally open, except for low-growing ferns or shrubs, an occasional thicket of bamboo or rattan, and tangles of vines. Although a Marine walking beneath the canopy could see a standing man as far as 50 yards away, a prone rifleman might remain invisible at a distance of just ten yards.

Only one of the three remaining kinds of vegetation seriously impeded military action. Second-growth forest, which often took over abandoned garden tracts, forced patrolling Marines to hack paths through the small trees, brush and vines. Grasslands posed a lesser problem; though the vegetation grew tall enough to conceal the Japanese defenders, it provided comparatively easy going for the Marines, unless the grass turned out to be wild sugar cane, with thick stalks that grew to a height of 15 feet. Cultivated tracts, whether coconut plantations or gardens, posed few obstacles to vision or movement.

By the time of the air action on the afternoon of D-Day, the 1st Marine Division had already established a beachhead. The assault battalions of the 7th Marines initially pushed ahead, capturing Target Hill on the left flank, and then paused to await reinforcements. During the day, two more battalions arrived. The 3d Battalion, 1st Marines—designated Landing Team 31 and led by Lieutenant Colonel Joseph F. Hankins, a Reserve officer who also was a crack shooter—came ashore at 0815 on Yellow Beach 1, passed through the 3d Battalion, 7th Marines, and veered to the northwest to lead the way toward the airfields. By 0845, the 2d Battalion, 7th Marines, under Lieutenant Colonel Odell M. Conoley, landed and began wading through the damp flat to take its place between the regiment's 1st and 3d Battalions as the beachhead expanded. The next infantry unit, the 1st Battalion, 1st Marines, reached Yellow Beach 1 at 1300 to join that regiment's 3d Battalion, commanded by Hankins, in advancing on the airfields. The 11th Marines, despite the accidental bombing, set up its artillery, an operation in which the amphibian tractor played a vital part. Some of the tractors brought lightweight 75mm howitzers from the LSTs directly to the battery firing positions; others broke trail through the undergrowth for tractors pulling the heavier 105mm weapons. Meanwhile, Army trucks loaded with supplies rolled ashore from the LSTs. Logistics plans called for these vehicles to move forward and function as mobile supply dumps, but the damp flat proved impassable by wheeled vehicles, and the drivers tended to abandon the trucks to avoid being left behind when the shipping moved out, hurried along by the threat from Japanese bombers. Ultimately, Marines had to build roads, corduroying them with logs when necessary, or shift the cargo to amphibian tractors. Despite careful planning and hard work on D-Day, the convoy sailed with about 100 tons of supplies still on board.

As the predicament of this truck and its Marine driver demonstrates, wheeled vehicles, like those supplied by the Army for mobile supply dumps, bog down in the mud of Cape Gloucester. Department of Defense (USMC) photo

While reinforcements and cargo crossed the beach, the Marines advancing inland encountered the first serious Japanese resistance. Shortly after 1000 on 26 December, Hankns's 3d Battalion, 1st Marines, pushed ahead, advancing in a column of companies because a swamp on the left narrowed the frontage. Fire from camouflaged bunkers killed Captain Joseph

A. Terzi, commander of Company K, posthumously awarded the Navy Cross for heroism while leading the attack, and his executive officer, Captain Philip A. Wilheit. The sturdy bunkers proved impervious to bazooka rockets, which failed to detonate in the soft earth covering the structures, and to fire from 37mm guns, which could not penetrate the logs protecting the occupants. An Alligator that had delivered supplies for Company K tried to crush one of the bunkers but became wedged between two trees. Japanese riflemen burst from cover and killed the tractor's two machine gunners, neither of them protected by armor, before the driver could break free. Again lunging ahead, the tractor caved in one bunker, silencing its fire and enabling Marine riflemen to isolate three others and destroy them in succession, killing 25 Japanese. A platoon of M4 Sherman tanks joined the company in time to lead the advance beyond this first strongpoint.

Japanese service troops—especially the men of the 1st Shipping Engineers and the 1st Debarkation Unit—provided most of the initial opposition, but Matsuda had alerted his nearby infantry units to converge on the beachhead. One enemy battalion, under Major Shinichi Takabe, moved into position late on the afternoon of D-Day, opposite Conoley's 2d Battalion, 7th Marines, which clung to a crescent-shaped position, both of its flanks sharply refused and resting on the marshland to the rear. After sunset, the darkness beneath the forest canopy became absolute, pierced only by muzzle flashes as the intensity of the firing increased.

On D-Day, among the shadows on the jungle floor, Navy corpsmen administer emergency treatment to a wounded Marine. Department of Defense (USMC) photo 69009

The Japanese clearly were preparing to counterattack. Conoley's battalion had a dwindling supply of ammunition, but amphibian tractors could not begin making supply runs until it became light enough for the drivers to avoid tree roots and fallen trunks as they navigated the damp flat. To aid the battalion in the dangerous period before the skies grew pale, Lieutenant Colonel Lewis B. Puller, the executive officer of the 7th Marines, organized the men of the regimental Headquarters and Service Company into carrying parties to load themselves down with ammunition and wade through the dangerous swamp. One misstep, and a Marine burdened with bandoliers of rifle ammunition or containers of mortar shells could stumble and drown. When Colonel Frisbie, the regimental commander, decided to reinforce Conoley's Marines with Battery D, 1st Special Weapons Battalion, Puller had the men leave their 37mm guns behind and carry ammunition instead. A guide from Conoley's headquarters met the column that Puller had pressed into service and began leading them forward, when a blinding downpour, driven by a monsoon gale, obscured landmarks and forced the heavily laden Marines to wade blindly onward, each man clinging to the belt of the one ahead of him. Not until 0805, some twelve hours after the column started off, did the men reach their goal, put down their loads, and take up their rifles.

Conoley's Marines had in the meantime been fighting for their lives since the storm first struck. A curtain of rain prevented mortar crews from seeing their aiming stakes, indeed, the battalion commander described the men as firing "by guess and by God." Mud got on the small-arms ammunition, at times jamming rifles and machine guns. Although forced to abandon water-filled foxholes, the defenders hung on. With the coming of dawn, Takabe's soldiers gravitated toward the right flank of Conoley's unit, perhaps in a conscious effort to outflank the position, or possibly forced in that direction by the fury of the battalion's defensive fire. An envelopment was in the making when Battery D arrived and moved into the threatened area, forcing the Japanese to break off the action and regroup.

The stumps of trees shattered by artillery and the seemingly bottomless mud can sometimes stymie even an LVT. Department of Defense (USMC) photo 72599

The Capture of the Cape Gloucester Airfields

The 1st Marine Division's overall plan of maneuver called for Colonel Frisbie's Combat Team C, the reinforced 7th Marines, to hold a beach head anchored at Target Hill, while Combat Team B, Colonel William A. Whaling's 1st Marines, reinforced but without the 2d Battalion ashore at Green Beach, advanced on the airfields. Because of the buildup in preparation for the attack on

Conoley's battalion, General Rupertus requested that Kreuger release the division reserve, Combat Team A, Colonel John T. Selden's reinforced 5th Marines. The Army general agreed, sending the 1st and 2d Battalions, followed a day later by the 3d Battalion. The division commander decided to land the team on Blue Beach, roughly three miles to the right of the Yellow Beaches. The use of Blue Beach would have placed the 5th Marines closer to Cape Gloucester and the airfields, but not every element of Selden's Combat Team A got the word. Some units touched down on the Yellow Beaches instead and had to move on foot or in vehicles to the intended destination.

While Rupertus laid plans to commit the reserve, Whaling's combat team advanced toward the Cape Gloucester airfields. The Marines encountered only sporadic resistance at first, but Army Air Forces light bombers spotted danger in their path—a maze of trenches and bunkers stretching inland from a promontory that soon earned the nickname Hell's Point. The Japanese had built these defenses to protect the beaches where Matsuda expected the Americans to land. Leading the advance, the 3d Battalion, 1st Marines, under Lieutenant Colonel Hankins, struck the Hell's Point position on the flank, rather than head-on, but overrunning the complex nevertheless would prove a deadly task.

Rain and Biting Insects

Driven by monsoon winds, the rain that screened the attack on Conoley's 2d Battalion, 7th Marines, drenched the entire island and everyone on it. At the front, the deluge flooded foxholes, and conditions were only marginally better at the rear, where some men slept in jungle hammocks slung between two trees. A Marine entered his hammock through an opening in a mosquito net, lay down on a length of rubberized cloth, and zipped the net shut. Above him, also enclosed in the netting, stretched a rubberized cover designed to shelter him from rain. Unfortunately, a gale as fierce as the one that began blowing on the night of D-Day set the cover to flapping like a loose sail and drove the rain inside the hammock. In the darkness, a gust of wind might uproot a tree, weakened by flooding or the effect of the preparatory bombardment, and send it crashing down. A falling tree toppled onto a hammock occupied by one of the Marines, who would have drowned if someone had not slashed through the covering with a knife and set him free.

The rain, said Lieutenant Colonel Lewis J. Fields, a battalion commander in the 11th Marines, resembled "a waterfall pouring down on you, and it goes on and on." The first deluge lasted five days, and recurring storms persisted for another two weeks. Wet uniforms never really dried, and the men suffered continually from fungus infections, the so-called jungle rot, which readily developed into open sores. Mosquito-borne malaria threatened the health of the Marines, who also had to contend with other insects—"little black ants, little red ants, big red ants," on an island where "even the caterpillars bite." The Japanese may have suffered even more because of shortages of medicine and difficulty in distributing what was available, but this was scant consolation to Marines beset by discomfort and disease. By the end of January 1944, disease or non-battle injuries forced the evacuation of more than a thousand Marines; more than one in ten had already returned to duty on New Britain.

The island's swamps and jungles would have been ordeal enough without the wind, rain, and disease. At times, the embattled Marines could see no more than a few feet ahead of them. Movement verged on the impossible, especially where the rains had flooded the land or turned the volcanic soil into slippery mud. No wonder that the Assistant Division Commander, Brigadier General Lemuel C. Shepherd, Jr., compared the New Britain campaign to "Grant's fight though the Wilderness in the Civil War."

oding caused by the monsoon deluge makes life serable even in the comparative comfort of the ar areas. Department of Defense (USMC) photo 463

Rupertus delayed the attack by Hankins to provide time for the division reserve, Selden's 5th Marines, to come ashore. On the morning of 28 December, after a bombardment by the 2d Battalion, 11th Marines, and strikes by Army Air Forces A-20s, the assault troops encountered another delay, waiting for an hour so that an additional platoon of M4 Sherman medium tanks could increase the weight of the attack. At 1100, Hankins's 3d Battalion, 1st Marines, moved ahead, Company I and the supporting tanks leading the way. Whaling, at about the same time, sent his regiment's Company A through swamp and jungle to seize the inland point of the ridge extending from Hell's Point. Despite the obstacles in its path, Company A burst from the jungle at about 1145 and advanced across a field of tall grass until stopped by intense Japanese fire. By late afternoon, Whaling abandoned the maneuver. Both Company A and the defenders were exhausted and short of ammunition; the Marines withdrew behind a barrage fired by the 2d Battalion, 11th Marines, and the Japanese abandoned their positions after dark.

Roughly 15 minutes after Company A assaulted the inland terminus of the ridge, Company I and the attached tanks collided with the main defenses, which the Japanese had modified since the 26 December landings, cutting new gunports in bunkers, hacking fire lanes in the undergrowth, and shifting men and weapons to oppose an attack along the coastal trail parallel to shore instead of over the beach. Advancing in a drenching rain, the Marines encountered a succession of jungle covered, mutually supporting positions protected by barbed wire and mines. The hour's wait for tanks paid dividends, as the Shermans, protected by riflemen, crushed bunkers and destroyed the weapons inside. During the fight, Company I drifted to its left, and Hankins used Company K, reinforced with a platoon of medium tanks, to close the gap between the coastal track and Hell's Point itself. This unit employed the same tactics as Company I. A rifle squad followed each of the M4 tanks, which cracked open the bunkers, twelve in all, and fired inside; the accompanying riflemen then killed anyone attempting to fight or flee. More than 260 Japanese perished in the fighting at Hell's Point, at the cost of 9 Marines killed and 36 wounded.

A 75mm pack howitzer of the 11th Marines fires in support of the advance on the Cape Gloucester airfields. Department of Defense (USMC) photo 12203

With the defenses of Hell's Point shattered, the two battalions of the 5th Marines, which came ashore on the morning of 29 December, joined later that day in the advance on the airfield. The 1st Battalion, commanded by Major William H. Barba, and the 2d Battalion, under Lieutenant Colonel Lewis H. Walt, moved out in a column, Barba's unit leading the way. In front of the Marines lay a swamp, described as only a few inches deep, but the depth, because of the continuing downpour, proved as much as five feet, "making it quite hard," Selden acknowledged, "for some of the youngsters who were not much more than 5 feet in height." The time lost in wading through the swamp delayed the attack, and the leading elements chose a piece of open and comparatively dry ground, where they established a perimeter while the rest of the force caught up.

Meanwhile, the 1st Battalion, 1st Marines, attacking through that regiment's 3d Battalion, encountered only scattered resistance, mainly sniper fire, as it pushed along the coast beyond Hell's Point. Half-tracks carrying 75mm guns, medium tanks, artillery, and even a pair of rocket-firing DUKWs supported the advance, which brought the battalion, commanded by Lieutenant Colonel Walker A. Reaves, to the edge of Airfield No. 2. When daylight faded on 29 December, the 1st Battalion, 1st Marines, held a line extending inland from the coast; on its left were the 3d Battalion, 1st Marines, and the 2d Battalion, 5th Marines, forming a semicircle around the airfield.

The Japanese officer responsible for defending the airfields, Colonel Kouki Sumiya of the 53d Infantry, had fallen back on 29 December, trading space for time as he gathered his surviving troops for the defense of Razorback Hill, a ridge running diagonally across the southwestern approaches to Airfield No. 2. The 1st and 2d Battalions, 5th Marines, attacked on 30 December supported by tanks and artillery. Sumiya's troops had constructed some sturdy bunkers, but the chest-high grass that covered Razorback Hill did not impede the attackers like the jungle at Hell's Point. The Japanese fought gallantly to hold the position, at times stalling the advancing Marines, but the defenders had neither the numbers nor the firepower to prevail. Typical of the day's fighting, one platoon of Company F from Selden's regiment beat back two separate banzai attacks, before tanks enabled the Marines to shatter the bunkers in their path and kill the enemy within. By dusk on 30 December, the landing force had overrun the defenses of the airfields, and at noon of the following day General Rupertus had the American flag raised beside the wreckage of a Japanese bomber at Airfield No. 2, the larger of the airstrips.

On 31 December 1943, the American flag rises beside the wreckage of a Japanese bomber after the capture of Airfield No. 2, five days after the 1st Marine Division landed on New Britain. Department of Defense (USMC) photo 71589

The 1st Marine Division thus seized the principal objective of the Cape Gloucester fighting, but the airstrips proved of marginal value to the Allied forces. Indeed, the Japanese had already abandoned the prewar facility, Airfield No. 1, which was thickly overgrown with tall, coarse kunai grass. Craters from American bombs pockmarked the surface of Airfield No. 2, and after its capture Japanese hit-and-run raiders added a few of their own, despite antiaircraft fire from the 12th Defense Battalion. Army aviation engineers worked around the clock to return Airfield No. 2 to operation, a task that took until the end of January 1944. Army aircraft based here defended against air attacks for as long as Rabaul remained an active air base and also supported operations on the ground.

Clearing the Shores of Borgen Bay

While General Rupertus personally directed the capture of the air fields, the Assistant Division Commander, Brigadier General Lemuel C. Shepherd, Jr., came ashore on D-Day, 26 December, and took command of the beachhead. Besides coordinating the logistics activity there, Shepherd assumed responsibility for expanding the perimeter to the southwest and securing the shores of Borgen Bay. He had a variety of shore party, engineer, transportation, and other service troops to handle the logistics chores. The 3d Battalion of Colonel Selden's 5th Marines—

the remaining component of the division reserve—arrived on 30 and 31 December to help the 7th Marines enlarge the beachhead.

During operations to clear the enemy from the shores of Borgen Bay, BGen Lemuel C. Shepherd, Jr., (left) the assistant division commander, confers with Col John T. Selden, in command of the 5th Marines. Department of Defense (USA) photo SC 188250

Shepherd had sketchy knowledge of
Japanese deployment west and south of the
Yellow Beaches. Dense vegetation concealed
streams, swamps, and even ridge lines, as
well as bunkers and trenches. The progress
toward the airfields seemed to indicate
Japanese weakness in that area and possible
strength in the vicinity of the Yellow Beaches
and Borgen Bay. To resolve the uncertainty
about the enemy's numbers and intentions,
Shepherd issued orders on 1 January 1944
to probe Japanese defenses beginning the
following morning.

In the meantime, the Japanese defenders,
under Colonel Kenshiro Katayama,
commander of the 141st Infantry, were
preparing for an attack of their own. General
Matsuda entrusted three reinforced
battalions to Katayama, who intended to hurl
them against Target Hill, which he considered
the anchor of the beachhead line. Since
Matsuda believed that roughly 2,500 Marines
were ashore on New Britain, 10 percent of the
actual total, Katayama's force seemed strong
enough for the job assigned it.

Katayama needed time to gather his strength,
enabling Shepherd to make the first move,
beginning at mid-morning on 2 January to
realign his forces. The 1st Battalion, 7th
Marines, stood fast in the vicinity of Target

Hill, the 2d Battalion remained in place along
a stream already known as Suicide Creek,
and the regiment's 3d Battalion began
pivoting to face generally south. Meanwhile,
the 3d Battalion, 5th Marines, pushed into
the jungle to come abreast of the 3d
Battalion, 7th Marines, on the inland flank.
As the units pivoted, they had to cross
Suicide Creek in order to squeeze out the 2d
Battalion, 7th Marines, which would become
Shepherd's reserve.

The change of direction proved extremely
difficult in vegetation so thick that, in the
words of one Marine: "You'd step from your
line, take say ten paces, and turn around to
guide on your buddy. And nobody there I
can tell you, it was a very small war, and a
very lonely business." The Japanese
defenders, moreover, had dug in south of
Suicide Creek, and from these positions they
repulsed every attempt to cross the stream
that day. A stalemate ensued, as Seabees
from Company C, 17th Marines, built a
corduroy road through the damp flat behind
the Yellow Beaches so that tanks could move
forward to punch through the defenses of
Suicide Creek.

Marines and Seabees struggle to build a corduroy road leading inland from the beachhead. Without the log surface trucks and tanks cannot advance over trails turned into quagmire by the unceasing rain. Department of Defense (USMC) photo 69013

While the Marine advance stalled at Suicide Creek, awaiting the arrival of tanks, Katayama attacked Target Hill. On the night of 2 January, taking advantage of the darkness, Japanese infantry cut steps in the lower slopes so the troops could climb more easily. Instead of reconnoitering the thinly held lines of Company A, 7th Marines, and trying to infiltrate, the enemy followed a preconceived plan to the letter, advanced up the steps, and at midnight stormed the strongest of the company's defenses.

Japanese mortar barrages fired to soften the defenses and screen the approach could not conceal the sound of the troops working their way up the hill, and the Marines were ready. Although the Japanese supporting fire proved generally inaccurate, one round scored a direct hit on a machine-gun position, killing two Marines and wounding the gunner, who kept firing the weapon until someone else could take over. This gun fired some 5,000 rounds and helped blunt the Japanese thrust, which ended by dawn of 3 January. Nowhere did the Japanese crack the lines of the 1st Battalion, 7th Marines, or loosen its grip on Target Hill.

The body of a Japanese officer killed at Target Hill yielded documents that cast new light on the Japanese defenses south of Suicide Creek. A crudely drawn map revealed the existence of Aogiri Ridge, an enemy strongpoint unknown to General Shepherd's intelligence section. Observers on Target Hill tried to locate the ridge and the trail network the enemy was using, but the jungle canopy frustrated their efforts.

Target Hill, where the Marines repulsed a Japanese counterattack on the night of 2-3 January, dominates the Yellow Beaches, the site of the main landings on 26 December. Department of Defense (USMC) photo 72292

While the Marines on Target Hill tabulated the results of the fighting there—patrols discovered 40 bodies, and captured documents, when translated, listed 46 Japanese killed, 54 wounded, and two missing—and used field glasses to scan the jungle south of Suicide Creek, the 17th Marines completed the road that would enable medium tanks to test the defenses of that stream. During the afternoon of 3 January, a trio of Sherman tanks reached the creek only to discover that the bank dropped off too sharply for them to negotiate. The engineers sent for a bulldozer, which arrived, lowered its blade, and began gouging at the lip of the embankment. Realizing the danger if tanks succeeded in crossing the creek, the Japanese opened fire on the bulldozer, wounding the driver. A volunteer climbed onto the exposed driver's seat and took over until he, too, was wounded. Another Marine stepped forward, but instead of climbing onto the machine, he walked along side, using its bulk for cover as he manipulated the controls with a shovel and an axe handle. By dark, he had finished the job of converting the impassable bank into a readily negotiated ramp.

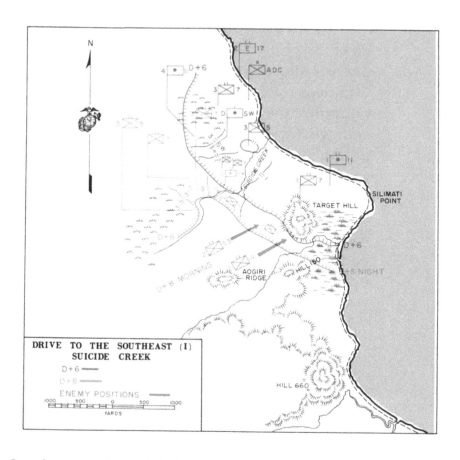

DRIVE TO THE SOUTHEAST (I)
SUICIDE CREEK

D+6 ━━━
D+8 ━━━
ENEMY POSITIONS ━━━

On the morning of 4 January, the first tank clanked down the ramp and across the stream. As the Sherman emerged on the other side, Marine riflemen cut down two Japanese soldiers trying to detonate magnetic mines against its sides. Other medium tanks followed, also accompanied by infantry, and broke open the bunkers that barred the way. The 3d Battalion, 7th Marines, and the 3d Battalion, 5th Marines, surged onward past the creek, squeezing out the 2d Battalion, 7th Marines, which crossed in the wake of those two units to come abreast of them on the far right of the line that closed in on the jungle concealing Aogiri Ridge. The 1st Battalion, 7th Marines, thereupon joined the southward advance, tying in with the 3d Battalion, 5th Marines, to present a four-battalion front that included the 2d Battalion and 3d Battalions, 7th Marines.

Once across Suicide Creek, the Marines groped for Aogiri Ridge, which for a time simply seemed to be another name for Hill 150, a terrain feature that appeared on American maps. The advance rapidly overran the hill, but Japanese resistance in the vicinity did not diminish. On 7 January, enemy fire wounded Lieutenant Colonel David S. MacDougal, commanding officer of the 3d Battalion, 5th Marines. His executive officer, Major Joseph Skoczylas, took over until he, too, was wounded. Lieutenant Colonel Lewis B. Puller, temporarily in command of the 3d Battalion, 7th Marines, assumed responsibility for both battalions until the arrival on the morning of 8 January of Lieutenant Colonel Lewis W. Walt, recently assigned as executive officer of the 5th Marines, who took over the regiment's 3d Battalion.

From Hell's Point, athwart the route to the airfields, to Suicide Creek near the Yellow Beaches, medium tanks and infantry team up to shatter the enemy's log and earthen bunkers. Dept. of Defense (USMC) photo 72283

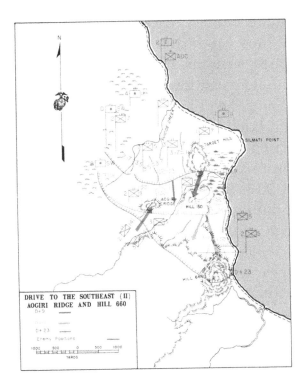

DRIVE TO THE SOUTHEAST (II)
AOGIRI RIDGE AND HILL 660

Upon assuming command of the battalion, Walt continued the previous day's attack. As his Marines braved savage fire and thick jungle, they began moving up a rapidly steepening slope. As night approached, the battalion formed a perimeter and dug in. Random Japanese fire and sudden skirmishes punctuated the darkness. The nature of the terrain and the determined resistance convinced Walt that he had found Aogiri Ridge.

Walt's battalion needed the shock action and firepower of tanks, but drenching rain, mud, and rampaging streams stopped the armored vehicles. The heaviest weapon that the Marines managed to bring forward was a single 37mm gun, manhandled into position on the afternoon of 9 January, While the 11th Marines hammered the crest of Aogiri Ridge, the 1st and 3d Battalions, 7th Marines, probed the flanks of the position and Walt's 3d Battalion, 5th Marines, pushed ahead in the center, seizing a narrow segment of the slope, its apex just short of the crest. By dusk, said the 1st Marine Division's special action report, Walt's men had "reached the limit of their physical endurance and morale was low. It was a question of whether or not they could hold their hard-earned gains." The crew of the 37mm gun opened fire in support of the afternoon's final attack, but after just three rounds, four of the nine men handling the weapon were killed or wounded. Walt called for volunteers; when no one responded, he and his runner crawled to the gun and began pushing the weapon up the incline. Twice more the gun barked, cutting a swath through the undergrowth, and a third round of canister destroyed a machine gun. Other Marines then took over from Walt and the runner, with new volunteers replacing those cut down by the enemy. The improvised crew kept firing canister rounds every few yards until they had wrestled the weapon to the crest. There the Marines dug in, as close as ten yards to the bunkers the Japanese had built on the crest and reverse slope.

At 0115 on the morning of 10 January, the Japanese emerged from their positions and charged through a curtain of rain, shouting and firing as they came. The Marines clinging to Aogiri Ridge broke up this attack and three others that followed, firing off almost all their ammunition in doing so. A carrying party scaled the muddy slope with belts and clips for the machine guns and rifles, but there barely was time to distribute the ammunition before the Japanese launched the fifth attack of the morning. Marine artillery tore into the enemy, as forward observers, their vision obstructed by rain and jungle, adjusted fire by sound more than by sight, moving 105mm concentrations to within 50 yards of the Marine infantrymen. A Japanese officer emerged from the darkness and ran almost to Walt's foxhole before fragments from a shell bursting in the trees overhead cut him down. This proved to be the high-water mark of the counterattack against Aogiri Ridge, for the Japanese tide receded as the daylight grew brighter. At 0800, when the Marines moved forward, they did not encounter even one living Japanese on the terrain feature they renamed Walt's Ridge in honor of their commander, who received the Navy Cross for his inspirational leadership.

LtCol Lewis W. Walt earned the Navy Cross leading an attack up Aogiri Ridge, renamed Walt's Ridge in his honor. Department of Defense (USMC) photo 977113

One Japanese stronghold in the vicinity of Aogiri Ridge still survived, a supply dump located along a trail linking the ridge to Hill 150. On 11 January, Lieutenant Colonel Weber's 1st Battalion, 7th Marines, supported by a pair of half-tracks and a platoon of light tanks, eliminated this pocket in four hours of fighting. Fifteen days of combat since the landings on 26 December, had cost the division 180 killed and 636 wounded in action.

The next objective, Hill 660, lay at the left of General Shepherd's zone of action, just inland of the coastal track. The 3d Battalion, 7th Marines, commanded since 9 January by Lieutenant Colonel Henry W. Buse, Jr., got the assignment of seizing the hill. In preparation for Buse's attack, Captain Joseph W. Buckley, commander of the Weapons Company, 7th Marines, set up a task force to bypass Hill 660 and block the coastal trail beyond that objective. Buckley's group—two platoons of infantry, a platoon of 37mm guns, two light tanks, two half-tracks mounting 75mm guns, a platoon of pioneers from the 17th Marines with a bulldozer, and one of the Army's rocket-firing DUKWs— pushed through the mud and set up a road block athwart the line of retreat from Hill 660. The Japanese directed long-range plunging fire against Buckley's command as it advanced roughly one mile along the trail. Because of their flat trajectory, his 75mm and 37mm guns could not destroy the enemy's automatic weapons, but the Marines succeeded in forcing the hostile gunners to keep their heads down. As they advanced, Buckley's men unreeled telephone wire to maintain contact with higher headquarters. Once the roadblock was in place and camouflaged, the captain requested that a truck bring hot meals for his men. When the vehicle bogged down, he sent the bulldozer to push it free.

Advancing past Hill 660, a task force under Capt Joseph W. Buckley cuts the line of retreat for the Japanese defenders. The 37mm gun in the emplacement on the right and the half-track mounted 75mm gun on the left drove the attacking enemy back with heavy casualties. Department of Defense (USMC) photo 71520

After aerial bombardment and preparatory artillery fire, Buse's battalion started up the hill at about 0930 on 13 January. His supporting tanks could not negotiate the ravines that scarred the hillside. Indeed, the going became so steep that riflemen sometimes had to sling arms, seize handholds among the vines, and pull themselves upward. The Japanese suddenly opened fire from hurriedly dug trenches at the crest, pinning down the Marines climbing toward them until mortar fire silenced the enemy weapons, which lacked overhead cover. Buse's riflemen followed closely behind the mortar barrage, scattering the defenders, some of whom tried to escape along the coastal trail, where Buckley's task force waited to cut them down.

Gaunt, weary, hollow-eyed, machine gunner PFC George C. Miller carries his weapon to the rear after 19 days of heavy fighting while beating back the Japanese counterattack at Hill 660. This moving photograph was taken by Marine Corps combat photographer Sgt Robert R. Brenner. Department of Defense (USMC) photo 72273

Apparently delayed by torrential rain, the Japanese did not counterattack Hill 660 until 16 January. Roughly two companies of

Katayama's troops stormed up the southwestern slope only to be slaughtered by mortar, artillery, and small-arms fire. Many of those lucky enough to survive tried to break through Buckley's roadblock, where 48 of the enemy perished.

With the capture of Hill 660, the nature of the campaign changed. The assault phase had captured its objective and eliminated the possibility of a Japanese counterattack against the airfield complex. Next, the Marines would repulse the Japanese who harassed the secondary beachhead at Cape Merkus and secure the mountainous, jungle-covered interior of Cape Gloucester, south of the airfields and between the Green and Yellow Beaches.

The Mopping-up Begins in the West

At Cape Merkus on the south coast of western New Britain, the fighting proved desultory in comparison to the violent struggle in the vicinity of Cape Gloucester. The Japanese in the south remained content to take advantage of the dense jungle and contain the 112th Cavalry on the Cape Merkus peninsula. Major Shinjiro Komori, the Japanese commander there, believed that the landing force intended to capture an abandoned airfield at Cape Merkus, an installation that did not figure in American plans. A series of concealed bunkers, boasting integrated fields of fire, held the lightly armed cavalrymen in check, as the defenders directed harassing fire at the beachhead.

Because the cavalry unit lacked heavy weapons, a call went out for those of the 1st Marine Division's tanks that had remained behind at Finschhafen, New Guinea, because armor enough was already churning up the mud of Cape Gloucester. Company B, 1st Marine Tank Battalion, with 18 M5A1 light tanks mounting 37mm guns, and the 2d Battalion, 158th Infantry, arrived at Cape Merkus, moved into position by 15 January and attacked on the following day. A squadron of Army Air Forces B-24s dropped 1,000-pound bombs on the jungle-covered defenses, B-25s followed up, and mortars and artillery joined in the bombardment, after which two platoons of tanks, ten vehicles in all, and two companies of infantry surged forward. Some of the tanks bogged down in the rain-soaked soil, and tank retrievers had to pull them free. Despite mud and nearly impenetrable thickets, the tank-infantry teams found and destroyed most of the bunkers. Having eliminated the source of harassing fire, the troops pulled back after destroying a tank immobilized by a thrown track so that the enemy could not use it as a pillbox. Another tank, trapped in a crater, also was earmarked for destruction, but Army engineers managed to free it and bring it back.

The attack on 16 January broke the back of Japanese resistance. Komori ordered a retreat to the vicinity of the airstrip, but the 112th Cavalry launched an attack that caught the slowly moving defenders and inflicted further casualties. By the time the enemy dug in to defend the airfield, which the Americans had no intention of seizing, Komori's men had suffered 116 killed, 117 wounded, 14 dead of disease, and another 80 too ill to fight. The Japanese hung on despite sickness and starvation, until 24 February, when Komori received orders to join in a general retreat by Matsuda Force.

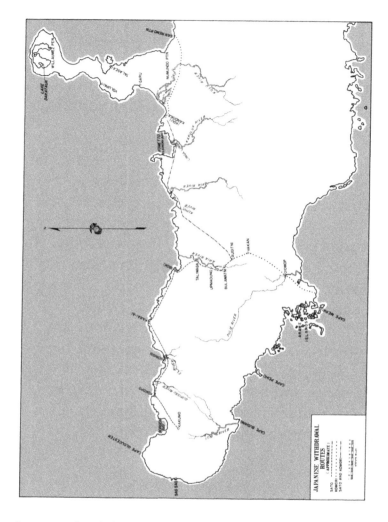

Across the island, after the victories at Walt's
Ridge and Hill 660, the 5th Marines
concentrated on seizing control of the shores
of Borgen Bay, immediately to the east. Major
Barba's 1st Battalion followed the coastal
trail until 20 January, when the column

collided with a Japanese stronghold at Natamo Point. Translations of documents captured earlier in the fighting revealed that at least one platoon, supported by automatic weapons had dug in there. Artillery and air strikes failed to suppress the Japanese fire, demonstrating that the captured papers were sadly out of date, since at least a company— armed with 20mm, 37mm, and 75mm weapons—checked the advance. Marine reinforcements, including medium tanks, arrived in landing craft on 23 January, and that afternoon, supported by artillery and a rocket-firing DUKW, Companies C and D overran Natamo Point. The battalion commander then dispatched patrols inland along the west bank of the Natamo River to outflank the strong positions on the east bank near the mouth of the stream. While the Marines were executing this maneuver, the Japanese abandoned their prepared defenses and retreated eastward.

Maj William H. Barba's 1st Battalion, 5th Marines, prepares to outflank the Japanese defenses along the Natamo River. Department of Defense (USMC) photo 75970

An officer of Maj Gordon D. Gayle's 2d Battalion, 5th Marines, displays a captured Japanese flag from a window of the structure that served as the headquarters of MajGen Iwao Matsuda. Department of Defense (USA) photo SC 188246

Success at Cape Gloucester and Borgen Bay enabled the 5th Marines to probe the trails leading inland toward the village of Magairapua, where Katayama once had his headquarters, and beyond. Elements of the regiment's 1st and 2d Battalions and of the

2d Battalion, 1st Marines—temporarily attached to the 5th Marines—led the way into the interior as one element in an effort to trap the enemy troops still in western New Britain.

In another part of this effort, Company L, 1st Marines, led by Captain Ronald J. Slay, pursued the Japanese retreating from Cape Gloucester toward Mount Talawe. Slay and his Marines crossed the mountain's eastern slope, threaded their way through a cluster of lesser outcroppings like Mount Langila, and in the saddle between Mounts Talawe and Tangi encountered four unoccupied bunkers situated to defend the junction of the track they had been following with another trail running east and west. The company had found the main east-west route from Sag Sag on the coast to the village of Agulupella and ultimately to Natamo Point on the northern coast.

The capture of Matsuda's headquarters provides Marine intelligence with a harvest of documents, which the enemy buried rather than burned, presumably to avoid smoke that might attract artillery fire or air strikes. Department of Defense (USMC) photo 77642

To exploit the discovery, a composite patrol from the 1st Marines, under the command of Captain Nickolai Stevenson, pushed south along that trail Slay had followed, while a composite company from the 7th Marines, under Captain Preston S. Parish, landed at Sag Sag on the west coast and advanced along the east-west track. An Australian reserve officer, William G. Wiedeman, who had been an Episcopal missionary at Sag Sag, served as Parish's guide and contact with the native populace. When determined opposition stopped Stevenson short of the trail junction near Mount Talawe, Captain George P Hunt's Company K, 1st Marines, renewed the attack.

On 28 January, Hunt concluded he had brought the Japanese to bay and attacked. For three hours that afternoon, his Marines tried unsuccessfully to break though a line of bunkers concealed by jungle growth, losing 15 killed or wounded. When Hunt withdrew beyond reach of the Japanese mortars that had scourged his company during the action, the enemy emerged from cover and attempted to pursue, a bold but foolish move that exposed the troops to deadly fire that cleared the way for an advance to the trail junction. Hunt and Parish joined forces and probed farther, only to be stopped by a Japanese ambush. At this point, Major William J. Piper, Jr., the executive officer of the 3d Battalion, 7th Marines, assumed command, renewed the pursuit on 30 January, and discovered the enemy had fled. Shortly afterward Piper's combined patrol made contact with those dispatched inland by the 5th Marines.

An Improvised Air Force

At Cape Gloucester, the 1st Marine Division had an air force of its own consisting of Piper

L-4 Cubs and Stinson L-5s provided by the Army. The improvised air force traced its origins to the summer of 1943, before the division plunged into the green inferno of New Britain. Lieutenant Colonel Kenneth H. Weir, the division's air officer, and Captain Theodore A. Petras, the personal pilot of Major General Alexander A. Vandegrift, then the division commander, concocted a plan for acquiring light aircraft mainly for artillery spotting. The assistant division commander at that time, Brigadier General Rupertus. had seen Army troops making use of Piper Cubs on maneuvers, and he promptly presented the plan to General MacArthur, the theater commander, who promised to give the division twelve light airplanes in time for the next operation.

When the 1st Marine Division arrived at Goodenough Island, off the southwestern tip of New Guinea, to begin preparing for further combat, Rupertus, now a major general and Vandegrift's successor as division commander, directed Petras and another pilot, First Lieutenant R. F. Murphy, to organize an aviation unit from among the Marines of the division. A call went out for volunteers with aviation experience; some sixty candidates stepped forward, and 12 qualified as pilots in the new Air Liaison Unit. The dozen Piper Cubs arrived as promised; six proved to be in excellent condition, three needed repair, and another three were fit only for cannibalization to provide parts to keep the others flying. The nine flyable planes practiced a variety of tasks during two months of training at Goodenough Island. The airmen acquired experience in artillery spotting, radio communications, and snagging messages, hung in a container trailing a pennant to help the pilot see it, from a line strung between two poles.

The division's air force landed at Cape Gloucester from LSTs on D-Day, reassembled their aircraft, and commenced operating. The radios installed in the L-4s proved too balky for artillery spotting, so the group concentrated on courier flights, visual and photographic reconnaissance, and delivering small amounts of cargo. As a light transport, a Piper Cub could drop a case of dry rations, for example, with pinpoint accuracy from an altitude of 200 feet. Occasionally, the light planes became attack aircraft when pilots or observers tossed hand grenades into Japanese positions.

Before the Marines pulled out of New Britain, two Army pilots, flying Stinson L-5s, faster and more powerful than the L-4s, joined the division's air arm. One airplane of each type was damaged beyond repair in crashes, but the pilots and passengers survived. All the Marine volunteers received the Air Medal for their contribution, but a specially trained squadron arrived from the United States and replaced them prior to the next operation, the assault on Peleliu.

Thus far, a vigorous pursuit along the coast and on the inland trails had failed to ensnare the Japanese. The Marines captured Matsuda's abandoned headquarters in the shadow of Mount Talawe and a cache of documents that the enemy buried rather than burned, perhaps because smoke would almost certainly bring air strikes or artillery fire, but the Japanese general and his troops escaped. Where had Matsuda Force gone?

LtCol Lewis H. Puller, left, and Maj William J. Piper discuss the route of a patrol from the village of Agulupella to Gilnit on the Itni River, a two-week operation. Department of Defense (USMC) photo 77436

Since a trail net led from the vicinity of Mount Talawe to the south, General Shepherd concluded that Matsuda was headed in that direction. The assistant division commander therefore organized a composite battalion of six reinforced rifle companies, some 3,900 officers and men in all, which General Rupertus entrusted to Lieutenant Colonel Puller. This patrol was to

advance from Agulupella on the east-west
track, down the so-called Government Trail
all the way to Gilnit, a village on the Itni
River, inland of Cape Bushing on New
Britain's southern coast. Before Puller could
set out, information discovered at Matsuda's
former headquarters and translated revealed
that the enemy actually was retreating to the
northeast. As a result, Rupertus detached the
recently arrived 1st Battalion, 5th Marines,
and reduced Puller's force from almost 4,000
to fewer than 400, still too many to be
supplied by the 150 native bearers assigned
to the column for the march through the
jungle to Gilnit.

Marine patrols, such as Puller's trek to Gilnit,
depended on bearers recruited from the villages of
western New Britain who were thoroughly familiar

with the local trail net. Department of Defense (USMC) photo 72836

During the trek, Puller's Marines depended heavily on supplies dropped from airplanes. Piper Cubs capable at best of carrying two cases of rations in addition to the pilot and observer, deposited their loads at villages along the way, and Fifth Air Force B-17s dropped cargo by the ton. Supplies delivered from the sky made the patrol possible but did little to ameliorate the discomfort of the Marines slogging through the mud.

Despite this assistance from the air, the march to Gilnit taxed the ingenuity of the Marines involved and hardened them for future action. This toughening-up seemed especially desirable to Puller, who had led many a patrol during the American intervention in Nicaragua, 1927-1933. The division's supply clerks, aware of the officer's disdain for creature comforts, were startled by requisitions from the patrol for hundreds of bottles of insect repellent. Puller had his reasons, however. According to one veteran of the Gilnit operation, "We were always soaked and everything we owned was likewise, and that lotion made the best damned stuff to start a fire with that your ever saw."

As Puller's Marines pushed toward Gilnit on the Itni River, they killed perhaps 75 Japanese and captured one straggler, along with some weapons and odds and ends of equipment. An abandoned pack contained an American flag, probably captured by a soldier of the 141st Infantry during Japan's conquest of the Philippines. After reaching Gilnit, the patrol fanned out but encountered no opposition. Puller's Marines made contact with an Army patrol from the Cape Merkus beachhead and then headed toward the north coast, beginning on 16 February.

To the west, Company B, 1st Marines, boarded landing craft on 12 February and crossed the Dampier Strait to occupy Rooke Island, some fifteen miles from the coast of New Britain. The division's intelligence specialists concluded correctly that the garrison had departed. Indeed, the transfer began on 6 December 1943, roughly three weeks before the landings at Cape Gloucester, when Colonel Jiro Sato and half of his 500-man 51st Reconnaissance Regiment, sailed off to Cape Bushing. Sato then led his command up the Itni River and joined the main body of the Matsuda Force east of Mount Talawe. Instead of committing Sato's troops to the defense of Hill 660, Matsuda directed him to delay the elements of the 5th Marines and 1st Marines that were converging over the inland trail net. Sato succeeded in checking the Hunt patrol on 28 January and buying time for Matsuda's retreat, not to the south, but, as the documents captured at the general's abandoned headquarters confirmed, along the northern coast, with the 51st Reconnaissance Regiment initially serving as the rear guard.

On 12 February 1944, infantrymen of Company B, from LtCol Walker A. Reaves's 1st Battalion, 1st Marines, advance inland on Rooke Island, west of New Britain, but find that the Japanese have withdrawn. Department of Defense (USMC) photo 79181

Once the Marines realized what Matsuda had in mind, cutting the line of retreat assumed the highest priority, as demonstrated by the withdrawal of the 1st Battalion, 5th Marines, from the Puller patrol on the very eve of the march toward Gilnit. As early as 3 February, Rupertus concluded that the Japanese could no longer mount a counterattack on the airfields and began devoting all his energy and resources to destroying the retreating Japanese. The division commander chose Selden's 5th Marines, now restored to three-battalion strength, to conduct the pursuit. While Petras and his light aircraft scouted the coastal track, landing craft stood ready to embark elements of the regiment and position them to cut off and destroy the Matsuda Force. Bad weather hampered Selden's Marines; clouds concealed the enemy from aerial observation, and a boiling surf ruled out landings over certain beaches. With about 5,000 Marines, and some Army dog handlers and their animals, the colonel rotated his battalions, sending out fresh troops each day and using 10 LCMs in attempts to leapfrog the retreating Japanese. "With few exceptions, men were not called upon to make marches on two successive days," Selden recalled. "After a one-day hike, they either remained at that camp for three or four days or made the next jump by

LCMs." At any point along the coastal track, the enemy might have concealed himself in the dense jungle and sprung a deadly ambush, but he did not. Selden, for instance, expected a battle for the Japanese supply point at Iboki Point, but the enemy faded away. Instead of encountering resistance by a determined and skillful rear guard, the 5th Marines found only stragglers, some of them sick or wounded. Nevertheless, the regimental commander could take pride in maintaining unremitting pressure on the retreating enemy "without loss or even having a man wounded" and occupying Iboki Point on 24 February.

Meanwhile, American amphibious forces had seized Kwajalein and Eniwetok Atolls in the Marshall Islands, as the Central Pacific offensive gathered momentum. Further to complicate Japanese strategy, carrier strikes proved that Truk had become too vulnerable to continue serving as a major naval base. The enemy, conscious of the threat to his inner perimeter that was developing to the north, decided to pull back his fleet units from Truk and his aircraft from Rabaul. On 19 February—just two days after the Americans invaded Eniwetok—Japanese fighters at Rabaul took off for the last time to challenge an American air raid. When the bombers returned on the following day, not a single operational Japanese fighter remained at the airfields there.

The defense of Rabaul now depended exclusively on ground forces. Lieutenant General Yusashi Sakai, in command of the 17th Division, received orders to scrap his plan to dig in near Cape Hoskins and instead proceed to Rabaul. The general believed that supplies enough had been positioned along the trail net to enable at least the most vigorous of Matsuda's troops to stay ahead of the Marines and reach the fortress. The remaining self-propelled barges could carry heavy equipment and those troops most needed to defend Rabaul, as well as the sick and wounded. The retreat, however, promised to be an ordeal for the Japanese. Selden had already demonstrated how swiftly the Marines could move, taking advantage of American control of the skies and the coastal waters, and a two-week march separated the nearest of Matsuda's soldiers from their destination. Attrition would be heavy, but those who could contribute the least to the defense of Rabaul seemed the likeliest to fall by the wayside.

The Japanese forces retreating to Rabaul included the defenders of Cape Merkus, where a stalemate had prevailed after the limited American attack on 16 January had sent Komori's troops reeling back beyond the airstrip. At Augitni, a village east of the Aria River southwest of Iboki Point, Komori reported to Colonel Sato of the 51st Reconnaissance Regiment, which had concluded the rear-guard action that enabled the Matsuda Force to cross the stream and take the trail through Augitni to Linga Linga and eastward along the coast. When the two commands met, Sato broke out a supply of sake he had been carrying, and the officers exchanged toasts well into the night.

Meanwhile, Captain Kiyomatsu Terunuma organized a task force built around the 1st Battalion, 54th Infantry, and prepared to defend the Talasea area near the base of the Willaumez Peninsula against a possible landing by the pursuing Marines. The Terunuma Force had the mission of holding out long enough for Matsuda Force to slip past on the way to Rabaul. On 6 March, the leading elements of Matsuda's column reached the base of the Willaumez Peninsula, and Komori, leading the way for Sato's rear guard, started from Augitni toward Linga Linga.

The Landings of Volupai

By coincidence, 6 March was the day chosen for the reinforced 5th Marines, now commanded by Colonel Oliver P. Smith, to land on the west coast of the Willaumez Peninsula midway between base and tip. The intelligence section of division headquarters believed that Japanese strength between Talasea, the site of a crude airstrip, and Cape Hoskins, across Kimbe Bay from Willaumez Peninsula, equaled that of the Smith's command, but that most of the enemy troops defended Cape Hoskins. The intelligence estimate proved correct, for Sakai had been preparing a last-ditch defense of Cape Hoskins, when word arrived to retreat all the way to Rabaul.

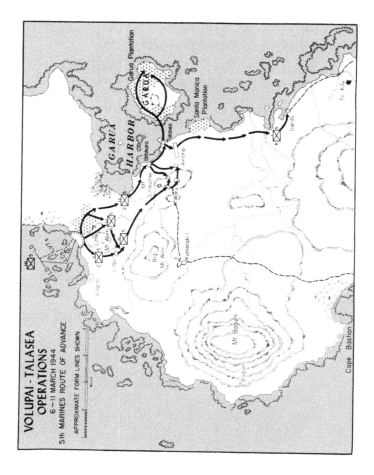

To discover the extent of Japanese preparations in the immediate vicinity of Volupai, a reconnaissance team landed from a torpedo boat at Bagum, a village about nine miles from Red Beach, the site chosen for the assault landing. Flight Lieutenant G. H. Rodney Marsland of the Royal Australian Air Force, First Lieutenant John D. Bradbeer— the division's chief scout, who had participated in three similar reconnaissance patrols of the Cape Gloucester area before the 26 December invasion—and two native bearers remained ashore for 24 hours and learned that Red Beach was lightly defended. Their sources, principally natives who had worked at a plantation that Marsland had operated in the area before the war, confirmed Marine estimates of Terunuma's aggregate force—some 600 men, two thirds of them located near Talasea, armed with mortars and artillery.

Bristol Beauforts of the Royal Australian Air Force based at Kiriwina Island bombed the Volupai Talasea region for three days and then conducted a last-minute strike to compensate for the absence of naval gunfire. Smith's force, designated Landing Team A, loaded into a small flotilla of landing craft, escorted by torpedo boats, and set out from Iboki Point. Lieutenant Colonel Robert Amory, Jr., an Army officer in command of an engineer boat unit, took command of the collection of small craft, some of them manned by his soldiers and the others by sailors. A storm buffeted the formation, and after the seas grew calm, the boat carrying the Army air liaison party broke down. Major Gordon D. Gayle, the new commander of the

2d Battalion, 5th Marines, who already was behind schedule, risked further delay by taking the disabled craft in tow. Gayle felt that Combat Team A's need for the liaison party's radio equipment justified his action.

At 0835 on 6 March, the first of the amphibian tractors carrying the assault troops clawed their way onto Red Beach. During the movement shoreward, Sherman tanks in Army LCMs opened fire with machine guns and stood ready to direct their 75mm weapons against any Japanese gunner who might oppose the landing. Aside from hard-to-pinpoint small-arms fire, the opposition consisted mainly of barrages from mortars, screened by the terrain from the flat-trajectory cannon of the tanks. When Japanese mortar shells began bursting among the approaching landing craft, Captain Theodore A. Petras, at the controls of one of the division's Piper Cubs, dived low over the mortar positions and dropped hand grenades from the supply he carried on all his flights. Natives had warned Marsland and Bradbeer of a machine-gun nest dominating the beach from the slopes of Little Mount Worri, but the men of the 1st Battalion, 5th Marines, leading the way, found it abandoned and encountered no serious opposition as they dug in to protect the beachhead.

Meanwhile, Gayle's Marines pressed their attack, with four medium tanks supporting Company E as it tried to push farther in land. One of the Shermans bogged down almost immediately in the soft sand of Red Beach, but the other three continued in column. The tank in the lead lost momentum on a muddy rise, and two Japanese soldiers carrying land mines burst from cover to attack it. Riflemen of Company E cut down one of them, but the other detonated his mine against the vehicle, killing himself and a Marine who tried to stop him. The explosion jammed the turret and stunned the crewmen, who were further shaken, but not wounded, when an antitank grenade exploded against the armor. The damaged Sherman got out of the way; when the other two tanks had passed, it returned to the trail only to hit a mine that disabled it.

Despite the loss of two tanks, one temporarily immobilized on the beach and the other out of action permanently, Gayle's battalion continued its advance. During the fighting on the approaches to the Volupai coconut plantation, the body of a Japanese soldier yielded a map showing enemy dispositions around Talasea. By mid-afternoon, Smith's regimental intelligence section was disseminating the information, which proved valuable in future operations.

At Volupai, as on Cape Gloucester, sand, mud, and land mines—sometimes carried by Japanese soldiers who detonated them against the sides of the vehicle—could immobilize even the Sherman M4 medium tank. Department of Defense (USMC) photo 79868

While Company E of Gayle's battalion followed the trail toward the plantation, Company G kept pace, crossing the western shoulder of Little Mount Worri. Five Army Air Forces P-39s from Airfield No. 2 at Cape Gloucester arrived overhead to support Gayle's attack, but the pilots could not locate the troops below and instead bombed Cape Hoskins, where there was no danger of hitting the Marines. Even without the aerial attack, the 2d Battalion, 5th Marines, overran the plantation by dusk and dug in for the night; the unit counted the bodies of 35 Japanese killed during the day's fighting.

On D-Day, Combat Team A lost 13 killed and 71 wounded, with artillery batteries rather than rifle companies suffering the greater number of casualties. The 2d Battalion, 11th Marines, set up its 75mm pack howitzers on the open beach, exposed to fire from the 90mm mortars upon which Petras had ineffectually showered his hand grenades. Some of the corpsmen at Red Beach, who went to the assistance of wounded artillerymen, became casualties themselves. Nine of the Marines killed on 6 March were members of the artillery unit, along with 29 of the wounded. Nevertheless, the gunners succeeded in registering their fires in the afternoon and harassing the enemy throughout the night.

While the Marines prepared to renew the attack on the second day, Terunuma deployed his troops to oppose them and keep open the line of retreat of the Matsuda Force. In doing so, the Japanese commander fell back from his prepared positions on the fringes of Volupai Plantation—including the mortar pits that had raised such havoc with the 2d Battalion, 11th Marines—and dug in on the northwest slopes of Mount Schleuther, overlooking the trail leading from the plantation to Bitokara village on the coast. As soon as he realized what the enemy had in mind, Gayle sent Company F uphill to thwart the Japanese plan, while Company E remained on the trail and built up a base of fire. On the right flank of the maneuver element, Company F, the weapons platoon burst from the undergrowth and surprised Japanese machine gunners setting up their weapon, killing them and turning the gun against the enemy. The advance of Company F caught the Japanese in mid-deployment and drove them back after killing some 40 of them. Gayle's battalion established a nighttime perimeter that extended from Mount Schleuther to the trail and embraced a portion of both.

Cpl Robert J. Hallahan, a member of the 1st Marine Division band, examines the shattered remains of a Japanese 75mm gun used in the defense of Mount Schleuther and rigged as a booby trap when the enemy withdrew. Department of Defense (USA) photo SC 260915

The action on 7 March represented a departure from plan. Smith had intended that both Barba and Gayle attack, with the 3d Battalion, 5th Marines, commanded since 12 January by Lieutenant Colonel Harold O. Deakin, assuming responsibility for the defense of the beachhead. The landing craft that had carried the assault troops departed from Red Beach during D-Day, some of them carrying the seriously wounded, in order to

pick up the 3d Battalion at Iboki Point and
bring it to Volupai. The day was waning by
the time enough landing craft were on hand
for Deakin's battalion. For the reinforcements
to arrive in time for an attack on the morning
of 7 March would require a dangerous
nighttime approach to Volupai, through
uncharted waters studded with sharp
outcroppings of coral that could lay open the
hull of a landing craft. Rupertus decided that
the risks of such a move outweighed the
advantages and canceled it at the last
moment. No boat started the return voyage to
Red Beach until after dawn on 7 March,
delaying the arrival of Deakin's battalion until
late afternoon. On that day, therefore,
Barba's 1st Battalion had only enough time
to send Company C a short distance inland
on a trail that passed to the right of Little
Mount Worri, enroute to the village of Liappo.
When the trail petered out among the trees
and vines, the Marines hacked their way
forward until they ran out of daylight short of
their objective.

On 8 March, the 1st Battalion, 5th Marines,
resumed the advance, Companies A and B
moving on parallel paths leading east of Little
Mount Worri. Members of Company A,
peering through dense undergrowth, saw a
figure in a Japanese uniform and opened fire.

The person was not a Japanese, however, but a native wearing clothing discarded by the enemy and serving as a guide for Company B. The first shots triggered an exchange of fire that wounded the guide, killed one Marine, and wounded a number of others. Afterward, the advance resumed, but once again the formidable terrain—muddy ravines choked with brush and vines—slowed the Marines, and the sun set with the battalion still on the trail.

Meanwhile, Gayle's 2d Battalion probed deeper into Terunuma's defenses. Patrols ranged ahead on the morning of 8 March and found the Japanese dug in at Bitokara Mission, but the enemy fell back before the Marines could storm the position. Gayle's troops occupied Bitokara and pushed as far as Talasea, taking over the abandoned airstrip. Other patrols from this battalion started up the steep slopes of Mount Schleuthen and collided with Terunuma's main strength. Fire from small arms, a 90mm mortar, and a 75mm field gun killed or wounded 18 Marines. Rather than press his attack in the gathering darkness, Gayle pulled back from the mountain and dug in at Bitokara Mission so artillery and mortars could hammer the defenses throughout the night, but he left one company to defend the Talasea airstrip.

Marines struggle to winch a tractor, and the 105mm howitzer it is towing, out of the mud of New Britain. The trails linking Volupai and Talasea proved as impassable for heavy vehicles as those on Cape Gloucester. Department of Defense (USMC) photo 69985

On the morning of 9 March, Company G of Gayle's battalion advanced up Mount Schleuthen while Companies B and C from Barba's command cleared the villages around the base. Company G expected to encounter intense opposition during its part of the coordinated attack, but Terunuma had decamped from the mountain top, leaving behind one dead, two stragglers, and an artillery piece. The enemy, however, had festooned the abandoned 75mm gun with vines that served as trip wires for a booby trap. When the Marines hacked at the vines to examine the weapon more closely, they released the firing pin and detonated a round in the chamber. Since the Japanese gun crew had plugged the bore before fleeing, the resulting explosion ruptured the breech block and wounded one of Gayle's men.

Besides yielding the dominant terrain, Terunuma chose not to defend any of the villages clustered at the base of the mountain. The 5th Marines thus opened a route across the Willaumez Peninsula to support further operations against Matsuda's line of retreat. Since 6 March, Colonel Smith's force had killed an estimated 150 Japanese at the cost of 17 Marines killed and 114 wounded, most of the casualties suffered on the first day. The final phase of the fighting that began on Red Beach consisted of securing Garua Island, abandoned by the Japanese, for American use, a task finished on 9 March.

The results of the action at the base of the Willaumez Peninsula proved mixed. The grass airstrip at Talasea lacked the length to accommodate fighters, but the division's liaison planes made extensive use of it, landing on either side of the carcass of a Japanese aircraft until the wreckage could be hauled away. The trail net, essentially a web of muddy paths, required long hours of hard work by Company F, 17th Marines, and Army engineers, who used a 10-ton wrecker to recover three Sherman tanks that had become mired during the fighting. By 10 March, the trails could support a further advance. Two days later, elements of Deakin's 3d Battalion, 5th Marines, having moved inland from the beachhead, provided a guard of honor as Colonel Smith and his executive officer, Lieutenant Colonel Henry W. Buse, raised over Bitokara the same flag that had flown over Airfield No. 2 at Cape Gloucester.

Final Combat and Relief

The flotilla of Army LCMs and Navy LCTs that supported the Volupai landings inflicted further damage on Japanese coastal traffic, already hard hit by air strikes. On 9 March, a convoy of landing craft carrying supplies around the tip of the peninsula for delivery to the advancing Marines at Talasea spotted four enemy barges, beached and sloppily camouflaged. An LCT took the barges under fire from its 20mm cannon and machine guns, destroying one of the Japanese craft.

Later that day, two LCMs used the 37mm gun of the Marine light tank that each was carrying, to fire upon another barge beached on the peninsula.

The enemy tried to make the best possible use of the dwindling number of barges, but the bulk of Matsuda's troops moved overland, screened by Terunuma's men during the transit of the base of the Willaumez Peninsula. About a hundred Japanese dug in at Garilli, but by the time Company K of Deakin's 3d Battalion, 5th Marines, attacked on 11 March, the enemy had fallen back to a new trail block about three miles distant. For four days, the Marines fought a succession of sharp actions, as the Japanese retreated a few hundred yards at a time, dragging with them a 75mm gun that anchored each of the blocking positions. On 16 March, Deakin himself joined Company K, arriving in an LCM that also carried a section of 81mm mortars. The Japanese turned their cannon seaward to deal with this threat but failed to hit the landing craft. Shortly after the Marine mortars landed and went into action, Terunuma's men again withdrew, but this time they simply faded away, since the bulk of Matsuda Force had escaped to the east.

Having secured the Red Beach-Garua Bay-Talasea area, the 5th Marines dispatched patrols southward to the base of the Willaumez Peninsula, capturing only the occasional straggler and confirming the departure of the main body of Matsuda's command. The 1st Marine Division established a comfortable headquarters, training sites, a hospital that utilized captured stocks of Japanese medicine, and a rest area that featured swimming off the Garua beaches and bathing in hot springs ashore. The Navy built a base on the Willaumez Peninsula for torpedo boats that harried the surviving Japanese barges. Unfortunately, on 27 March, the second day the base was operating, Allied aircraft mistook two of the boats for Japanese craft and attacked, killing five sailors and wounding 18.

One of the courses taught at the new Garua training center sought to produce amphibious scouts for the division's future operations. The school's headquarters decided that a reconnaissance of Cape Hoskins would serve as a suitable graduation exercise, since aerial observers had seen no sign of enemy activity there. On 13 April, Second Lieutenant Richard R. Breen, accompanied by Lieutenant Marsland of the Royal Australian Air Force, embarked with 16 trainees, two native guides, and a rifle platoon from the 2d Battalion, 5th Marines, in a pair of LCMs. While two instructors stood by in one of the landing craft, the platoon established a trail block, and the future scouts advanced toward the Cape Hoskins airfield, no longer used by the Japanese. En route to the objective, however, the patrol encountered fire from small arms and mortars, but the Marines had apparently learned their lessons well, for they succeeded in breaking off the action and escaped without suffering casualties.

Before the building of a rest area at Garua Bay, with its hot springs and bathing beaches, these Marines relax in one of the crystal clear streams running into the sea from New Britain's

mountainous interior. Department of Defense (USMC) photo 78381

Meanwhile, the Japanese retreat continued. Komori's troops, blazing the trail for Sato's command from Augitni to the northern coast, encountered a disheartening number of hungry stragglers as they marched toward a supply depot at Kandoka, roughly 10 miles west of the Willaumez Peninsula. Crossing the Kuhu River, Komori's soldiers came under ineffectual fire from an American landing craft. The rain-swollen Via River, broader than the Kuhu, proved a more serious obstacle, requiring a detour lasting two days to reach a point where the stream narrowed. Komori's provisions ran out on 17 March, forcing the soldiers to subsist on taro, birds and fish, and vegetables from village garden plots, supplemented by some welcome coconuts gathered from a plantation at Linga Linga. After losing additional time and a dozen lives crossing yet another river, the Kapaluk, Komori's troops straggled into Kandoka on the 24th, only to discover that the food and other supplies had been carried off toward Rabaul. Despite this crushing disappointment, Komori pressed on, his men continuing to live off the land as best they could. Five more men drowned in the fast-moving waters of the Kulu River, and a native hired as a guide defected. Already weakened physically, Komori came down with an attack of malaria, but he forced himself to continue.

The survivors struggled onward toward Cape Hoskins and ultimately Rabaul. On 9 April, Easter Sunday, four half-starved Japanese wandered onto the San Remo Plantation, where Gayle's battalion had bivouacked after pursuing the enemy eastward from the Willaumez Peninsula. The Marine unit was preparing to pass in review for the regimental commander later that day, when a sentry saw the intruders and opened fire. The ensuing skirmish killed three of the enemy. One of the dead proved to be Major Komori; his pack contained a rusty revolver and a diary describing the sufferings of his command.

Colonel Sato, with the rest of the rear guard for the Matsuda Force, set out from Augitni on 7 March, one day after Komori, who sent back word on the 19th that patrols from the 5th Marines had fanned out from the Willaumez Peninsula, where the reinforced regiment had landed almost two weeks earlier. When Sato reached Linga Linga and came across a bivouac abandoned by a Marine patrol, his force had dwindled to just 250 men, less than half the number that started out. He received a shock the following day when American landing craft appeared as his men prepared to cross the Kapaluk River.

He immediately set up a perimeter to beat back the expected attack, but the boats were carrying elements of the 2d Battalion, 1st Marines, under Major Charles H. Brush, Jr. A patrol from Brush's Company F landed on a beach beyond Kandoka, the former site of a Japanese supply cache, and dispatched one platoon, led by First Lieutenant William C. Schleip, westward along the coastal track, even as Sato, aware only of the general location of the landing, groped eastward toward the village. On 26 March, the two collided, the Japanese surprising the Marines in the act of crossing a small stream and pinning them down for some three hours until the approach of reinforcements from Company F forced the enemy to break off the action, take to the jungle, and bypass Kandoka.

As the head of Sato's column disappeared in the jungle, one of the division's light airplanes, scouting landing sites for Brush's battalion, sighted the tail near Linga Linga. The pilot, Captain Petras, turned over the controls to Brigadier General Earl C. Long, also a pilot, sketched the location of the Japanese, and dropped the map to one of the troop-laden landing craft. Petras then led the way to an undefended beach, where Brush's Marines waded ashore and set out in pursuit of Sato. On 30 March, Second Lieutenant Richard B. Watkins, at the head of an eight-man patrol, spotted a pair of Japanese, their rifles slung, who turned out to be members of a 73-man patrol, far too many for Watkins to handle.

Once the enemy column had moved off, Watkins and his men hurried to Kandoka, where he reported to Major Brush and obtained mortars and machine guns before again taking to the trail. Brush followed, bringing a reinforced rifle platoon to increase the Marine fire power. Meanwhile, the Japanese encountered yet another Marine patrol, this one led by Sergeant Frank Chliek, which took up a position on high ground that commanded the trail. When they heard Chliek's group open fire, Watkins and Brush hurried to its aid; the resulting slaughter killed 55 Japanese, including Colonel Sato, who died sword in hand, but the Marines did not suffer even one casualty.

On 9 April, the 3d Battalion, 1st Marines, under Lieutenant Colonel Hankins, replaced Brush's 1st Battalion and continued the search for enemy stragglers. The bulk of the Matsuda Force, and whatever supplies it could transport, had by this time retreated to Cape Hoskins and beyond, and Army troops were taking over from the Marines. Almost four months had elapsed since the landing at Cape Gloucester; clearly the time had come for the amphibious troops to move on to an operation that would make better use of their specialized training and equipment. The final action fought by the Leathernecks took place on 22 April, when an ambush sprung by the 2d Battalion, 5th Marines, killed 20 Japanese and resulted in the last Marine fatality of the campaign. In seizing western New Britain as part of the isolation of Rabaul, the division suffered 310 killed in action and 1,083 wounded, roughly one-fourth the estimated Japanese casualties.

Early in February 1944, after the capture of the Cape Gloucester airfields but before the landing at Volupai. General Rupertus, warned that his 1st Marine Division might remain on New Britain indefinitely. Having the unit tied down for an extended period alarmed the recently appointed Commandant of the Marine Corps, General Vandegrift. "Six months there," he remarked, referring to an extended commitment in New Britain, "and it will no longer be a well-trained amphibious division." Vandegrift urged Admiral Ernest J. King, the Chief of Naval Operations, to help pry the division from MacArthur's grasp so it could again undertake amphibious operations. Admiral Chester W. Nimitz,

Commander in Chief, Pacific Ocean Areas, wanted the division for the impending invasion of the Palau Islands, the capture of which would protect the flank of MacArthur's advance to the Philippines. In order to obtain the Marines, Nimitz made the Army's 40th Infantry Division available to MacArthur, in effect swapping a division capable of taking over the New Britain campaign for one that could spearhead the amphibious offensive against Japan. MacArthur, however, briefly retained control of one component of the Marine division—Company A, 1st Tank Battalion. That unit's medium tanks landed on 22 April at Hollandia on the northern coast of New Guinea, but a swamp just beyond the beachhead prevented the Shermans from supporting the advance inland.

New Weapons in the Division's Arsenal

During the period of rehabilitation following the Guadalcanal campaign, the 1st Marine Division received two new weapons—the M4 medium tank, nicknamed the Sherman in honor of William Tecumseh Sherman whose Union troops marched from Atlanta to the sea, and the M-1 rifle. The new rifle, designed by John C. Garand, a civilian employee of the Springfield Armory in Massachusetts, was a semi-automatic, gas-operated weapon, weighing 9.5 pounds and using an eight-round clip. Although less accurate at longer range than the former standard rifle, the M-1903, which snipers continued to use, the M-1 could lay down a deadly volume of fire at the comparatively short ranges typical of jungle warfare.

In addition, the division received the M4A1, an early version of the Sherman tank, which MacArthur valued so highly that he borrowed a company of them from the 1st Marine Division for the Hollandia operation. The model used by the Marines weighed 34 tons, mounted a 75mm gun, and had frontal armor some three inches thick. Although a more formidable weapon than the 16-ton high tank, with a 37mm gun, the medium tank had certain shortcomings. A high silhouette made it a comparatively easy target for Japanese gunners, who fortunately did not have a truly deadly anti-tank weapon, and narrow treads provided poor traction in the mud of New Britain.

The commanding general of the Army's 40th Infantry Division, Major General Rapp Brush, arrived at New Britain on 10 April to arrange for the relief. His advance echelon arrived on the 23d and the remainder of the division five days later. The 1st Marine Division departed in two echelons on 6 April and 4 May. Left behind was the 12th Defense Battalion, which continued to provide antiaircraft defense for the Cape Gloucester airfields until relieved by an Army unit late in May.

In a campaign lasting four months, the 1st Marine Division had plunged into the unforgiving jungle and overwhelmed a determined and resolute enemy, capturing the Cape Gloucester airfields and driving the Japanese from western New Britain. A number of factors helped the Marines defeat nature and the Japanese. Allied control of the air and the sea provided mobility and disrupted the coastal barge traffic upon which the enemy had to depend for the movement of large quantities of supplies, especially badly needed medicines, during the retreat to Rabaul. Warships and landing craft armed with rockets—supplemented by such improvisations as tanks or rocket-equipped amphibian trucks firing from landing craft—supported the landings, but the size of the island and the lack of fixed coastal defenses limited the effectiveness of the various forms of naval gunfire. Using superior engineering skills, the Marines defied swamp and undergrowth to bring forward tanks that crushed enemy emplacements and added to the already formidable American firepower. Although photo analysis, an art that improved rapidly, misinterpreted the nature of the damp flat, Marine intelligence made excellent use of captured Japanese documents throughout the campaign. In the last analysis, the courage and endurance of the average Marine made victory possible, as he braved discomfort, disease, and violent death during his time in the green inferno.

Sources

Three books have proved essential to this account of the fighting on New Britain. Lieutenant Colonel Frank O., Hough, USMCR, dealt at length with the campaign in The Island War: The United States Marine

Corps in the Pacific (Philadelphia: J. B. Lippincott, 1947). With Major John Crown, USMCR, he wrote the official Marine Corps historical monograph: The New Britain Campaign (Washington: Historical Branch, G-3 Division, HQMC, 1952). The third of these essential volumes is Henry I. Shaw, Jr., and Major Douglas T. Kane, USMC, Isolation of Rabaul—History of U. S. Marine Corps Operations in World War II, vol 2 (Washington: Historical Branch, G-3 Division, HQMC, 1963.)

Other valuable sources include: Wesley Frank Craven and James Lea Cate, eds., The Pacific: Guadalcanal to Saipan, August 1942-July 1944—The Army Air Forces in World War II, vol 4 (Washington: Office of Air Force History, reprint 1983); George McMillan, The Old Breed: A History of the First Marine Division in World War II (Washington: Infantry Journal Press, 1949); John Miller, Jr., The United States Army in World War II; The War in the Pacific: CARTWHEEL, The Reduction of Rabaul (Washington: Office of Chief of Military History, 1959); Samuel Eliot Morison, Breaking the Bismarcks Barrier, 22 July 1942-1 May 1944—A History of United States Naval Operations in World War II, vol 6 (Boston: Little, Brown, and Company, 1950).

The Marine Corps Gazette printed four articles analyzing aspects of the New Britain campaign: Lieutenant Colonel Robert B. Luckey, USMC, "Cannon, Mud, and Japs," vol 28, no 10 (October 1944); George McMillan, "Scouting at Cape Gloucester," vol 30, no 5 (May 1946); and Fletcher Pratt, "Marines Under MacArthur: Cape Gloucester," vol 31, no 12 (December 1947); and "Marines Under MacArthur: Willaumez," vol 32, no 1 (January 1947).

Of the Marine Corps oral history interviews of participants in the New Britain fighting, the most valuable were with Generals Lemuel C. Shepherd, Jr., and Edwin A. Pollock and Lieutenant Generals Henry W. Buse, Lewis J. Fields, Robert B. Luckey, and John N. McLaughlin.

Almost three dozen collections of personal papers deal in one way or another with the campaign, some of them providing narratives of varying length and others photographs or maps. The most enlightening commentary came from the papers of Major Sherwood Moran, USMCR, before the war a missionary in Japan and during the fighting an intelligence specialist with the 1st Marine Division, who discussed everything from coping with the weather to understanding the motivation of the Japanese soldier.

About the Author

Bernard C. Nalty served as a civilian member of the Historical Branch, G-3 Division, HQMC, from October 1956 to September 1961. In collaboration with Henry I. Shaw, Jr., and Edwin T. Turnbladh, he wrote Central Pacific Drive, volume 3 of the History of U.S. Marine Corps Operations in World War II, and he also completed a number of short historical studies, some of which appeared as articles in Leatherneck or Marine Corps Gazette. He joined the history office of the Joint Chiefs of Staff in 1961, transferring in 1964 to the Air Force history program, from which he retired in January 1994.

THIS PAMPHLET HISTORY, one in a series devoted to U.S. Marines in the World War II era, is published for the education and training of Marines by the History and Museums Division, Headquarters, U.S. Marine Corps, Washington, D.C., as a part of the U.S. Department of Defense observance of the 50th anniversary of victory in that war.

WORLD WAR II COMMEMORATIVE SERIES

DIRECTOR OF MARINE CORPS HISTORY AND MUSEUMS

Brigadier General Edwin H. Simmons, USMC (Ret)

GENERAL EDITOR,

WORLD WAR II COMMEMORATIVE SERIES

Benis M. Frank

CARTOGRAPHIC CONSULTANT

George C. MacGillivray

EDITING AND DESIGN SECTION, HISTORY AND MUSEUMS DIVISION

Robert E. Struder, Senior Editor; W. Stephen Hill, Visual Information Specialist;

Catherine A. Kerns, Composition Services Technician, R.D. Payne, Volunteer—Web Edition

Marine Corps Historical Center

Building 58, Washington Navy Yard

Washington, D.C. 20374-5040

1994 - PCN 190 003128 00

First Marine Division Special Action Report: Cape Gloucester

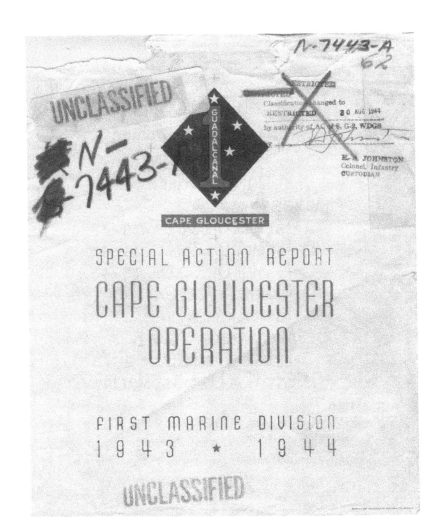

N-7443-A
62

N-7443-

RESTRICTED

Classification changed to
RESTRICTED   30 AUG 1944
by authority of AC of S, G-2, WDGS

E. B. JOHNSTON
Colonel, Infantry
CUSTODIAN

GUADALCANAL

1

CAPE GLOUCESTER

SPECIAL ACTION REPORT

CAPE GLOUCESTER
OPERATION

FIRST MARINE DIVISION
1943 ★ 1944

PHASE I

Planning and Training
Part I - Training.
Part II - Planning.

Annexes:

A - 1st. Mar. Div. Op. O. 16-43
B - 1st. Mar. Div. Op. O. 14-43
C - 1st. Mar. Div. Op. O. 15-43
D - Alamo Force G-3 Plan
E - Task Alamo Force
F - Alamo Force FO # 5
G - 1st. Mar. Div. Op. O. # 2-43
H - Station List - 1st. Mar. Div.

PHASE I

PLANNING AND TRAINING

PART I - TRAINING

The First Marine Division arrived at Melbourne, Victoria, Australia, on 12 January, 1943. Arrangements had been made by the Army Base Section Four in conjunction with the Marine Advance Echelon to billet the Division in the general area around Melbourne. Units of the Division were assigned to various camps as follows:

Melbourne Metropolitan Area

Camp Murphy	1st Mar
	Co D 1st Med Bn
Camp Robinson	Div Hq Bn (less Det and Cas Co)
	1st MT Bn (less Co B and Co C).
	1st Serv Bn
	Hq and Serv Co 1st Med Bn
Camp Pell (Convalescent)	Co E 1st Med Bn
	Cas Co Div Hq Bn (later transferred to Mt. Martha).

Balcombe - Mount Martha Area

Balcombe	Det Div Hq Bn
	5th Mar
	1st Amph Trac Bn
	Co A 1st Med Bn
	Co D 1st Tk Bn (Sct)
Mount Martha	7th Mar
	17th Mar
	Co B and Co C 1st MT Bn
	Co C 1st Med Bn

Ballarat Area

Ballarat	11th Mar
	1st Tk Bn (less Co D)
	1st Spl Wpns Bn
	Co B 1st Med Bn

The training phase in Australia began on 18 January, 1943. During the first period of four weeks emphasis was placed on disciplinary drills, reorganize, reequipment and recreation. Training during the second period February 1 to 27 March 1943, continued along the same lines as prescribed for the first period with the addition of small unit tactics. Particular emphasis was placed on physical conditioning of all personnel. During the month of April landing exercises were conducted by the Fifth Marines and Seventh Marines in Port Shillip Bay. In the reequipment of the Division the M-1 rifle was issued in place of the 1903 Springfields. Range qualification by personnel armed with this weapon was conducted during the months April, May and June at the Williamstown Range. During the third period 10 April to 30 June, tactical training was progressive and culminated in large scale Landing Team and Combat Team exercises, using live ammunition for all weapons. Due to the restricted training camp was established during May in the vicinity of Rowville, about 30 miles from the City. This was occupied by the First Marines (less 1 Battalion). The Battalion remaining at Camp Murphy rotated duty with those in the field.

Training for the period 1 July to 30 September, consisted of a review of the elementary phases and additional exercises of ten days duration in the field by Combat Teams employing all supporting units. In the final phases of the field exercises, supporting overhead fires augmenting rifle and machine gun and mortar fires by infantry units added realism to the operations.

On August 31, 1943, the Division was alerted for movement to staging areas in New Guinea and the Ferguson Island Group. During the latter part of September and the first part of October this movement was effected as follows:

Combat Team A (Fifth Marines Reinforced) - To Milne Bay, New Guinea.
Combat Team C (Seventh Marines Reinforced) - To Oro Bay, New Guinea.
First Marine Division (less Combat Teams A and C) - To Goodenough Island.

For the next two months, units conducted advanced training in the staging areas. This period was most beneficial to the troops as it was possible to conduct training under climatic conditions similar to that which would be encountered in future operations. Training in shore-to-shore operations, new to this Division, using LST's, LCI's, LCT's, Amphibian Tractors, and Amphibian Trucks, was conducted during this period. While it is not deemed necessary to conduct all of the training of organizations in areas where climatic and terrain conditions similar to those of the theatre of operations, it is strongly recommended that a period of approximately two months of advanced training under these conditions be included for units going into combat.

- 2 -

PART II - PLANNING

Planning for the Western New Britain campaign began in June 1943, when certain Division Staff Officers were ordered to GHQ at Brisbane to collaborate in the formation of the initial plans. On 31 August Division Operations Orders were issued forming the Amoeba Force (Annex A Division Operation Order 16-43), the Lazaretto Force (Annex B Division Operation Order 14-43 and the Backhander Force (Annex C Division Operation Order 15-43). These forces were all a part of the Alamo Force under the Command of Lieutenant General Krueger, U. S. Army, Commanding General, Sixth U. S. Army. The mission of the Amoeba Force was to occupy Western New Britain to include the general line Gasmata - Talasea and by combined airborne and overwater operations to establish airdromes therein for subsequent operations against Rabaul. For the initial Sixth Army Plan See Annex D G-3 Plan and Annex E.

As the situation in Western New Britain developed these initial plans were drastically revised. The landing on the south coast in the vicinity of Gasmata (Lazaretto Force) was abandoned and the First Marine Division was assigned the primary task of seizing Cape Gloucester and rapidly developing the airdrome facilities in that area coincident therewith to extend control over Western New Britain to include the general line Borgen Bay - Itni River.

Briefly the Cape Gloucester Plan of operations was developed as follows:

(a) "To land one Combat Team (less one landing team) to the east and one landing team to the west of the airdrome with one airborne parachute regiment landing to the south". This plan was subsequently revised due to the reported growing strength of the Japanese in the Gloucester area.

(b) "To land one Combat Team to the east and one landing team to the west of the airdrome with one Combat Team (less LT) in reserve. One airborne parachute regiment landing in the kunai patches south of yellow beach after the beachhead had been secured. Due to the difficulties of transporting such a large body of paratroopers and dropping them in the limited areas available, the Commanding General, First Marine Division, recommended that this unit be replaced by Combat Team A, First Marine Division. This recommendation was approved by the Commanding General, Sixth U. S. Army on 15 December and the final plan was agreed upon.

(c) "To land one Combat Team in assault with one Combat Team (less 1 LT) in close support to the east and simultaneously to land one landing team to the west of the airdrome. The remaining Combat Team of the Division to be in reserve". For details of this plan see FO #5 Alamo Force and Operation Order 2-43, First Marine Division, Annexes F and G. The execution of this plan is given in detail in Phase II of this Special Action Report.

ANNEX A.

1st Marine Division Operation Order 16-43

00392
180/cmb

First Marine Division,
Fleet Marine Force,
C/O Fleet Post Office, San Francisco, Calif.

31 August, 1943.

OPERATION ORDER
NUMBER   16-43

1.   The AMOEBA FORCE is hereby constituted consisting
of the following units of this division:

TASK ORGANIZATION:-

(a) <u>Whaling Group</u>   Colonel Wm. J. Whaling, USMC
                1st Mar
                3d Bn 11th Mar
                Co B 1st Tk Bn (less 1st Plat)
                1st Plat Co D (Sct) 1st Tk Bn
                Co A 1st MT Bn
                Btry C 1st Spl Wpns Bn
                2nd Plat Btry A 1st Spl Wpns Bn
                Co D 1st Med Bn
                Co B 1st Amph Trac Bn
                Co B 1st Bn 17th Mar
                Co E 2nd Bn 17th Mar
                Det S&S Co 1st Ser Bn
                2nd Plat Ord Co 1st Ser Bn
                2nd Plat 1st MP Co

b) <u>McDougal Group</u>   LtCol David S. McDougal, USMC
                3d Bn 5th Mar

c) <u>Meints Group</u>   LtCol C. G. Meints, USMC
                Div Hq Bn (less Dets Div Hq Co, 1st Sig Co (less
                    dets) and 1st, 2nd, 3d Plats 1st MP Co)
                1st MT Bn (less Cos A, B, & C)
                1st Tk Bn (less Cos A, B, & 1st, 2nd & 3d Plats
                    Co D (Sct))
                17th Mar (less Cos A,B,C,D,E, & F)
                11th Mar (less 1st, 3d, 4th & 5th Bns)
                Spl Wpns Bn (less Btrys B, C. D & 1st, 2d 3d Plats
                    Btry A)
                1st Med Bn (less Cos A, C & D)
                1st Ser Bn (less Ord Co (less Dets), and dets S&S Co)
                1st Amph Trac Bn (less Cos A, B, & C)

3.   Colonel Robert H. PEPPER, USMC, is designated
Commander AMOEBA FORCE.

BY COMMAND OF MAJOR GENERAL RUPERTUS:

AMOR LeR. SIMS,
Colonel, U. S. Marine Corps,
Chief of Staff.

O-F-F-I-C-I-A-L:

E. A. POLLOCK,
LtCol., USMC,
   D-3

ANNEX B.

1st Marine Division Operation Order 14-43

First Marine Division,
Fleet Marine Force,
C/o Fleet Post Office, San Francisco, Calif.

 UNCLASSIFIED 31 August, 1943.

OPERATION ORDER
NUMBER 14-43.

1.   The LAZARETTO FORCE consisting of the following troops of this DIVISION is hereby constituted for purposes of operation against the enemy in the Southwest Pacific Area:

```
ADC Comd Grp
5th Mar (less 3d Bn)
5th Bn, 11th Mar
Btry B, 1st Sol Wpns Bn
1st Plat, Btry A, 1st Sol Wpns Bn
Co. B, 1st MT Bn
Co. A, 1st Med Bn
Co. A, 1st Amph Trac Bn
Co. A, 1st Bn, 17th Mar
Co. D, 2nd Bn, 17th Mar
2nd Plat, Co. D (Sct), 1st Tk Bn
1st Plat, 1st MP Co
Det, S&S Co, 1st Ser Bn
1st Plat, Ord Co, 1st Ser Bn
2d Plat, Co. B 1st Tk Bn
```

2.   The CG 6th Army will assign the following Army troops to the LAZARETTO FORCE:

```
Btry B 104th CA Bn (AW) (40mm)
Hq & Hq Btry 209th CA Bn (AA)
Btry B 743d CA Bn (Gun)(90mm)
Btry A 104th CA Bn (AW)(40mm)
Btry A 236th AAA SL Bn
1 Btry FA - 155mm guns
Det ESB
Port Detachment
```

3.   A Navy Shore Establishment will be assigned by ComPhib For 7th Fleet.

4.   Brigadier General Lemuel C. SHEPHERD, JR., is designated Commander LAZARETTO FORCE.

BY COMMAND OF MAJOR GENERAL RUPERTUS:

AMOR LeR. SIMS,
Colonel, U. S. Marine Corps,
Chief of Staff.

O-F-F-I-C-I-A-L:

E. A. POLLOCK,
LtCol., USMC,
D-3

ANNEX "B"   **UNCLASSIFIED**

ANNEX C

First Marine Division Operation Order 15-43.

First Marine Division,
Fleet Marine Force,
C/o Fleet Post Office, San Francisco, Calif.

31 August, 1943.

OPERATION ORDER:
NUMBER   15-43:

UNCLASSIFIED

1.   The BACKHANDER FORCE consisting of the following units of this DIVISION is formed for purpose of operation against the enemy in the Southwest Pacific Area:

> Det Div Hq Co
> 7th Mar
> 4th Bn 11th Mar
> 1st Bn 11th Mar
> Co A 1st Tk Bn
> 3d Plat Co D (Sct) 1st Tk Bn
> Co C 1st MT Bn
> Btry D 1st Spl Wpns Bn
> Co C 1st Med Bn
> Co C 1st Amph Trac Bn
> Co C 1st Bn 17th Mar
> Co F 2nd Bn 17th Mar
> 3d Plat 1st MP Co
> 1st Sig Co (less dets)
> Det S&S Co 1st Serv Bn
> Ord Co 1st Serv Bn (less dets)
> 3d Plat Btry A 1st Spl Wpns Bn

2.   The CG 6th Army will assign the following units to the BACKHANDER FORCE:

> 503d Parachute Regt.
> 12th Marine Defense Bn.
> 1 Engr Avn Bn.

3.   Major General W. H. RUPERTUS assumes command of the BACKHANDER FORCE.

BY COMMAND OF MAJOR GENERAL RUPERTUS:

AMOR LeR. SIMS,
Colonel, U.S. Marine Corps,
Chief of Staff.

O-F-F-I-C-I-A-L:

E. A. POLLOCK,
LtCol., USMC.,
   D - 3.

UNCLASSIFIED

ANNEX D
ALAMO FORCE
G-3 PLAN

G-3 PLAN

1. **MISSION.**

   a. General:

   Occupy western New Britain, to include the general line Gasmata-Talasea, by combined airborne and overwater operations and establish airdromes thereon for subsequent operations against Rabaul.

   b. Specific Missions:

   (1) Capture Gasmata by overwater operations; extend present air strip or build new strip; maintain strip in stand-by condition.

   (2) Capture Cape Gloucester by a combined airborne-amphibious operation and establish airdromes to accommodate two groups of fighters and 1½ groups of medium bombardment.

   (3) By subsequent shore-to-shore operations consolidate the Cape Gloucester area and establish control over the north coast of New Britain to include Talasea and the nearby island groups to the northeast and west.

   c. D-day for the operation will be the date of the initial landing of the Gasmata Force.

2. **AVAILABLE FORCES:**

   1st Marine Division
   32d Infantry Division
   503d Parachute Infantry

3. **COMPOSITION OF TASK FORCES:**

   a. Gasmata Force:
   1 RCT (less 1 Inf Bn)
   1 Btry FA, 155mm Guns
   1 Hq, AA Bn (AW)
   1 Btry AA, Gun
   2 Btrys AA (AW)
   1 Pl, AA (SL)
   Det ESB
   Navy Shore Establishment
   Port Detachment

   b. Gloucester Force:
   Advanced Echelon, Division Hq
   503d Parachute Regiment
   1 RCT (with 105mm howitzers)
   1 Hq AA Bn (AW)
   3 Btrys AA (AW)
   1 Engr Av Bn
   1 Additional battalion of field artillery if landings are planned for widely separated beaches.

c. Reserves and additional garrison elements are as proposed in Marfa Plan.

4. STAGING PLAN:

a. Command Post New Britain Force: Goodenough Island.

b. 1st Marine Division (less Gasmata Force and less Gloucester Force): Goodenough Island.

c. Gasmata Force: Milne Bay.

d. Gloucester Force: Oro Bay.

e. 32d Infantry Division (less 2 Rcts): Goodenough Island.

f. L RCT, 32d Infantry Division: Milne Bay until relieved by elements of the 1st Cavalry Division; thence Goodenough Island.

g. 1 RCT, 32d Infantry Division: Oro Bay.

h. 503d Parachute Infantry: Port Moresby until November 10; thence Dobodura.

i. All units will close in staging areas prior to October 10.

j. Discussion:

(1) This plan contemplates the use of the Marine Division in assault and the 32d Division in reserve. From the standpoint of both combat efficiency and morale, the Marine Division is probably the better of the two; however, both Divisions contain many officers and men with combat experiences. The Marine Division was returned to the mainland from Guadalcanal several months prior to the return of the 32d Division from New Guinea; and recurrent malaria cases have been relieved by replacements from the States. In contrast, the progress of training of the 32d Division is still being hindered by approximately 1700 cases of recurrent malaria; otherwise, its training efficiency is steadily on the increase, and by early September it will have completed amphibious training. The early relief of the Gloucester Force by elements of the 32d Division is contemplated in order that the Marine Division may have sufficient time to prepare for the final assault on Rabaul. The relief of the Gasmata Force by units other than 32d Division is under consideration.

k. Pertinent advantages of this staging plan are:

(1) Adequate dispersion of forces during the final preparatory phase without loss of close supervision and control.

(2) The staging of Task Forces at bases designated to supply them during operations.

- 2 -

(3) The establishment of a pool of labor at each base for emergency use.

(4) The headquarters of both divisions would be convenient to the CP of the New Britain Force, thus insuring close coordination and control of all operational matters.

(5) Both Task Forces receive final preparatory tra... climate and training closely akin to that of objective areas.

(6) The embarkation of task forces would be at points nearest to respective objectives thus reducing the time required for overwater movements.

(7) Ad advanced location of task force reserves. Running time of LCI's to Gasmata is less than 24 hours; that to Cape Gloucester approximately 48 hours.

(8) Location of Gloucester Force near Dobodura convenient to combined training with Parachute Regiment.

b. TRAINING OF TASK FORCES:

a. Training in staging areas will be designed to prepare units physically, tactically and mentally for battle. Emphasis will be placed on:
   (1) The perfection of amphibious training to include APD's.
   (2) Combat exercises over terrain approximating that of the objective areas.
   (3) Day and night landing operations, in conjunction with supporting air and naval elements with full participation of service units.
   (4) Perfection of communications.
   (5) Final rehearsal of respective operations with all elements participating.

b. Training of the Parachute Regiment will include:
   (1) Participation in exercises at Port Moresby with those air elements designated for the Cape Gloucester operation.
   (2) Training with supporting artillery in the Dobodura area.
   (3) Full participation in the final rehearsal for the Cape Gloucester operation.

6. ESTIMATE OF TRANSPORT:

a. For Gasmata Force:
   (1) Initial: 4 APD's; 4 APD's 5 LCM's; 50 LCV's.
   (2) Re-supply; 1 LST.

b. For Gloucester Force:
   (1) Initial: 4 APD's; 4 APD's; 20 LCI's; 40 LCM's; 2½ Groups T.C.
   (2) Re-supply: 7 additional LST's.

SECRET

7. **MOVEMENT TO OBJECTIVES:**

a. Gasmata Force:
  (1) 4 APD's:
   Lv Milne Bay D-1
   Ar Gasmata D-Day

  (2) 4 AP's:
   Lv Milne Bay D-2
   Ar Kiriwina D-1
   Lv Kiriwina D-1
   Ar Gasmata D-Day

b. Gloucester Force:
  (1) 4 APD's:
   Lv Oro Bay D-2
   Ar Lae D-1
   Lv Lae D-1
   Ar Cape Gloucester D-Day

  (2) 20 LCI's:
   Lv Oro Bay D-3
   Ar Morobe D-2
   Lr Morobe D-2
   Ar Finschaffen D-1
   Lv Finschaffen D-1
   Ar Cape Gloucester D-Day.

  (3) 40 LCM's:
   Lv Oro Bay D-3
   Ar Morobe D-2
   Lv Morobe D-2
   Ar Finschaffeh D-1
   Lv Finschaffen D-1
   Ar Cape Gloucester D-Day

  (4) 4 LST's:
   Lv Oro Bay D-1
   Ar Lae D-Day
   Lv Lae D-Day
   Ar Cape Gloucester D/1.

  (5) 2½ Groups T. C.
   Lv Dobodura D-Day 0530
   Ar Cape Gloucester D-Day 0700

c. Consideration must be given to the location of an additional staging point for the Gloucester Force at some point on Rooke Island.

8. **SCHEMES OF MANEUVER:**

a. Gasmata Force - Plan one.
  (1) Heavy bombing of Gasmata airdrome and defensive installations prior to darkness D-1.
  (2) Bombing of Rabaul airdromes prior to dawn on D-Day, and again just after dawn on D-Day.
  (3) Bombardment of Gasmata airdrome just prior to dawn on D-Day by Naval gun fire.
  (4) Effect landing at Lindenhafen Plantation just prior to dawn on D-Day. Initiate shore to shore operation against Gasmata as soon as heavy gun battery can be emplaced.

b. Gasmata Force - Plan Two.

  (1) (2) and (3) same as Plan One.
  (4) Effect landing directly east of Gasmata airdrome, sup-

- 4 -

ported by Naval gun fire, bombers and fighter planes, and making
maximum use of smoke; push forward rapidly and seize the narrow
sector of the Gasmata Peninsula.

c. Discussion:
     Plan One has the advantage of landing away from hostile
position and siezing the probable site for the airfield but loses the
advantage of an immediate follow-up of bombing and Naval gun fire, and
permits the enemy, should he so desire, to scatter into the jungle in
small groups, thus becoming the source of nuisance raids for many weeks.
     Plan Two has the disadvantage of attempting a landing against
hostile opposition. But this opposition should be considerably nullified
by the tremendous effect of prior bombing and shelling. Blocking off
Gasmata Peninsula would prevent any chance of escape into the jungle and
place the enemy in an unfavorable position with his back to the sea.
The losses to be expected from Plan Two should be little, if any, greater
than the shore-to-shore and mopping up operations necessitated by Plan
One. If initially successful, the time saved would materially reduce
the air and Naval operations necessary and insure the launching of the
Gloucester operation on schedule.

     d. Gloucester Force - Plan One.
     (1) Heavy bombing of Cape Gloucester airfields and defensive
installations prior to darkness on D/5.
     (2) Periodic bombing of Cape Gloucester area throughout the
night of D/5 and early morning of D/6 with heaviest concentrations
between 0300 and 0500.
     (3) Heavy shelling of Cape Gloucester defensive installations
by naval gun fire from escorting destroyers commencing at 0500 D/6
with particular attention to landing beaches.
     (4) Under cover of darkness D/6 land one infantry battalion
from APDs east of the airdrome area with supporting fire furnished
by APDs.
     (5) Under cover of darkness D/6 land the RCT (less one bn)
west of the airfield in the order:
          (a) One battalion of infantry in LCMs.
          (b) One battalion of field artillery in LCMs.
          (c) One company of Engrs in LCMs.
          (d) Remainder of RCT in LCIs.
     (6) Just after dawn D/6, preceded by a heavy bombing attack
and with maximum fighter coverage, land the Parachute Regiment
south of the airfield.
     (7) Deliver a coordinated, convergent attack on the airfield
with all three landing forces as soon as supporting artillery is
in position.

     e. Gloucester Force - Plan Two.
     This plan differs from Plan One in that the Parachute Regiment
remains at Dobodura on ground alert until the success of the amphibious
landings can be foreseen. In the interim between beach landings and
Parachute landings, it is anticipated that the enemy outposts will
have been driven in and his main defensive positions uncovered. A
coordinated attack supported by bombers, ground artillery and naval

-5-

gun fire should be initiated as soon as the parachute troops are ready for the assault.

    f. Gloucester Force - Plan Three.
      (1) and (2) same as Plan One.
      (3) Heavy shelling of airdrome and landing beaches commencing at 0500 0500 D-Day by APDs and escorting warships.
      (4) Land assault elements east of the airfield in the following sequence:
          (a) One battalion of infantry from APDs and one battalion of infantry from LCMs on adjacent beaches.
          (b) One battalion of field artillery from LCMs.
          (c) One engineer company from LCMs.
          (d) Remainder of RCT from LCIs.
      (5) The Parachute Regiment will remain at Dobodura on ground alert until the beach head is safely established. On call, it will land within the beach head and participate in a coordinated attack on the airfield. This attack should be supported by coordinated action of bombers, naval gun fire and ground artillery.

    g. In all of the above plans it is contemplated that AA units and the Engr Av Bn will land prior to daybreak on D/7, if the attack appears to be nearing a successful conclusion. Otherwise, these units remain on LSTs in Finschafen Harbor until called forward.

    h. After debarkation of personnel and equipment, all landing craft of assault waves will immediately return to nearest staging point.

    i. Shore-to-shore operations to establish control of Talasea and the outlying islands will be initiated as soon as the local defense of the Gloucester area has been firmly established.

    j. Discussion:
      Plans One and Two take advantage of the convex shoreline of Cape Gloucester, which permits of a convergent attack from the east and west, and utilizes open terrain south of the airdrome for parachute landings. Both Plans are designed to place the enemy with his back to the sea, thereby eliminating all chances of escape and reinforcement.
      Plan One has the distinct advantage of a sudden powerful thrust, striking the enemy with the full force of one concerted action before he has sufficient time to recover from the shock of bombing and shelling. On the other hand, it offers the grave risk of losing the entire Parachute Regiment if landing operations are not initially successful. It is the more daring of the three plans presented but offers the best chance of an immediate success.
      Plan Two lacks the advantage of early, concerted action; but it eliminated the risk involved in landing the Parachute Regiment prior to the successful establishment of a beachhead. The time required for organizing a coordinated attack, after a landing under cover of darkness, might possibly bridge the delay caused by withholding the Para-

-6-

chute Regiment and thus avoid any relaxation of pressure against the
enemy.

The adoption of Plan Three may be forced by the necessity of
using the route north of Rooke Island. It has the advantage of cen-
tralized control and of providing a protected landing area for the
Paratroopers. But it permits the enemy to concentrate his forces against
an attack from one direction, and exposes the rear of our forces to a
possible run of a "Tokio Express".

With present information, neither the detailed plan of operation nor the landing beaches can be definitely determined. However,
all three of the plans appear feasible and do not differ radically in
any respect. Any Plan adopted will require a strong Naval escort in
the Bismarck Sea for protection against a possible "Tokio Express"
from Rabaul.

9. COORDINATION OF OPERATIONS:

a. A simultaneous attack on each objective is precluded by lack
of sufficient air forces to support concurrent operations and by the
necessity for employing all available APDs in both landings.

b. The capture of Gasmata should definitely block any attempts
by the enemy to reinforce Cape Gloucester from the south and make the
sea route northward to Finschhafen reasonably safe from attacks by enemy
surface ships. Moreover, the simpler operation of the two would be
accomplished first, leaving available for the Cape Gloucester attack
a maximum concentration of planes and shipping. The Gasmata operation
may delude the enemy into believing that an early movement against
Rabaul will follow along the south coast; but it might well create
the opposite effect and result in a rush of reinforcements to Cape
Gloucester and Talasea.

c. Initiating operations against Cape Gloucester would crack
the hardest nut first and better utilize the advantage of surprise.
However, as the capture of Cape Gloucester is only the beginning of
operations along the north coast, it might be difficult to determine
just when planes and ships could be diverted for the attack on
Gasmata. The proximity of Gasmata to Rabaul makes it far less difficult for the enemy to reinforce than Cape Gloucester.

d. In view of the above considerations, it is believed that the
Gasmata operation should precede the attack on Cape Gloucester. But
the intervening time should be reduced to the minimum in order to
forestall any attempts of the enemy to rush adequate reinforcements
to Cape Gloucester. This interval can best be determined by the time
necessary for APDs to proceed from Gasmata to Oro Bay, refuel, load
troops and then proceed to Cape Gloucester. It is believed that five
days would suffice for this process, thus permitting the assault on
Cape Gloucester to be initiated on D/6.

 -7-

SECRET

10. **COMPARISION WITH MARFA PLAN:**

The plan proposed herein does not adhere to the "Marfa" Plan proposed by GHQ in the following respects:

a. The Gasmata Force is staged at Milne Bay instead of Townsville.

b. The Reserve of the Gasmata Force is located at Goodenough Island instead of Milne Bay.

c. In lieu of staging the entire 32d Division at Milne Bay, the Division (less 2 RCTs) is staged at Goodenough Island, one RCT at Milne Bay and one RCT at Oro Bay.

d. The organization of the Gasmata Force is simplified by substituting an RCT (less one inf bn) in lieu of one inf regt (less 1 bn), one FA Bn (less 1 Btry), 1 Engr Company (C) and CT detachments. The "Marfa" Plan fails to definitely account for the 105mm battery withdrawn.

e. Eight LCMs and 50 LCVs are substituted for 10 LCMs and 40 LCVs due to the fact that only eight LCMs can probably be deck loaded on four APs.

f. The Gloucester Force is staged at Oro Bay instead of Goodenough Island.

g. The Parachute Regiment is moved to Dobodura for the final week of training.

h. D-day is determined as the date of the initial landing at Gasmata; not at Cape Gloucester.

-8-

ANNEX E

TASK — ALAMO FORCE

(GHQ DIRECTIVE)

GHQ DIRECTIVE

TASK

(a) The task assigned to ALAMO force is:

Occupy western NEW BRITAIN to include general line GASMATA-TALASEA by combined airborne and over water operations and establish airdromes therein for subsequent operations against RABAUL.

(b) The objective of these operations is to provide, from western NEW BRITAIN, effective general and direct air support for subsequent operations against RABAUL and KAVIENG.

(c)(1) At initiation of this operation it is expected that SOUTHWEST PACIFIC forces will have the shores of HUON GULF and FINSCHAFEN, with fighter and bomber aviation operation from LAE-MARCHAN VALLEY area. SOUTH PACIFIC forces will hold BUIN-FAIST area. Both forces, by coordinated air operations, will have established air superiority over NEW BRITAIN, south NEW IRELAND, and north coast of NEW GUINEA, to include MADANG. Enemy fighter protection will probably remain active in RABAUL and KAVIENG areas. WEWAK will be principal advance operations base of enemy air force, and there may be a minor air base on MANUS ISLAND. The SOLOMON SEA will be effectively denied to enemy naval forces, although barge traffic will undoubtedly continue. Water borne supply to RABAUL will be seriously hampered by our air forces. Enemy will have effected limited reinforcement of his garrison in western NEW BRITAIN to probably minima of:

CAPE GLOUCESTER	1200-1500
GASMATA	800-1000
TALASEA	500- 800
ARAWE	300

Reserves of supplies at these garrisons will be limited.

(2) Establishment of our air forces in the CAPE GLOUCESTER area will require denial to the enemy of western NEW BRITAIN as far as the line TALASEA-GASMATA; the VITU ISLAND, ROOKE ISLAND, TOLOQUIN and LONG ISLAND as base from which to hamper our operations. An air strip on GASMATA area is required, during subsequent operations against RABAUL, for air cover of convoy movements.

-1-

SECRET

(3) This operation will be assisted by coordinated operation by SOUTH PACIFIC force to eliminate enemy occupied areas in central BOUGAINVILLE and to neutralize BUKA and by NEW GUINEA force to consolidate its position in the HUON PENINSULA. The occupation of, or neutralization of, enemy forces in MADANG may precede, be concurrent with, or follow this operation.

(4) This operation must be economically conducted in order to conserve forces for assault upon RABAUL. In addition, employment of troop carrying assault landing craft must be closely coordinated with requirements of the MADANG operation. Necessary coordination of means and timing will be provided by GHQ as the situation develops during operation IIa. For planning purposes, it may be assumed that timely allotment of amply equipment as estimated herein will be made by GHQ for the minimum period required to accomplish the various phases of the operation.

(d)(1) Combat elements allotted to ALAMO:

> 1 Division in Assault.
> 1 Division in Reserve.
> 503 Parachute Infantry.

(2) Over water transportation support of the operation will be provided by AMPHIBIOUS FORCE - 7th FLEET.

2. (1) Scheme of Maneuver.
The general concept is one of a quick stroke which neutralizes GASMATA followed by an attack in force to take CAPE GLOUCESTER.

(2) GASMATA will be initially neutralized by an overseas landing operation, employing APA's to place airdrome under fire of long range artillery, later taken by shore to shore operation employing 1 Boat Company, Engineers Special Brigade, when resistance is weakened permitting occupation with minor loss. The expedition will land one Regiment, 1 Combat Team less one Battalion in the LINDENHAFEN-RING RING PLANATION area, 8 to 11 miles eastward of present airdrome. Close air support will be provided from KIRWINA, DOBODURA and LAE. An airstrip will be constructed (or the present enemy strip extended) and maintained in stand-by condition to provide convoy cover as required during the RABAUL operation. The operation will base on MILNE BAY and be initially maintained therefrom by amphibious transportation. Eventually supply will be by SOS from MILNE BAY.

- 2 -

SECRET

(3) Preceded by heavy air neutralization of RABAUL and KAVIENG by SOUTH PACIFIC forces and of LORENGAU and WEWAK by SOUTHWEST PACIFIC general support elements, a combined airborne amphibious operation will seize CAPE GLOUCESTER. This operation will base on ORO BAY - DOBODURA and will require forward Army staging bases for light amphibious equipment in the FINSCHAFEN - ROOKE ISLAND area. As visualized, the over water compenents will land one regiment prior to dawn in the immediate vicinity, east and west of the present Jap landing strips, main effort on the west, concurrently artillery will be landed further to the westward to establish fire support of the ensuing action. At dawn one parachute regiment will be launched onto the airdrome to accompany assault by the landing forces. The parachute attack will be preceded by a major concentration of close air support and protected by maximum use of smoke. Heavy supporting elements will be brought in by air and water at maximum rate. Reinforcements to bring the protective garrison to a Division (less 1 CT) will be contingent upon the enemy situation at the time. Subsequently the CAPE GLOUCESTER position will be consolidated by minor shore to shore operations therefrom, employing one Boat Bn., Engr. Special Brigade, to establish control over the north coast of NEW BRITAIN to include TALASEA and the nearby island groups to the northeast and west. Airdrome will be developed to accomodate two groups fighters, 1-1/2 groups medium bombardment. Garrison will be maintained by SOS transportation from ORO BAY.

(4) ARAWE not being required in our operation, will be neutralized by our light naval force if it interferes with our operations.

(b) D-day for the operation will be the landing in force of the amphibious operation in the vicinity of CAPE GLOUCESTER airdrome. The GASMATA operation will precede by about six days the D-day attack on CAPE GLOUCESTER, in order to permit concentration of maximum close air and naval support for each. Establishment of covering forces for CAPE GLOUCESTER can be initiated by about D/7. Target date for D-day is 15 November. Exact date to be announced.

3. Estimate of forces:

(a) North Force (CAPE GLOUCESTER)
(1) Assault elements - (Stripped units)

1 Hq Div	100
503 Para Regt	2000
1 Regt CT	4000
1 Hq AA Bn	140
3 Btrys AA	480
1 Bn Engrs.	800
	7520

- 3 -

(2) Reserve:
    1 CT (GOODENOUGH) *(1)

(3) Major Supporting Elements*(2)
    2-1/2 groups TC
Assault amphibious equipment to float
approximately 4500 with minimum equipment and supplies. Naval and air support
as required.

(4) Additional garrison *(3)

*NOTES: (1) Later included as garrison unit.
       (2) Later withdrawn.
       (3) Includes covering forces established
           as 2 Bns. and services.

(b) South Force (GASMATA):
    (1) Assault elements:

1 CT (less 1 Bn)	2850
1 Btry 155mm	150
1 Hq AA Bn	140
1 Btry AA	150
2 Btrys AA	320
1 Pl AA (SL)	120
1 Co Engrs, Combat	180
CT Dets.	100
Det Engr (Spec Brig Boat) *(4)	200
Navy Shore Det	50
Port Det	150
	4410

(2) Reserve:
    1 Bn CT MILNE

(3) Supporting Elements
    Ship to shore equipment to float 4400
with minimum equipment and supplies. Air and naval support
as assigned.

(4) Additional garrison elements:

1 Airdrome Squadron	300
1 Bn Engrs	800
Army Service	600
	1700

(5) Total eventual garrison 6110

SECRET

    c. Island Force
       Garrison elements

WOODLARK	6000
KIRIWINA	9000
GOODENOUGH	5000
	20000

*NOTE: (4) lOL 40 L

   4. Logistic arrangements:

     (a) ALAMO Force responsible for supply.

     Supply and Evacuation:
      (1) Bases
        (a) North Force — ORO BAY
        (b) South Force — MILNE BAY

      (2) Supply Scale:
        (a) Initial
          1. North Force
            3 units fire
            20 days at 15 lbs per man
          2. South Force
            5 units fire
            30 days at 15 lbs per man

        (b) Eventual
          Ammunition — 5 units fire except AA
                10 units fire AA
                30 days at 20 lbs per man
                    per day

      (3) Equipment Scale:
        (a) Assault Force Motor Transport except-
ing Engrs, not to exceed 25% TBA appropriate increments forwarded with garrison echelon.

        (b) Heavy tent with garrison echelon.

      (4) Monthly Maintenance
        (a) North Force
          (1) Land and air service elements
at 20 lbs. per man per day.

        (b) South force.

- 5 -

ANNEX F
Field Order No. 5
ALAMO FORCE

S E C R E T

UNCLASSIFIED

HEADQUARTERS ESCALATOR
A.P.O. 712
1800 30 November 1943

FO 5
(Supercedes FO 4 Hq Escalator 18 Oct 1943)

Maps: WD Corps of Engineers Map ARABIC, 1" - 4 miles. 3 sheets.
4 mile Strategical Map, CENTRAL, 1" - 4 miles. COCKNEY sheet.
WD Corps of Engineers Provisional Map, ARABIC, 1:63,360.
WD Corps of Engineers SP Map, 1:20,000, BACKHANDER 7 sheets.

1. a. Hostile dispositions are as shown in intelligence summaries
and in Annex No. 1 (Intelligence).

b. Forces of the Southwest Pacific continue offensive operations
with the strategical support of South Pacific air and naval
forces.

(1) Phosphorus continues assigned missions.

(2) Allied Air Force Supports the operations of Escalator
by:

(a) Denying seaborne reinforcement and supply of enemy
occupied areas in western ARABIC by an intensive
blockade established in conjunction with the
Allied Naval Forces at the earliest practicable
date.

(b) Providing intensive preliminary aerial bombardment
of the DIRECTOR and BACKHANDER areas and close
air support of operations to seize objectives.

(c) Neutralizing hostile air and naval operations along
the south coast of ARABIC.

(d) Providing anti-submarine escort and air protection
of over-water troop and supply movements of
Escalator.

(3) Allied Naval Forces support the operations of Escalator
by:

(a) Destroying threatening hostile naval forces and providing naval protection of areas occupied.

UNCLASSIFIED

-1-

S-E-C-R-E-T

FO 5 Cont'd.

        (b) Transporting and landing troops and supplies at times and places designated by the Commanding General, Escalator.

(c) Denying seaborne reinforcement and supply of enemy occupied areas in western ARABIC by an intensive blockade established in conjunction with the Allied Air Force at the earliest practicable date.

        (d) Establishing light naval facilities in the DIRECTOR area for the protection of the southeastern flank of overwater operations in BOILINGPOINT.

        (e) Protecting lines of communication.

2. a. Escalator:

        (1) Will by overwater operations seize and defend a suitable location for the establishment of light naval facilities in the DIRECTOR area, and will occupy and consolidate such other areas to the westward thereof as may be essential.

        (2) Will assist the Commander, Allied Naval Forces, in the establishment of light naval facilities in the DIRECTOR area.

        (3) Will by overwater - operations seize, occupy and defend the BACKHANDER area, and will establish control over such adjacent islands and minimum portions of western ARABIC as may be required to insure uninterrupted operations of our air force from the BACKHANDER area.

        (4) Will establish airdrome facilities in the BACKHANDER area to accommodate two groups fighters and two groups medium bombardment; facilities to accommodate one group fighters (intercept) will be established with the least practicable delay.

        (5) Will assist Commander, Allied Air Force, in the establishment of air warning and radio navigational facilities in the general area of Escalator operations.

        (6) Will arrange overwater transportation at the earliest practicable date as required by the Commander, Allied Air Force, for the movement of Air Force elements from final staging areas to objective areas.

b. Task Forces:

        (1) Director Task Force:

           (a) Commander:

S-E-C-R-E-T

FO 5 Cont'd.

Brigadier General Julian W. Cunningham, USA.

Effective date of organization:

25 November 1943.

(c) Units and staging:

ASSAULT UNITS – DIRECTOR TASK FORCE

Unit	Staging Area
112th Cav Regt	Amoeba
148th FA Bn	Amoeba
59th Engr Co (C)(Sep)	Amoeba
Hq & Hq Btry, 256th AAA SL Bn	Amoeba
Btry C, 470th AAA AW Bn	Amoeba
Btry D, 470th AAA AW Bn	Amoeba

SUPPORTING GARRISON UNITS – DIRECTOR TASK FORCE

Det 93d Cml Comp Co	Amoeba
Prov Surv Det, 8th Engr Sq	Amoeba
Co "B" & H&S Det, 841st Engr Bn (Avn)	Amoeba
29th Evac Hosp	Amoeba
Co C (Coll) 135th Med Regt	Amoeba
1st Plat, 670th Clr Co	Amoeba
3469th Ord MM Co	Amoeba
Det 622d Ord Am Co	Amoeba
2d Plat, Co A, 207th Gas Sup Bn	Amoeba
1st Plat, 558th QM Rhd Co	Amoeba
1 Sec 3d Plat, 601st QM Graves Reg Co	Amoeba
Prov Sig Det	Amoeba
4th Combat Asgmt Unit (Photo)	Amoeba
Pigeon Det	Amoeba
Det ANGAU	Amoeba

(2) Backhander Task Force:

(a) Commander:

Major General W. H. Rupertus, USMC.

(b) Effective date of organization:

20 October 1943.

(c) Units and staging:

S-E-C-R-E-T

FO 5 Cont'd.

ASSAULT UNITS - BACKHANDER TASK FORCE

Unit	Staging Area
Det Hq 1st Marine Div	Penumbra
Combat Team "C" 1st Marine Div	
reinforced by 1 bn 105mm how	Penumbra
Combat Team "B".	Amoeba
12th Defense Bn USMC	
Det Hq & Serv Btry	Penumbra
Special Weapons Gp	Penumbra
90mm Gp	Penumbra
1913th Engr Avn Bn	Penumbra

SUPPORTING GARRISON UNITS - BACKHANDER TASK FORCE

Unit	Staging Area
1st Marine Div (less Combat Team "A" and	
assault units of Backhander Task Force)	Amoeba
Combat Team "A", 1st Marine Div	Pemmican
12th Def Bn USMC	
Hq & Serv Btry (dets)	Penumbra
2 Btrys 155mm Gp	Penumbra
469th AAA AW Bn	Penumbra
Det 93d Cml Comp Co	Penumbra
1 plat, 453d Engr Dep Co	Pemmican
864th Engr Avn Bn	Stilo
5th Malaria Control Unit	Pemmican
21st Med Sup Plat (Avn)	Amoeba
26th Malaria Survey Unit	Penumbra
30th Evac Hosp	Pemmican
58th Evac Hosp	Pemmican
Co A (Coll) 135th Med Regt	Penumbra
Co B (Coll) 135th Med Regt	Pemmican
Co G (Clr) 135th Med Reft	Penumbra
263d Ord MM Co	Penumbra
622d Ord Am Co (less det)	Penumbra
123d QM Bkry Co (less 1 plat)	Pemmican
Co A, 207th QM Gas Sup Bn (less 1 plat)	Pemmican
1 Co, 543d QM Serv Bn	Penumbra
558th QM Rhd Co (less 1 plat)	Pemmican

S-E-C-R-E-T

FO 5 Cont'd.

SUPPORTING GARRISON UNITS - BACKHANDER TASK FORCE - Cont'd.

Unit	Staging Area
1998th QM Trk Co (Avn) (less 1 plat)	Pemmican
1 Radar Rep Team	Pemmican
Co A, 99th Sig Bn (less dets)	Amoeba
22d Rad Sta Sec, 832d Sig Serv Co	Amoeba
23d Rad Sta Sec, 832d Sig Serv Co	Amoeba
244th Port Co	Pemmican
Survey Plat, 69th Engr Topo Co	Amoeba
Trailing Dog Det	Amoeba
Det ANGAU	Amoeba

UNCLASSIFIED

  (3) <u>Escalator Reserve</u>:

    (a) Commander:

      Major General William H. Gill, USA.

    (b) Effective date of organization:

      15 December 1943.

    (c) Units and Staging:

Unit	Staging Area
32d Inf Div (less 126th & 127th RCTs)	Amoeba
126th, 127th RCTs, 32d Inf Div	Pemmican

    (4) Command of units assigned to a Task Force passes to the Task Force Commander on the date his Task Force organization becomes effective, or upon arrival of the unit in its staging area if that arrival is subsequent to the date of organization of the Task Force.

  <u>c</u>. (1) Z-Day will be the date of the initial landing in the DIRECTOR area and for planning purposes is designated as 15 December 1943. The exact date will be announced later.

    (2) D-Day will be the date of the initial landing in the BACKHANDER area and for planning purposes is designated as 26 December 1943. The exact date will be announced later.

3. <u>a</u>. <u>The Director Task Force</u>:

UNCLASSIFIED

    (1) Will by overwater operations, land assault elements in the DIRECTOR AREA on Z-Day and will seize, occupy and defend that area. Security toward SADSACK and

- 5 -

S-E-C-R-E-T

FO 5 Cont'd.

along the trail toward ROSEMONT is important.

(2) Will, after consolidation of the DIRECTOR area:

    (a) Push reconnaissance westward to the mouth of CORNFIELD and up that river to DISCUS (exclusive) with a view to determining feasibility of developing a supply line to and establishing contact with the Backhander Task Force.

    (b) Occupy and consolidate areas so reconnoitered as may be essential.

(3) Will assist the Commander, Allied Naval Forces, in the establishment of light naval facilities in the DIRECTOR area.

(4) Will arrange overwater transportation for air warning units to the DIRECTOR area as requested by Commander, Allied Air Force, and will assist Commander, Allied Air Force, in the establishment of radar stations in that area.

b. The Backhander Task Force:

(1) Will move Combat Team "B" to the STILO – REDHERRING area; movement to be completed prior to D-Day in accordance with schedule to be furnished by Commander, Allied Naval Forces.

(2) Will by combined overwater – operations land assault elements in the BACKHANDER area on D-Day and will attack and capture the BACKHANDER airdrome and defenses.

(3) Will establish airdrome facilities in the BACKHANDER area to accomodate two groups fighters and two groups medium bombardment; facilities to accommodate one group fighters (intercept) will be established with the least practicable delay. Coincident therewith, will rapidly extend control over the western tip of ARABIC to include the general line CORNFIELD – GREYHOUND, and will defend the area so occupied.

(4) Will arrange overwater transportation for fighter sector and air warning units to the BACKHANDER area and will assist Commander, Allied Air Force, in the establishment of air warning and radio navigational facilities in areas occupied by the Backhander Task Force.

S-E-C-R-E-T

FO 5 Cont'd.

    (5) 1 Bn 128th Def. to REDHERRING prior to D-Day in accordance with schedule furnished by Commander, Allied Naval Forces. This Bn will be prepared by D-Day for overwater operations to seize and BOU and SOUO.

    (6) Will secure early information as to feasibility of developing a supply line south to DISCUS (inclusive). Commander, Director Task Force, will secure information as to feasibility of its development from the mouth of CORNFIELD to DISCUS (exclusive).

  c. The Escalator Reserve:

    (1) Will maintain close liaison with the Director and Backhander Task Forces.

    (2) Will be prepared to relieve units of the 1st Marine Division in any or all objective areas, if and as directed by the Commanding General, Escalator, and to assume responsibility for completion of any or all missions previously assigned to the Backhander Task Force in those areas.

x. (1) Director and Backhander Task Force Commanders and the Commander, Escalator Reserve, will submit their respective plans to this headquarters on or before 5 December 1943.

    (2) Director and Backhander Task Force Commanders will arrange details of air bombardment and naval gunfire support directly with the respective commanders of air and naval forces assigned to support their operations.

    (3) Recognition signals will be arranged by mutual agreement between Commanders of Director and Backhander Task Force for the purpose of establishing the identity of reconnaissance parties.

    (4) Commanding General, Escalator, will:

      (a) Arrange for movement of all units to staging areas.

      (b) Arrange for naval and air liaison to assist Task Forces in training and operational planning.

      (c) Arrange with Allied Air Force to furnish each Task Force with a weather party and sufficient air liaison parties.

-7-

SECRET

FO 5 Cont'd.

(d) Arrange directly for supporting air and naval forces, including the small landing craft in each objective area necessary for subsequent shore to shore movements.

(e) Arrange with the Commander, Phosphorus, for the use of adequate temporary staging areas in the STILO - REDHERRING area and in other localities in CENTRAL as may be required for Dexority.

(5) All troops will be utilized as required for loading, unloading and dispersal of equipment and supplies at destination.

(6) Except in emergencies, engineer construction units will be employed on airfields, docks and related activities only, with priority in the order named.

(7) When an enemy attack on any of the areas in ARABIC, occupied by Escalator, is imminent, or in progress, the operational control of all forces of the SWPA in the threatened area will pass to the local Escalator Commander in the threatened area.

(8) All persons will observe the greatest secrecy in all phases of the planning for this operation. Distribution of orders will be strictly limited to those who must know the complete operational plan. Each echelon will divulge only such parts of its instructions and at such times as deemed essential for action by next subordinate units.

4. Adm O 4.

5. Command Posts:

a. Escalator: AMOEBA.

Advance Echelon: To be reported.

b. Director Task Force: AMOEBA.

Opens DIRECTOR on Z-Day.

c. Backhander Task Force: PENUMBRA.

Opens BACKHANDER on D-Day.

S-E-C-R-E-T

FO 5 Cont'd.

   d. **Escalator Reserve**: AMOEBA.

WALTER KRUEGER,
Lieutenant General, U. S. Army,
Commanding.

1-Incl.
  List of Code Names.

UNCLASSIFIED

ANNEXES:
  1. Intelligence.
  2. Artillery.
  3. Antiaircraft Artillery.
  4. Engineer.
  5. Communications.

DISTRIBUTION:

CinC SWPA	(3)
CG USAFFE	(1)
Comdr ANF	(1)
CTF 76	(1)
Comdr AAF	(1)
CG Advon 5	(1)
Comdr Director Task Force	(2)
Comdr Backhander Task Force	(2)
Comdr Escalator Reserve	(2)
CG USASOS	(2)
CG Inter Sec USASOS	(1)
CG Sixth Army	(11)
C/S Escalator	(1)
G-1 Escalator	(1)
G-2 Escalator	(25)
G-3 Escalator	(3)
G-4 Escalator	(1)
QM Escalator	(1)
Ord Escalator	(1)
Surg Escalator	(1)
Sig Escalator	(1)
Engr Escalator	(1)
Cml Escalator	(1)
FA Escalator	(1)
AA Escalator	(1)
AG Escalator	(1)
Naval Liaison Officer.	(1)
Air Liaison Officer	(1)
CO 503d Prch Inf Regt	(1)

UNCLASSIFIED

S-E-C-R-E-T

```
            Copy No. 8
........................
:  S-E-C-R-E-T         :
:Auth: CG ESCALATOR    :
:Init:                 :
:Date:  15 Dec 1943    :
........................
```

HEADQUARTERS ESCALATOR
A. P. O. 712
1800 15 December 1943.

AMENDMENT NO. 1

TO FO 5

1. FO 5, Headquarters Escalator, 30 November 1943, is amended as follows:

  <u>a</u>. Delete paragraph 1<u>b</u>(2)(e).

  <u>b</u>. Paragraph 2<u>a</u>(3) is amended to read:

    Will by overwater operations seize, occupy and defend the BACKHANDER area, and will establish control over such adjacent islands and minimum portions of western ARABIC as may be required to insure uninterrupted operations of our air force from the BACKHANDER area.

  <u>c</u>. Paragraph 2<u>b</u>(2)(c) <u>ASSAULT UNITS - BACKHANDER TASK FORCE</u>.

    Delete: 1 bn landing team CT"B"
             503d Prcht Inf Regt

    Substitute: Combat Team "B", 1st Marine Div.

  <u>d</u>. Delete paragraph 2<u>c</u>(2) and substitute the following:

    D-Day will be the date of the initial landing in the BACKHANDER area and for planning purposes is designated as 26 December 1943. The exact date will be announced later.

  <u>e</u>. Delete paragraph 3<u>b</u>(1) and sub-paragraphs (a) and (b) and substitute the following:

    Will move Combat Team "B" to the STILO - REDHERRING area; movement to be completed prior to D-Day in accordance with schedule to be furnished by Commander, Allied Naval Forces.

  <u>f</u>. Paragraph 3<u>b</u>(2) is amended to read as follows:

    Will be overwater operations land assault elements in the BACKHANDER area on D-Day and will attack and capture the BACKHANDER airdrome and defenses.

- 1 -

S-E-C-R-E-T

g. Delete Paragraph 3b(5) and substitute the following:

Will move Combat Team "A" from BENEVOLENT to CELLULOID on D-Day in accordance with schedule provided by Commander, Allied Naval Forces. Upon arrival at CELLULOID Combat Team "A" will tranship on amphibious transportation and move to REDHERRING where it will be at the disposal of the Commanding General, Escalator.

(1) Combat Team "A" (less 1 battalion landing team), will be prepared to reinforce the assault elements in their attack on BACKHANDER, if and when ordered by the Commanding General, Escalator.

(2) The excepted battalion landing team will be prepared for overwater operations to seize and occupy BARNYARD and SANATOGEN, or to participate in the assault on BACKHANDER, whichever may be directed by the Commanding General, Escalator.

h. Delete paragraph 3x(4)(f).

WALTER KRUEGER,
Lieutenant General, U.S. Army,
Commanding.

DISTRIBUTION:

CinC SWPA	(3)	G-3 Escalator	(25)
CG USAFFE	(1)	G-4 Escalator	(3)
Comdr ANF	(1)	QM Escalator	(1)
CTF 76	(1)	Ord Escalator	(1)
Comdr AAF	(1)	Surg Escalator	(1)
CG Advon 5	(1)	Sig Escalator	(1)
Comdr Director Task Force	(2)	Engr Escalator	(1)
Comdr Backhander Task Force	(2)	Cml Escalator	(1)
Comdr Escalator Reserve	(2)	FA Escalator	(1)
CG USASOS	(2)	AA Escalator	(1)
CG Inter Sec USASOS	(1)	AG Escalator	(1)
CG Sixth Army	(11)	Naval Liaison Officer	(1)
C/S Escalator	(1)	Air Liaison Officer	(1)
G-1 Escalator	(1)	Comdr NGF	(1)
G-2 Escalator	(1)	CO 503d Prcht Inf Regt	(1)

[redacted]

S-E-C-R-E-T

UNCLASSIFIED

```
.........................
:   S E C R E T          :
:Auth: CG ESCALATOR      :
:Init:                   :
:Date:   30 Nov 43       :
.........................
```

HEADQUARTERS ESCALATOR
A. P. O. 712
1800 30 November 1943

ANNEX 1 to FO 5, INTELLIGENCE
(Supercedes ANNEX 1 to FO 4, INTELLIGENCE, Hq Escalator 18 Oct 1943)

1. SUMMARY OF ENEMY SITUATION:

    See current Intelligence Summaries and Estimates.

2. ESSENTIAL ELEMENTS OF INFORMATION:

    a. What is the strength, composition and disposition of the enemy occupying western ARABIC to include the general line: APPEASE-LAZARETTO and the NORTHPOLE and BOILING-POINT Islands?

    b. Will the enemy defend western ARABIC by making a determined stand at BACKHANDER?

    c. Will the enemy withdraw from the BACKHANDER area? If so, what will be his method and routes of withdrawal and to what area will he withdraw?

    d. Will the enemy launch a counteroffensive to retake the DIRECTOR and BACKHANDER areas and attempt to reestablish his control over them? If so, when, where and with what forces?

    e. Will the enemy interfere with our concentration of troops, supplies and transportation by aerial or naval attacks on our staging areas? If so, when, where, in what force and from what bases?

    f. Will the enemy interdict our waterborne movements by naval and aerial attacks? If so, when, where and with what strengths?

    g. Will the enemy employ naval forces for bombardment of our positions in DIRECTOR and BACKHANDER, in order to support his defenses, counteroffensive, reinforcement, or withdrawal?

- 1 -

S-E-C-R-E-T

UNCLASSIFIED

3. RECONNAISSANCE AND OBSERVATION MISSIONS:

   a. Commander, Director Task Force Will:

     (1) Initiate not more than 48 hours prior to landing operations such reconnaissance as he may deem necessary in his operational area.

     (2) As soon as practicable after landing, recruit, organize and train an appropriate detachment of native scouts for reconnaissance purposes.

     (3) Establish such system of coastwatchers, air-spotters and patrols as will enable him to report enemy movements in ARABIC south of the water-shed running east and west along the Island and between SADSACK on the east and first river north of GIGGLE on the west, also such portion of the sea as is visible from the above area.

     (4) Reconnoiter the trail running from lower SADSACK north to ROSEMONT and report on its condition and the feasibility of its further development.

     (5) Maintain a patrol in the vicinity of ROSEMONT and report all enemy activities in that locality.

   b. Commander, Backhander Task Force will:

     (1) Initiate not more than 48 hours prior to landing operations such reconnaissance as he may deem necessary in his operational area.

     (2) As soon as practicable after landing, recruit, organize and train an appropriate detachment of native scouts for reconnaissance purposes.

     (3) Establish such system of coastwatchers, air-spotters and patrols as will enable him to report enemy movements in the vicinity of SANATOGEN, BARNYARD, BOILINGPOINT, TRAJECTORY, NORTHPOLE, BACKHANDER area and along the north coast of ARABIC to include APPEASE.

     (4) Reconnoiter and report on the condition and feasibility of further development of the following tracks:

       (a) Coastal track from GREYHOUND to TORTILLA.

       (b) Overland track from HAMILTON to DISCUS.

       (c) Overland track from STONEFACE and COCKNEY to GUILD.

- 2 -

S-E-C-R-E-T

  (5) Investigate the navigational possibilities of the CORNFIELD from DISCUS to its mouth.

MEASURES FOR HANDLING PRISONERS AND CAPTURED DOCUMENTS:

 a. See Intelligence SOP and ADMINISTRATIVE ORDER 4.

 b. Four interrogators (Nisei) will be attached to Director Task Force.

 c. One Interrogator Team (Nisei) composed of 10 EM attached to Backhander Task Force.

5. MAPS AND PHOTOGRAPHS:

 a. Maps:

  (1) Small Scale – 1,1,000,000.

   (a) Australian Aeronautical Series, Sheets A-8, A-9, B-8, B-9, C-9.

  (2) Intermediate Scale – 1:253,440.

   (a) Provisional 1" to 4 mi map of ARABIC, Sheets: Western ARABIC, Central ARABIC and WOODCHUCK.

   (b) CENTRAL Strategical Series 1" to 4 mi, Sheets: Nos. 4, 5, 6, 7, to cover islands not included in (a) above.

  (3) Medium Scale – 1:63,360.

   (a) Provisional Map 1" to 1 mi, covering all of ARABIC west of the line APPEASE – CUMBERLAND, consisting of 41 sheets.

   (b) Provisional Map 1" to 1 mi, covering BARNYARD in 4 series.

  (4) Large Scale – 1:20,000.

   (a) Photo map 1:20,000 covering operational area of DIRECTOR, 6 sheets.

   (b) Photo map 1:20,000 covering operational area of BACKHANDER, 7 sheets.

   (c) Battle map (contoured) 1:20,000, covering same area as, and printed on reverse side of (b) above.

S-E-C-R-E-T

(5) Maps and Place Names:

Place names and localities included within the areas covered by the 1:20,000 photo map of DIRECTOR and the 1:20,000 line and photo map of BACKHANDER will be referred to as designated thereon regardless of variance from any other maps. Place and locality names on existing maps will be used as shown. Local place names will not be used in lieu of the names as designated on maps. In the event a village or other locality is found to be located in a place different from that shown on maps, or a new village or other locality is found bearing the same name as one shown on maps, then the new village or other locality will be referred to as village (given name) No. 2, No. 3, etc.

b. Photographs:

(1) Objective Folder #75, lithorgraphed obliques covering GREYHOUND to TORTILLA, now available.

(2) Objective Folder, lithographed obliques covering ZIMMERMAN to DIRECTOR will be available 1 December 1943.

(3) Requests for all contact prints and lithographed copies of aerial photography of operational areas will be submitted through Task Force Headquarters to AC of S, G-2, Escalator.

6. COUNTERINTELLIGENCE:

See Intelligence SOP.

7. PROPAGANDA:

Each Task Force Commander will be responsible for propaganda within his assigned area subject to the coordinating supervision of this and higher headquarters.

8. REPORTS AND DISTRIBUTION:

See Intelligence SOP.

By command of Lieutenant General KRUEGER:

EDWIN D. PATRICK,
Brigadier General, G.S.C.,
Chief of Staff.

OFFICIAL:

G - 2

- 4 -
S-E-C-R-E-T

S-E-C-R-E-T

```
: . . . . . . . . . . . . . . . . . . . . . :
:    S-E-C-R-E-T              :
: Auth: GG ESCALATOR          :
: Init:                       :
: Date: 30 November 43:
: . . . . . . . . . . . . . . . . . . . . . :
```

UNCLASSIFIED

HEADQUARTERS ESCALATOR
A. P. O. 712
1800 30 November 1943.

ANNEX 2 to FO 5, ARTILLERY.
(Supercedes ANNEX 2 to FO 4, ARTILLERY, Hq Escalator 18 Oct 1943)

FIELD ARTILLERY:

1. Field Artillery Intelligence Summary - Annex 2 a.

2. Special Instructions:

   a. Coordinate artillery employment with naval supporting
      fires to include composition and employment of shore
      fire control parties.

   b. Prepare and furnish naval supporting ships with plan of
      artillery fires.

   c. Be prepared to utilize field artillery fire from landing
      craft to provide close artillery support during shore
      to shore operations.

   d. Coordinate survey with Task Force Engineer.

3. Ammunition:

   a. Amounts.

      (1) Three units of fire will accompany assault troops.

      (2) Three additional units of fire will be dispatched so
          as to arrive in each objective area within 48 hours
          after the initial landing.

      (3) Escalator will establish and maintain a level of six
          units of fire.

   b. Proportions:

      10% Shell, Smoke, W.P., w/Fuze P.D., M57.
      30% Shell, H.E., M1 w/Fuze P.D., M54.
      60% Shell, H.E., M1 w/Fuze P.D., M48 or M48A1.

- 1 -

S-E-C-R-E-T

S-E-C-R-E-T

ANNEX 2 TO FO 5, Cont'd.

SEACOAST ARTILLERY:

1. **Special Instructions:**

   The Seacoast Artillery Commander w

   a. Be responsible for identification of war vessels and fire direction against those determined as hostile.

   b. Support illumination of anti-aircraft searchlights on request of Anti-aircraft Officer, if not engaged with sea-borne targets.

   c. Obtain clearance of Anti-aircraft Officer before placing searchlights in action.

2. **Ammunition:**

   a. Amounts:

   (1) 3 u/f will accompany assault elements.

   (2) Escalator will build up to and maintain level of 6 u/f.

   b. Proportions:

   75% Shell, H.E., MK III Al unfuzed, w/Fuze P.D., M51, w/Booster M21.
   25% Shell, A.P., M112, w/Fuze BD M60.
   125% Primers, percussion, 21-grain, MK II Al.
   Charges, propelling:
   110% - if in sealed fiber containers.
   100% - if in sealed metal containers.

   BY Command of Lieutenant General KRUEGER:

   EDWIN D. PATRICK,
   Brigadier General, G.S.C.,
   Chief of Staff.

OFFICIAL:

G - 3.

ANNEX 2a - Intelligence Summary.

- 2 -

ANNEX G

1st Marine Division Operation Order 2-43

00519
1990-5-80
160/283

Headquarters Backhander Force
A.P.O. 320

November 14, 1943.   1000

UNCLASSIFIED

Opn O
No. 2-43

MAPS: Special Map - ISLAND of ARABIC, 1;20,000, BACKHANDER
AIRDROMES, DAISYMAE, RANDOLPH, GOLDBERG, COCKNEY Sheets.
Annex D (Opn Overlay)

TASK ORGANIZATION

(a) Greyhound Gp   Col Julian N. Frisbie, USMC
    CT "C"
    4th Bn 11th Mar
    2d Bn 17th Mar (less Co F)
    3d Plat 1st MP Co
    Det S&S Co 1st Serv Bn
    3d Plat Ord Co
    Det Co C 583d Sig Bn (Det 20th Fi Sub Sector)
    Det 15th Wea Sq
    Det 2d ESB
    Det Sp Wpns Gp 12th Def Bn

(b) Wild Duck Gp   Col W. J. Whaling, USMC
    CT "B" (less LT 21, 3d Bn 11th Mar (less Btry H), Co B
                        1st Tk Bn)
    2d Bn 11th Mar
    Det 2d ESB
    Det Co C 583d Sig Bn (Det 20th Fi Sub Sector)
    Det H&S Btry 11th Mar

(c) Stoneface Gp   LtCol James M. Masters, Sr., USMC
    LT 21 (less 2d Plat Co B 1st Tk Bn and 2d Plat Co A 1st MT
                        Bn)
    4th Plat Btry A 1st Sp Wpns Bn
    1 Plat (Surg) Co B 1st Med Bn
    Det Co C 583d Sig Bn (Det 20th Fi Sub Sector)
    Det ANGAU
    Det 2d ESB

(d) AA Gp   Col W. H. Harrison, USMC
    Det H&S Btry 12th Def Bn
    90mm Gp 12th Def Bn
    Det Sp Wpns Gp 12th Def Bn
    One gun Sec 155mm Gp 12th Def Bn

SECRET

(e) <u>Engr Gp</u>   Col H. E. Rosecrans, USMC
    17th Mar (less 2d Bn & Cos A, B, & C)
    Co E 1st Med Bn
    Base Engr Hq

(f) <u>Res Gp</u>   Col J. T. Selden, USMC
    CT "A"

(g) <u>Garrison Gp</u>   LtCol J. M. Clark, USMC
    Det Co C 583d Sig Bn (Det 20th Fi Sub Sector)
    1913th Engr Avn Bn
    Det ANGAU
    Co Hqs Co F 565th Sig AW Bn (Det 20th Fi Sector)
    Plotting Plat F., Co F 565th Sig AW Bn (Det 20th Fi Sector)
    RS 414 19th Rep Plat Co F 565th Sig AW Bn (Det 20th Fi Sector)
    RS 473 4th Rep Plat Co A 565th Sig AW Bn (Det 20th Fi Sector)
    Surv Plat 69th Engr Topo Co
    Det H&S 12th Def Bn
    155mm Gp (less 2 gun sec) 12th Def Bn
    469th AAA AW Bn
    Radar Rep Team
    Co G (Clr) 135th Med Regt
    Co A 99th Sig Bn (less Dets)
    22d Rad Sta Sec 832d Sig Serv Co
    23d Rad Sta Sec 832d Sig Serv Co
    622d Ord AM Co (less dets)
    1 Co 543d QM Serv Bn (less 1 Plat)
    558th QM Rhd Co (less 1 Plat)
    26th Malaria Surv Unit
    864th Engr Avn Bn
    1 Plat 453d Engr Dep Co
    1998th QM Trk Co (Avn)(less 1 Plat)
    244th Port Co
    263d Ord MM Co
    Co A 207th QM Gas Sup Bn (less 1 Plat)
    21st Med Sup Plat (Avn)
    5th Malarial Control Unit
    Co B (Coll) 135th Med Regt
    Co A (Coll) 135th Med Regt
    1 Plat 123d QM Bkry Co
    Det 93d Cml Comp Co
    30th Evac Hosp
    58th Evac Hosp
    Hq Co E 565th Sig AW Bn (Det 20th Fi Sector)
    14th Rept Plat 565th Sig AW Bn (Det 20th Fi Sector)
    15th Rept Plat 565th Sig AW Bn (Det 20th Fi Sector)
    16th Rept Plat 565th Sig AW Bn (Det 20th Fi Sector)
    20th Fi Sub-sector Co C 583d Sig AW Bn
      (less 17th & 18th LW Rept Plat)
    Rad Sta 636 17th LW Rept Plat Co C 583d Sig AW Bn
      (Det 20th Fi Sub Sector)

-2-

Rad Sta 637 18th LW Rept Plat Co C 583d Sig AW Bn
(Det 20th Fi Sub Sector)

(h) Amoeba Gp   LtCol E. F. Doyle, USMCR
Div Hq Bn (less dets)
Hq Co 1st Med Bn (less dets)
Co B 1st Med Bn (less dets)
1st Serv Bn (less dets)
Det H&S Co 1st MT Bn
Det H&S Co 17th Mar
Rr Ech 12th Def Bn
Pers dets of all units of 1st MarDiv

1. See Annex A (Int) to Opn O No. 1-43.
Escalator will by overwater Opns seize, occupy, and defend
the BACKHANDER Area, and will establish control over such
adjacent islands and minimum portions of Western ARABIC
as may be required to insure uninterrupted Opns of our
air force from the BACKHANDER Area.
Director Task Force will seize DIRECTOR prior to D-day
for the establishment of light naval facilities in that
area. Director Task Force will push reconnaissance westward to the mouth of CORNFIELD and up that river to DISCUS
(exclusive) to determine feasibility of developing a
supply line to and establishing contact with the Backhander
Force.
Naval Attack Force provides escort for landing craft and
naval gunfire on landing beaches and designated targets.
See Annex B (Naval Gunfire Support Plan).
5th AF provides air protection for landing craft, supports
landing by strafing and bombing missions. See Annex C
(Air Support Plan).

2. (a) Backhander Force will:
PHASE I - By overwater Opns land in the GREYHOUND -
STONEFACE Areas, establish beachheads, and
capture the BACKHANDER Adrm and defenses;
PHASE II - Immediately initiate and expedite the
preparation and extension of air-landing
facilities at BACKHANDER; coincident therewith rapidly extend control over Western ARABIC
to include the general line CORNFIELD -
GREYHOUND and defend the area so occupied;
PHASE III - Assist the Commander Allied Air Force, in
establishing fighter sector, air warning,
and radio navigational facilities in areas
occupied by the Backhander Force; secure
early information as to feasibility of
developing a supply line to DISCUS,
(inclusive).

-3-

Time of landing: D-day H-hour. For transport area, line of departure, beaches, direction of attack, phase lines, objectives. Annex D (Opn Overlay).

3. (a) <u>Greyhound Gp.</u>- Land on BEACHES YELLOW 1 & 2 at H-hour; clear area of Japanese as shown on Opn Overlay; seize beachhead line MM and organize for defense; cover landing of the remainder of the force; pay particular attention to Hill 450; one (1) Bn on right (W) sector of beachhead be prepared to assemble in Force Res. Annex D (Opn Overlay).

(b) <u>Wild Duck Gp.</u>-
   (1) Land assault elements on BEACH YELLOW - 1 on AM of D-day; pass through beachhead, Atk to the W on a front of 500 yards with right resting on shore line, seize phase line 1; protect own left (S) flank during Adv; be prepared for further Adv on order. Annex D (Opn Overlay).
   (2) Land Wild Duck Gp (less assault elements) on BEACHES YELLOW 1 & 2 on PM of D-day; assemble in area as shown on Opn Overlay. Annex D (Opn Overlay).
   (3) On order Wild Duck Gp resume Atk to W on a front of 500 yards with right resting on shore line; seize objective OO; be prepared for further Atk. Annex D (Opn Overlay).

(c) <u>Stoneface Gp.</u>- Land at H-hour on BEACH GREEN, seize beachhead and organize for defense; block Japanese withdrawal to SW and Japanese Adv from SW. Be prepared to Adv on order. Annex D (Opn Overlay).

(d) <u>AA Gp.</u>- Augment and coordinate the AA defense of landing craft. Land on BEACHES YELLOW 1 & 2 on D/1 day, establish AA and seacoast defense of beach areas and BACKHANDER Area occupied by force troops. Annex F (AA Defense).

(e) <u>Engr Gp.</u>- Land on BEACHES YELLOW 1 & 2, on PM of D/1 day prepared to assist the landing, Adv, and capture of airfield at BACKHANDER. Annex G (Engr).

(f) <u>Res Gp.</u>-
   (1) Res Gp (less 1 LT) be prepared to reinforce assault elements in their Atk on BACKHANDER.
   (2) One (1) LT be prepared to seize and occupy BARNYARD and SANATOGEN by overwater Opns or to participate in assault on BACKHANDER on order.

(g) <u>Garrison Gp.</u>- Be prepared to move from staging area on order in accordance with priority as listed in "TASK ORGN" - Sub-paragraph (g).

-4-

UNCLASSIFIED

    (h) **Amoeba Gp.**- Establish Rr Ech as directed in 1st MarDiv SOP.

    (x) (1) Following units upon landing pass to control Force Comdr and carry out following duties:
      (a) Art units of Greyhound and Wild Duck Gps - Support the Atk and be prepared to mass fires in Z of action of CT "B". Be prepared to place fires in all sectors covering avenues of approach to the beachhead. Annex H (Art).
      (b) Dets Co C 583d Sig Bn - Carry out normal duties.
      (c) 2d Bn 17th Mar - Carry out duties of Force Shore Party on BEACHES YELLOW 1 & 2. Be prepared to assemble in Force Res.
      (d) Det 15th Wea Sq - Carry out normal duties.
      (e) Dets 2d ESB of Greyhound and Wild Duck Gps - Carry out assigned duties.
      (f) All Cos 1st Med Bn - Carry out normal duties.
      (g) Co C 1st Tk Bn - Assemble in area as shown on Opn Overlay and carry out assigned duties.

      (2) Attach two (2) Plats Co C 1st Amph Trac Bn to Art Units of Greyhound Gp.
      (3) Land 1st Bn 11th Mar on BEACH YELLOW - 2, 4th Bn 11th Mar BEACH YELLOW - 1.
      (4) All AA units upon landing pass to control Force AA O. Annex F (AA Defense).
      (5) Upon capture of line OO be prepared for Atk on airfield at BACKHANDER.
      (6) Land bridging equipment on BEACH YELLOW - 1.
      (7) Upon seizure of phase lines resume Atk without further orders. See Annex D (Opn Overlay).
      (8) Secret Code names will NOT be used in Opn O of subordinate units.
      (9) Recognition signals have been arranged by mutual agreement between Comdrs of Director and Backhander Task Forces for the purpose of establishing the identity of reconnaissance parties. Annex E (Sig Com).
      (10) H-hour and D-day to be announced later.
      (11) Essential elements of information:
        (a) Will the Japanese defend in force at the landing area?
        (b) Will the Japanese conduct an active defense by providing light defenses of the landing areas, observing the coast line, and withholding a strong mobile Res, or a strong defense of the Adrm?
        (c) Will the Japanese conduct a series of delaying actions withdrawing to a final defensive position in the vicinity of the Adrm?

SECRET

```
Res Gp (CT "A") - - - - - - - - -        to be reported
Garrison Gp - - - - - - - - - - -        to be reported
(c) Ax Sig Com:
CP Afloat - report location ashore.
```

BY COMMAND OF MAJOR GENERAL RUPERTUS:

AMOR LeR. SIMS,
Colonel, U. S. Marine Corps,
Chief of Staff.

ANNEXES:

```
*A - Intelligence
*B - Naval Gunfire Support Plan
 C - Air Support Plan
 D - Operation Overlay
 E - Signal Communication
 F - AA and Seacoast Defense
*G - Engineer
 H - Artillery
 I - Landing Schedule
*K - List of Code Names
 T - Naval Gunfire (ALTERNATE PLAN)
 *  Annexes to Opn O No. 1-43 applicable to this order.
```

DISTRIBUTION: Special

O-F-F-I-C-I-A-L:

E. A. POLLOCK,
Colonel, USMC,
    D-3.

UNCLASSIFIED

S E C R E T

Headquarters Backhander Force
A.P.O. 320

00591
1990-5-80
160/283

December 19, 1943.   1000

Amendment No. 1 to

Opn O
No. 2-43

Operation Order No. 2-43, Backhander Force, is amended to read as follows: Delete paragraph 3 (f) (1) and (2) and substitute the following:

(1) Res Gp (less 1 LTO will be prepared to reinforce the assault elements in their attack on BACKHANDER, if and when ordered by the Commanding General, Escalator.

(2) The excepted Bn LT will be prepared for overwater operations to seize and occupy BARNYARD and SANATOGEN, or to participate in the assault on BACKHANDER, whichever may be directed by the Commanding General, Escalator.

BY COMMAND OF MAJOR GENERAL RUPERTUS:

AMOR LeR. SIMS,
Colonel, U. S. Marine Corps,
Chief of Staff.

DISTRIBUTION: Special

O-F-F-I-C-I-A-L:

E. A. POLLOCK,
Colonel, USMC,
D-3.

UNCLASSIFIED

SECRET

ANNEX "A" TO OPERATION ORDER No. 1 - 43, BACKHANDER FORCE

INTELLIGENCE

00591
1990-5-
168/29 UNCLASSIFIED

Headquarters, Backhander Force,
A. P. O. 320,
14 November, 1943   1000.

MAPS   : Special Map and photo map, 1:20,000, BACKHANDER.
                  Special Map, 1:63,360 BACKHANDER.

CHARTS   : Australian Aeronautical Chart, Third Edition, CENTRAL -
                  ARABIC Area.

PHOTOGRAPHS   : Aerial Mosaic, 5" - 1 mile, N coast ARABIC.
                  Aerial Mosaic, 5" - 1 mile, W Coast ARABIC.
                  Stereo Pairs GREYHOUND Area, ARABIC.
                  Stereo Pairs STONEFACE Area, W Coast ARABIC.
                  Vectographs - same areas.
                  Objective Folder Number 75, CIU.

TERRAIN STUDIES : Terrain Estimate, BACKHANDER, G-2 Alamo Force.
                  Handbook BACKHANDER Area, Allied Geographical
                  Section.

REFERENCES   SOP, A.P.I., Division Intelligence Section, dated
                  26 February, 1943.
                  SOP, Division Intelligence, dated 30 August, 1943.
                  SOP, Division Intelligence Command Post, dated 26
                  April, 1943.
                  SOP, Military Intelligence, 17 September, 1943,
                  (Division General Order Number 100-43).

1.   SUMMARY OF ENEMY SITUATION.

          See Appendix "1".

2.   ESSENTIAL ELEMENTS OF INFORMATION.

          a.   Will the Japanese attempt interference by air
               and/or naval action:

               (1) At staging areas and our forward bases?

                    The Japanese can attack our staging areas
                    at PENUMBRA and in the vicinity of BINOCULAR
                    from the airfields at EQUILIBRIUM and PIP-
                    SQUEAK in CENTRAL, from SOMNAMBULIST in
                    ARABIC and from FOREARM in CARDIAC. The
                    possibility of carrier borne aircraft
                    attack is remote.

UNCLASSIFIED

-1-

Medium bombers, light bombers and fighters
operate from these airfields. Seaplanes
operate from SOMNAMBULIST and night sneak
attacks in addition to daylight attacks by
aircraft are possible.

Dawn, dusk and night attacks are possible
from the Japanese air bases in this area.
Our forward bases at AMOEBA, MANTLESHELF,
BYPRODUCT and PEMMICAN may be subject to
such attacks but in a lesser degree of
intensity.

Naval action against these bases and staging areas is possible but improbable.

(2) While enroute?

Attacks upon our forces by aircraft while
enroute from forward bases to staging
areas and from staging areas to the operational area is not only possible but very
probable. Aircraft dive bombing, torpedo
and strafing attacks from the Japanese
bases at SOMNAMBULIST and CENTRAL, while
our shipping is enroute from staging areas
to the BACKHANDER beachhead, is very probable. The usual time for such attacks is:
dive bombing from out of the sun while the
sun is overhead; torpedo or strafing attacks
at dawn or dusk. If weather is overcast
with scattered open places, attacks may be
expected at any time during the day from
torpedo and strafing planes.

Time and distance factors from BACKHANDER
are as shown appendix "7".

Naval action against BACKHANDER including
submarine attack is possible and probable.
The most probable direction from which
such attacks will come is the BOILING
POINT area and the seaward approaches to
the landing beaches. Submarine attacks
are possible at any time while afloat.
Dawn and dusk are the usual times of
attack by submarines.

(3) During landing?

Air and naval attack is possible during
disembarkation and landing on the beaches.
Air attack at this time appears certain.

S E C R E T   -3-

Time and distance factors are as shown in
appendix "7". Aircraft identification must
be accurate during landing.

Naval action against us during landing operations is possible but once inside the reefs,
attacks from surface ships will be improbable. Small boats can operate almost at
will within the reefs surrounding BACKHANDER.

(4) In support of their own land operations?

The airfields at BACKHANDER should be render-
ed unserviceable prior to our landing. Japanese air support therefor must come from
the airfields in SOMNAMBULIST, FOREARM,
CENTRAL or carrier borne aircraft. This
possiblity must be considered and until
such time as BACKHANDER Task Force captures
the airfield and gets it into operation,
aircraft attack by the Japanese may materially affect our operations and help theirs.

b. Will the Japanese defend the area by:

(1) Established beach defenses?

The Japanese have established beach defenses
in the vicinity of RUNYON consisting of
gun emplacements, unoccupied at present.

There are gun emplacements on the North
coast of BACKHANDER (see operational overlay). There are persistent reports by
pilots that light AA fire has been received
along the coast of GREYHOUND and West to
point "F". (See terrain study map). This
area is covered, almost to the beach, with
rain forest. Machine guns, and other defensive installations may well be concealed
from aerial observation. The possibility
of guns emplaced throughout the beach area
should not be overlooked. All located
Japanese guns and possible defensive locations are as shown on the operational overlay.

(2) Static perimeter defense?

To date no definite perimeter defense has
been located but it must be considered that
the Japanese may have static defenses. The
most probable locations are as shown on
operational overlay. Their defenses, con-

-4-

structed in depth, are usually mutually
supporting strong points consisting of
machine guns emplaced in bunkers.

The location of AA guns are as shown on
operational overlay. Most of these guns
are dual purpose and have personnel shelters located in the immediate vicinity.

The strength of the Japanese defenses can
be determined by the overall figure of about
6,500 personnel in the BACKHANDER area.

(3) Series of strong points in depth?

The Japanese will probably use a system of
strong points in depth once their positions
are attacked. The area to the East of the
airfield is well adapted to this type of
defense as is the area to the west of the
airfield. With their available weapons
(see Summary of Enemy Situation) they can
develop successive positions which will be
hard to overcome. Bunker emplacements constructed of heavy logs and well camouflaged
are the type most commonly used. These
bunkers are normally in groups of four,
mutually supporting and in addition are
covered by sniper fire from surrounding
trees. See operational overlay for the
most likely positions.

(3) Maneuver?

The BACKHANDER area is well adapted to movement of troops and motorized equipment. The
well developed coastal road both east and west
of the airfield is indicative of the intended
use of motor transport. To date no mechanized
organizations have been identified in this
area. There are tanks at SOMNAMBULIST which
could be used against us in about three to
four days. There are indications of some
motorized dual purpose AA which are a potent-
ial threat. Ground troops could be moved from
the airfield area in a matter of a few hours
to deny specific areas to us. Much activity
in the HAMILTON area and the existence of a
coastal road in this area also indicates that
the Japanese might be capable of quickly bringing a sizeable force against us from that area.

-4-

-5-

The most probable routes for Japanese troop movements against us are (1) the coastal road or (2) inland over the wooded area. The wooded inland route will be difficult but not impassable although it is very hilly and thick with undergrowth. Here the Japanese have undoubtedly familiarized themselves with existing trails.

c. Will the Japanese attempt to reinforce or supply the area, if so, how and with what forces:

(1) By barge?

Barge traffic may be expected to start almost immediately with seizure of the beachhead. While it is not probable that barges will operate into the BACKHANDER area, it can be expected that they will attempt to land troops at known barge hideouts in the nearby areas.

(2) By ship?

Same as (1) above.

(3) By land?

Troops may be landed from barges or surface vessels at spots known to be used in the past. GREYHOUND, PALMOLIVE, COCKNEY and TORTILLA are locations that may be used and troops from these areas can be moved overland to the BACKHANDER area. The GREYHOUND area is the nearest and most probable area from which land reinforcements might come. In a matter of hours the enemy could bring troops across the coastal flat from this area. The Japanese strength in this area is unknown at present.

In the TORTILLA area the Japanese have an estimated 300 to 400 troops which could be used as reinforcements. The probable route would be the overland trail from DISCUS to HAMILTON. From best information available to a minimum of two days would be required to make the trip by foot troops.

Reinforcement by land is improbable from any other area in ARABIC, due to undeveloped roads and trails into the BACKHANDER area. The coastal roads in ARABIC other than the BACKHANDER area are not completed but reports indicate work is progressing.

-6-

-6-

BACKHANDER area are not completed but reports indicate work is progressing.

(4) By air?

The Japanese have parachute troops at SOMNAM-
BULIST. The one battalion identified (574
troops) could be dispatched from there and
landed within about two days. This statement presupposes that there are enough
transport planes available and allows 36
hours to prepare and fly to BACKHANDER.
The airstrips at BACKHANDER should be unserviceable. The landing of airborne troops
from transport planes is therefore improbable. However, the Japanese will, in all
probability, supply their troops by air if
it becomes necessary. Supply planes could
come from their CENTRAL, ARABIC or CARDIAC
bases. See overlay, appendix "7".

(5) By submarine?

The Japanese have regular submarine reinforcement and supply routes in this area. Submarines from SOMNAMBULIST or FOREARM could
reach BACKHANDER area in about 25 to 30 hours
and begin discharging cargo. It is known
that the Japanese have about 7 submarines
being used for this purpose (at SOMNAMBULIST).
(However, they are subject to limitations due
to coral reefs extending along the coast
north of BACKHANDER).

d. Will the Japanese withdraw:

(1) By sea?

If the Japanese should attempt withdrawal by
sea, they would probably use barges and/or
destroyers. Once a beachhead is established
by our forces, this withdrawal by sea from
BACKHANDER will be restricted. The most probable place for Japanese embarkation would be
the beach area near RUNYON or by the overland
route to TORTILLA then by sea.

(2) By land?

The only land routes by which the Japanese
can withdraw are the coastal tracks East and
West of the airfield or overland to TORTILLA,

-6-

-7-

then on Eastward. With the two coastal tracks denied to them, they would have only the overland trail to DISCUS. Small detachments and stragglers may take to the bush by way of existing but difficult trails. However, the probability of withdrawal by land is remote.

e. To what extent will the weather influence our plans:

The NW season begins about December 15. From that date the seas on the North coast are likely to be high and rough making it difficult to land from small boats. The NW season also brings heavy rain (15 to 25 rain days per month). The coastal flats become water soaked and the streams are subject to sudden and quick rises which subside just as quickly. The coastal flat absorbs this excess rainfall rather well and even in the NW season is passable for troops and motor transport.

Bad weather which accompanies the NW season may impose restrictions on our air effort. Therefore bombing and strafing by our forces may be impossible during the initial stages of attack.

f. To what extent will the weather influence the Japanese plans:

The NW season may materially help the Japanese insofar as it may hinder our amphibious operations in the area. The excessive rain will, however, hinder the Japanese operations as well as our own. The bad weather that accompanies the NW season will restrict the Japanese air operations to the same degree as it restricts ours.

g. To what extent will the Japanese use the terrain against us:

(1) The numerous streams, ridges and forest covered areas give the Japanese successive obstacles to use against us. They will initially have observation advantages. They will be able to take up natural defensive positions and maneuver their forces against us. The flat coastal area immediately East of the airfield provides a maneuver ground in which they can move at will, thus disposing their forces to best advantage..

-7-

-8-

The high ground to the South of the airfield provides them with OPs which overlook the TRAJECTORY area and the sea to the North of the airfield. These OPs also provide good ground observation.

The secondary forest in the area lends itself to Japanese defense tactics in that it provides them with areas in which they may construct well concealed positions, dug in and mutually defensive.

They will probably booby trap the area and put riflemen in trees. Infiltration of small parties through and behind our lines may be expected.

They will probably use reverse slopes fox holes in which they can protect themselves from our artillery and mortar fire and re-occupy the defensive positions in the ridge lines upon the fire lifting.

The Japanese have a great advantage in their knowledge of the existing road and trail nets and the possibilities therof through-out the whole of the BACKHANDER area.

(2) The Japanese reinforcement of the GREYHOUND area apparent from recent aerial photographs, indicates that they could quickly counter-attack against our landing forces from the East. Construction of trails, roads, and possibly bridges across the streams and this intimate knowledge of the surrounding terrain makes this possibility an immediate threat to our operations.

(3) Japanese activity on the west coast of ARABIC, particularly in the vicinity of COCKNEY and DAISYMAE, indicates a possible threat against our landing forces from these areas. The terrain between BACKHANDER and DAISYMAE is adaptable to quick movement by the coastal road and numerous trails inland. From DAISYMAE South the going gets more difficult.

From COCKNEY North to our landing beach is difficult terrain for troops but the Japan-ese could move via the coastal road or by barge up the coast.

-8-

SECRET   -9-

MEASURES TO OBTAIN INFORMATION.

3. a. Supporting Intelligence Agencies.

FIFTH AIR FORCE

(1) After landing, visual air reconnaissance
GREYHOUND and in area adjacent to beachhead.

See Appendix "2".

S.I.O.

(1) Advise by radio all Japanese aircraft sightings, troops movements, or surface vessel
sightings.

b. Reconnaissance Missions.

COMBAT TEAM "C"

(1) Reconnoiter coast road to West and to GREY-
HOUND. Keep contact with Japanese by aggres-
sive patrolling to front. Establish OPs.

(2) Establish OP on hill at 7300-9020. Report
all Japanese information to Combat Team Intelligence Officer. When Division Headquarters is ashore, to D-2.

(3) Upon landing of assault echelons report to
Division CP (D-2) as observed, otherwise
submit negative reports upon the following:

The Japanese reaction to the advance, the
location, strength and direction of all Japanese troop movements and concentrations, the
location and type of artillery fire received,
the location, extent and nature of Japanese
defensive organizations of the ground, amount,
location and type of Japanese air activities,
demolition, road-blocks and mines encountered
within Z of action.

Report to TF Comdr. immediately any indication of Japanese counterattack or a Japanese
withdrawal.

MT BOATS

(1) Make offshore reconnaissance of the BACKHANDER -
GREYHOUND area. Warn TF Commander of approaching barges, boats, submarines, etc., and of any
significant movement by the Japanese along

-9-

S E C R E T   -10-

the coast. Boats to have proper communication system for warning service.

LANDING TEAM 21

Upon landing submit reports to TF Commander at two hour intervals of essential items as listed for CT "C".

Reconnoiter coastal road to North and South of beachhead. Establish OPs.

DIVISION INTELLIGENCE

(1) Reconnoiter and establish OP at 7300-9020; establish OP in vicinity of front lines where observation of airfield area is possible. Report all Japanese information to D-2.

(2) Upon order after landing D-2 will recruit, organize and train an appropriate detachment of native scouts for reconnaissance purposes.

(3) Upon order, establish such systems of coast watchers, air spotters and patrols to furnish reports of Japanese movements in the vicinity of SANATOGEN, BARNYARD, BOILING POINT, TRAJECTORY, NORTHPOLE, BACKHANDER area and along the North coast of ARABIC to include APPEASE.

(4) Using available boats make shore to shore reconnaissance in BACKHANDER-GREYHOUND area to locate Japanese concentrations of troops, stores, dumps and other activity. Boats to have proper communication system for warning service.

(5) Special reconnaissance missions after landing as directed.

11th MARINES

Reconnoiter to flanks and front lines, establish OPs and report all Japanese information to D-2.

12th DEFENSE BATTALION

(1) Reconnoiter occupied area, establish OPs, set up warning net and tie into Task Force, warning net. Report all information to D-2.

DETACHMENT COMPANY "C" 583RD SIGNAL BATTALION

(1) Set up master air raid control station,

-11-

establish direct communication with D-2.
Report all air raid warnings or attacks direct to D-2.

reconnoiter and report immediately by
installations, trails, roads, etc.,
Reference 1/20,000 operational map.

All OPs will be particularly on the alert and
will immediately report indications of Japanese
counterattacks or withdrawal.

Radio intelligence as allocated by higher authority.

c. Existing censorship regulations remain in effect.
Unit Intelligence Officers to control censorship
within their units. All Press and Public Relations
will be controlled by Division Public Relations
Officer. (See Division Circular 171-43).

All units strictly enforce security measures.
Report all suspicious movements, conversations
or actions on the part of natives, prisoners and
our own troops.

No diaries, personal letters, personal or unit
identification or material identification (such
as pictures of guns and equipment), except identification tags will be taken forward of staging
areas by any personnel. Prior to embarkation
from staging areas, Combat Team Commanders will
ascertain by inspection that these security
instructions are carried out. All such items
found will be confiscated and destroyed.

No operational orders, marked operational maps
or photographs, operational notes, artillery or
other fire plans, technical pamphlets, training
pamphlets or notes, personnel rosters or any
other similar documents will be taken forward
of battalion CPs.

d. The presence or suspected use of chemical agents,
including smoke, will be reported immediately to
D-2 and Division Chemical Officer.

x. When Japanese aircraft are shot down, crash, or
otherwise land within or close to our occupied
area, the unit in whose area they fall will establish a guard to protect the craft and will make
immediate report to D-2. If plane is destroyed
or otherwise cannot be kept intact, unit intell-

-11-

SECRET   -12-

UNCLASSIFIED

igence officers will remove all documents,
camera equipment, sights, magnetos, name plates,
(There will be an air intelligence party attached
to BACKHANDER Task Force to study and dispose of
such material.

All air raid warnings, warnings of mechanized
attacks, etc., will be disseminated by D-2 to all
units. Information of Japanese naval action,
bombardments or aircraft reinforcement will be
disseminated by D-2 to all units.

4.   PRISONERS OF WAR, DESERTERS, STRAGGLERS, ETC.:

     a.   Prisoners of war, Japanese deserters and stragglers
will be immediately reported to Combat Team Intelligence Officer and then taken to the prisoner
compound. When Division CP opens ashore, send
reports of prisoners to D-2. All subordinate
commanders will be impressed with the importance
of capturing prisoners.

           Initially all intelligence information will be
reported to Combat Team Intelligence Officer, and
to D-2 when Division CP opens ashore. (See SOP,
Division Intelligence.)

     b.   Send all documents, maps, and identifications
initially to Combat Team Intelligence Officer;
to D-2 when Division CP opens ashore. Send
captured material to Force Salvage Dump. Salvage Officer notify D-2. D-2 Section will
identify, mark and direct disposition. Force
QM furnish D-2 with shipping list.

5.   MAPS, CHARTS AND AERIAL PHOTOGRAPHS:

           All maps and aerial photos will be distributed
by D-2. Operational maps distributed prior to
D-day. Requests for reproduction and maps to
D-2. (See SOP, Division Intelligence.)

           Special aerial photos and vectographs to units
prior to D-day, thereafter as requested.

6.   REPORTS AND DISTRIBUTION:

     a.   Routine reports will commence upon landing on
beach and close at 2400. Thereafter from 0000
to 2400 daily.

     b.   Special reports as directed. D-2 and D-3 com-
bined combat reports to be submitted, as soon
as beachhead is established, to Combat Team

UNCLASSIFIED

-12-

SECRET

-13-

Intelligence Officer; to D-2 when Division CP opens ashore and thereafter as situation warrants.

All other reports as in SOP Division Intelligence.

c. All reports sent in by most expeditious means. Telephone first and send written report of confirmation at earliest opportunity.

d. Priority of reporting information: telephone, special messenger, radio, message center.

e. Daily reports distributed by D-2 to lower units at 1800. Other reports as prepared.

f. Each unit will keep situation map using regular operational map (1/20,000). Reports and overlays must refer to this map. Other situation maps as desired by lower unit commanders.

g. Intelligence Officers report either in person or by telephone to D-2 daily, to get available information.

BY COMMAND OF MAJOR GENERAL W. H. RUPERTUS:

AMOR LeR. SIMS,
Colonel, U. S. Marine Corps,
Chief of Staff.

APPENDICES:
1. Summary of Enemy Situation and Enemy Order of Battle.
2. Request for aerial reconnaissance.
3. List of passwords.
4. Sunrise and sunset tables.
5. Moonrise and moonset tables.
6. Barge and ship routes.
7. Air distance chart.

DISTRIBUTION: Same as Operation Order 1 - 43.

O F F I C I A L :

E. J. BUCKLEY,
Lt. Col., USMC.
D-2

-13-

APPENDIX "1" TO ANNEX "A"

t o

UNCLASSIFIED OPERATION ORDER 1 - 43

SUMMARY OF ENEMY SITUATION AND ENEMY ORDER OF BATTLE

1. SUMMARY OF ENEMY SITUATION.

The Japanese occupied BACKHANDER in December, 1942. Since that time they have greatly developed the area in roads, defensive emplacements and have completed two air strips.

The estimated strength of the Japanese in the BACKHANDER and adjacent areas is as follows:

BACKHANDER area proper 6,500 of all arms.

MABEL estimated to have 200 Japanese w/artillery and a radio station.

TORTILLA estimated at 300 to 400 with a radio station. This area is connected to BACKHANDER by a road and trail beginning at DISCUS and ending in the vicinity of HAMILTON. This trail is passable for foot troops.

COCKNEY area unknown number of Japanese and a radio station.

BARNYARD known to have been a barge staging area. There is a radio station and searchlight at the southern end of BARNYARD. Searchlight also reported at CHICORY. 520 Japanese at BARNYARD.

DIRECTOR plantation estimated to have 100 Japanese.

LAZARETTO area is estimated to have 1,500 Japanese. There is evidence that a full infantry regiment might be in the area.

A headquarters is reported to be in the vicinity of TRACY.

In the vicinity of BLONDIE on 23-24 October, a possible Japanese force of 1,000 reported to have landed.

APPEASE area estimated to have 1,500 Japanese. Airfield is capable of use by fighters and light bombers.

b. REAR AREAS:

(1) ARABIC.

a. The large naval and air base at SOMNAMBULIST

-2-

is estimated to contain 55,000 Japanese with reinforcement proceeding. This does not include 3,800 Army air personnel and 6,200 Navy air personnel. There are five (5) airfields in the vicinity and a seaplane anchorage in SOMNAMBULIST. The largest aircraft known to have operated from these fields are medium bombers.

The five fields are:

VUNAKANAU	-	Fighters, medium bombers.
LAKUNAI	-	Fighters, medium bombers.
RAPOPO	-	Fighters, light & medium bombers.
TOBERA	-	Fighters, medium bombers.
KERAVAT	-	Fighters, medium bombers.

In the past six months there has been an average of 130,000 tons of merchant shipping present in the SOMNAMBULIST harbor. In addition there has been warships, including cruisers and destroyers, seaplane tenders and submarines.

b. The naval and air base at FOREARM, is estimated to contain 8,000 Japanese.

c. GOODRICH is estimated to contain 1,000 Japanese and is principally a staging station and seaplane anchorage.

(2) CENTRAL.

a. The coastal area between DIMINISH and EQUILIBRIUM estimated to contain 12,000 Japanese most of these are engaged with Allied forces in that area.

b. The large naval, and air, base at EQUILIBRIUM estimated to contain 16,000 Japanese. There are three airfields in this area.

c. The large air-naval supply base at PIPSQUEAK, the main supply and staging area in CENTRAL area, is estimated to contain 30,000 Japanese. There are four airdromes in this area.

(3) Reinforcement Possibilities.

Well developed barge routes along the coast of CENTRAL and both North and South coast of ARABIC make the quick reinforcement of the BACKHANDER area a very likely probability.

The barge staging time from EQUILIBRIUM is about two days, from SOMNAMBULIST Northern route about four days, Southern route about eight days. These barges can bring troops, supplies, artillery, ammunition and transportation.

The large barge (53 to 69 feet long) can carry

-2-

S E C R E T   -3-

170 equipped men, 6 artillery pieces or 22 tons ammunition; the medium size barge (50 feet long) can carry about 50 to 80 equipped men or 3 artillery pieces or 20 tons ammunition; the small barge (30 - 35 feet long) can carry 35 to 45 equipped men or 3.6 tons ammunition.

Reinforcement be destroyers or transports respectively. Destroyers usually carry about 150 to 200 equipped troops, transports as many as 2,000 to 5,000 equipped troops. Time to unload from destroyers about one hour, from transports six hours to a day or more.

Reinforcement and supply is possible by submarine. The Japanese have well developed submarine routes from SOMNAMBULIST. Large submarines can carry 20 to 30 tons of supplies or 100 to 150 troops. Time necessary to reach BACKHANDER from 25 to 30 hours.

    c. Terrain as it affects the Japanese.

Weather; BACKHANDER is located in the tropical belt, lat. $5°30'S$ - Long. $146°30'E$, approximately. This area has definite NW and SE seasons with doldrums (periods of calm) in between. The NW season extends from December to April. SE season from April to October. The doldrums extend from mid-October to Mid-December and from mid-February to mid-April. Invasion of the North Coast during the NW season is hazardous. During the SE season and the doldrums, invasion is possible from a weather standpoint.

During the NW season heavy rainfall is predominant there being about 15 to 25 rain days during the month. The prevailing winds during this season are NW to W. This period is very favorable to the enemy for defensive action and unfavorable to us for invasion, because of heavy and unpredictable seas.

During the doldrums and NW season the atmosphere is hazy but it does not interfere with observation throughout the area. OPs on Mts. Talawe and Tange can observe all the TRAJECTORY, ROITAN group and seaward to the West and Northwest of BACKHANDER. OPs on Mt Langia can observe all the GREYHOUND area.

Tides vary from 2 to 3 feet. Low tide about 6 or 7 a.m., and high tide about 6 or 7 p.m. During the doldrums a small false tide, of about 1 foot rises, occasionally appears between low and high tide. The reefs are usually dry during the day.

Reefs: Incomplete study, from aerial photographs, shows a decided reef formation extending from an Easterly to generally Westerly direction approximately ten thousand yards from shore on the North coast of BACKHANDER.

The terrain in this area adapts itself to all around defense in that there is good observation from the high ground to the South of the airfield and unfavorable landing beaches in the

-3-

S E C R E T   -4-

immediate vicinity of the airfields, due to high banks, shingle and off-lying reefs. There are good landing beaches near COCKNEY, STONE-FACE, RUNYON and from the prominent point (H) (See terrain study BACK-HANDER) Eastwards to HAMILTON. There is also a small but good landing beach at METRO.

UNCLASSIFIED

CRITICAL AREAS:

There is a landing beach at HAMILTON where the road or trail comes across from DISCUS on South coast near TOR-TILLA. This area is a critical point for Japanese reinforcement or withdrawal by land.

Landing beaches point (F) to (G) to (H) (BACKHANDER terrain study) are good. Beach defenses are as shown on operational overlay. A fair motor road runs along the coast from the airfield Eastwards to HAMILTON varying from a few yards to one hundred yards inland from the beach.

From (G) to (H) (same reference) there is a coastal flat (which is damp during NW season), extending inland for about one mile. This area is fairly dry during the doldrums. During the NW season this area is damp but will support motor transport. This area is covered with secondary growth but has only light under-growth. Inland from this damp area the ground begins to rise gradually and for the most part is not suitable for transport other than tracked vehicles. From (H) to the airfield area (strip #2) the coastal flat extends inland about one mile, is flat and dry, suitable for all types of motor transport.

The kunai around the airfield and surrounding area provides a maneuver area for the Japanese which is adaptable to the use of motor transport.

Most streams can be forded, throughout the most of their courses, in the plains area.

There is both rain forest and secondary growth throughout the area. The beach area and the back hilly areas are fringed in the main with rain forest (which presents no great obstacle to foot troops). Secondary growth covers most of the stream bed areas and valleys that have been previously cultivated or burned over. The secondary growth provides an advantage to the Japanese in that it is practically impassable except for foot troops and for them it is hard going.

The landing beach beginning about one-half mile North of STONEFACE is fringed with off lying reefs varying from 25 to 50 yards at the Southern extremity to as much as 200 yards at some points. The reef is awash at low tide and is covered with about 2 to 3 feet of water at high tide. The reef is solid coral.

-4-

UNCLASSIFIED

-5-

At the mouth of CORNFIELD large barges could be landed at high tide. Entrance to the river mouth can only be made during the day or excellent light conditions. DIRECTOR natives are best guides for this job. Barges can go up CORNFIELD to DISCUS. It is questionable whether they can unload before reaching DISCUS. Estimated time for foot troops to go from DISCUS to HAMILTON; at least two days.

2.   CONCLUSIONS:

UNCLASSIFIED

a.   Japanese capabilities.

(1) To defend, in strength, the airfield area and the surrounding beaches.

(2) Concentrate troops and supplies in the HAMILTON - METRO area to quickly counterattack against our landing forces.

(3) To withdraw towards APPEASE fighting a delaying action awaiting reinforcements from SOMNAMBULIST, FOREARM or CENTRAL, then to counterattack.

(4) To withdraw to the hinterland, reorganize then counterattack.

(5) To evacuate prior to a landing made by Allied forces.

b.   Most Probable line of action.

(1) The most probable line of action for the Japanese is (1) above to defend in strength the airfield area and the surrounding beaches.

The study of aerial photographs, reports of Japanese action, barge traffic, etc., definitely shows a move towards reinforcing this area. In view of the loss, to the Japanese, of the coast of CENTRAL and BILL STICKING, the BACKHANDER area has become an important area to them. They will probably defend this area at all costs.

There is a very extensive anti-aircraft defense system around the airfields and the high ground to the South.

There is light, medium and heavy AA located as shown on operational overlay.

Bunker type personnel shelters are built near most of the gun emplacements. There is a possible defense system located to the South and Southwest of the airfields approximately ½ to 1 mile from number 1 strip, extending from the beach at number 1 strip in a Southeasterly direction. This system follows the ridge line and generally the high ground.

UNCLASSIFIED

-6-

-6-

Previous experience indicates that the Japanese will defend to the last man and hold tenaciously to any area occupied by him.

(2) The second most probable line of action for the Japanese is (2) above, <u>concentrate troops and supplies in the HAMILTON - METRO area then to counterattack immediately.</u>

The increase of activity in the HAMILTON - METRO area, in the past few weeks indicates that the Japanese are moving troops and supplies in quantity into this area. From API study, new clearings, trails and the construction of buildings indicate bivouac areas, supply dumps and possible defensive installations.

Using the existing road and trail systems the Japanese could quickly counterattack by moving West along the coast.

Also the Japanese could go inland and attempt a counterattack by an enveloping movement. The intimate knowledge of the trail systems, the capabilities of the streams, etc., would help the Japanese in such a course of action.

(3) The third most probable line of action open to the Japanese is (3) above, that is, <u>retire Eastwards awaiting reinforcements then to counterattack</u>.

The Japanese could do this quite easily (unless blocked at critical points), using the barge route and the existing road and trail systems. The coastal flat, which will take motor transport, is the probable line of withdrawal and the Japanese will probably make maximum use of this area. Critical areas to frustrate such a move are stream crossings near HAMILTON on the coastal road, and the points of land along the North coast known to be barge hide-outs (HAMILTON - TRACY, etc.).

The unnamed rivers at HAMILTON and between HAMILTON and METRO are unfordable except at the mouth and at low tide and are not bridged along the coastal track, except two known foot bridges. This presents a definite obstacle to withdrawal by land in this direction except for foot troops.

The present increase at GOODRICH from 400 to 1,000 indicates that the Japanese probably intends this island to be a supply and fueling area for light naval units.

The unwillingness, on the part of the Japanese, to use their air strength in force, suggests that they are withholding it to use as a counter offensive weapon when their bases in ARABIC are attacked.

The recent increase in Japanese warship activity,

-7-

staging out of SOMNAMBULIST, would indicate a sizeable naval force
that is available to harass and attack our shipping when we move to
attack ARABIC.

It is believed that the Japanese, placing great
value on this area, will strike back quickly with air, naval and
ground forces. With the available forces at their disposal this will
probably be an all out attack.

JAPANESE ORDER OF BATTLE

Presently available information puts the Japanese strength in
the BACKHANDER area at approximately 6,500. This figure has been
derived from a close cross-check of captured documents, prisoners of
war statements, Japanese Tables of Organization and aerial photographic interpretation.

The 65th Division, a well-seasoned unit which took part in the
Bataan campaign, appears to be the defender of the BACKHANDER area
together with supporting units. One of its infantry regiments, the
141st is definitely located here the there is an indication that
another, the 142nd may also be in the area. Supporting units include
anti-aircraft, artillery, shipping engineers, service troops, etc.,
and augment the infantry force to bring the Japanese strength to the
6,500 figure.

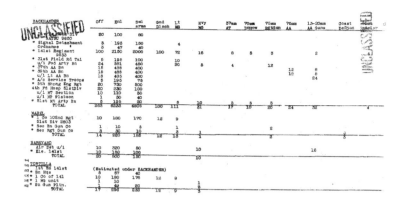

BACKHANDER	Off	Enl	Sml arms	Gnd Disch	Lt MG	Hvy MG	37mm AT	70mm Bngw	75mm BtlGun	75mm AA	13-20mm AA Guns	Coast DefGun	
KATSU 9850	20	100	80										
* Signal Detachment	5	195	150		4								
* Ordnance	3	47	40										
* 141st Regiment	100	2150	2000	100	72	15	8	5	3		2		
9833													
* 31st Field Rd Tai	5	195	100		10								
u/1 Fod Arty Bn	24	581	450		20	5	4		12				
* 37th AA Bn	15	488	400							12	8		
* 39th AA Bn	15	488	400							12	8		
u/1 Lt AA Bn	15	485	400								24		
* A/c Service Troops	5	195	75										
* 5th Shpng Eng Rgt	20	730	500										
4th Fd Hosp 51stDiv	20	230	100										
u/1 MT Section	10	110	50										
u/1 MP Platoon	1	50	40										
* 51st MT Arty Bn	5	195	20		5	10	5	5	5				
TOTAL	263	6233	4905	100	111	31	17	10	20	24	32		4
MABEL													
* 1 Co 102nd Rgt	10	180	170	12	9								
51st Div 2803													
* Sec Bn Gun Co	1	10	5		1				2				
* Sec Rgt Gun Co	3	30	10		3	1						3	
TOTAL	14	220	185	12	13	1			2			3	
BARNYARD													
* Air Det u/1	10	320	80			10					12		
* Ele. 141st	10	180	100										
TOTAL	20	500	180			10							
TORTILLA													
1st Bn 141st	(Estimated under BACKHANDER)												
* Bn Hqs	5	57	40										
* 1 Co of 141	10	180	178	12	9								
* 1 MG unit	1	10				1							
* Bn Gun Pltn.	1	49	20			2							
TOTAL	17	296	238	12	9	3							

BACKHANDER	Off	Enl	Sml Arms	Gnd Disch	Lt MG	Hvy MG	37mm AT	70mm Howow	75mm Regun	75mm AA	13-20mm AA Guns	Coast DefGun	81mm Mortar	5/1
GOODRICH														
Ele 65th Div	5	100												
Air Def Unit	10	320	50			10					12			2
w/i reinforcements	15	550												
TOTAL	30	970	50			10					12			2
TRACY														
Hdqtrs.	10	40												
TOTAL	10	40												

OVERALL JAPANESE STRENGTH BACKHANDER SECTOR:

BACKHANDER	6,896
KASEL	234
BARNYARD	313
TORTILLA	1,000
GOODRICH	50
TRACY	
	8,713
Less 20% sickness, casualties	1,742
GRAND TOTAL	7,371

Note: This excludes the possible 1,000 troops landed at BLONDIE and approximately 2,500 of the 142nd Regiment, 65th Division.

S E C R E T

Also to be considered in an Order of Battle in regard to possible reinforcements are the Japanese troops in such "rear areas" as SOMNAM-BULIST and CENTRAL.

At SOMNAMBULIST there are an estimated 67,400 troops, 10,000 of which are air personnel. This figure can be broken down as follows:

Hdqts. 8th Army Group	250
Hdqts. 17th Army	200
Hdqts. 18th Army	200
Hdqts. 8th Fleet	200
2nd Division	
38th Division	14,000
8th Tank Regiment	900
Parachute Battalion	674
35th Brigade	4,000
Army Air Personnel	3,800
Navy Air Personnel	6,200
Anti aircraft Personnel	3,200
Engineer Regiment	1,200
Shipping Engineer Regiment	1,075
Q.M. Personnel	1,000
L of C Personnel	2,000
Signal Personnel	1,000
Military Police Personnel	500
Motor Transport Personnel	2,500
SNLP	2,500
Replacements	5/10,000

TOTAL 67,400

In CENTRAL the following strengths are estimated for the below named locations:

EQUILIBRIUM   16,000

8th Shipping Engineer Regiment
37th   "   "   "
3rd   "   "   "
96th   "   "   "
36th   "   "   "
41st Inpt. AA Btry.
6th Airdrome Const. Unit
81st Land Duty Unit
27th Field Ordnance Depot
3rd Field Transport Unit
27th Field Supply Depot
Elements of the 5th Division
78th Regt., 30th Division

-10-

PIPSQUEAK   31,600

54th Division
Elements of the 41st Division
Elements of the 5th Division
Detachments of the SASEBU 5th SLF
49th Anchorage Tai
39th Indpt. MT Co.
4th Searchlight Co.
40th Indpt. AA Btry.

DIMINISH   6,000

Elements of the 79th Regiment
Elements of the 80th Regiment
Elements of the 26th Field Arty. Regt.
Hdqts. 20th Division
Elements 41st Division
Elements of 20th Engr. Regt.
Battalion of SNLP

OFFICIAL:

E. J. BUCKLEY,
Lt.Col., USMC,
D-2.

S E C R E T

APPENDIX "2" TO ANNEX "A"

of

OPERATION ORDER Number... 1 - 43.

(00541)
164/292 **UNCLASSIFIED**

BACKHANDER TASK FORCE,
AMOEBA,
18 November, 1943.

From: The Commanding General.
To : The Commanding General, Alamo Force.

Subject: Aerial reconnaissance, request for.

1. It is requested that this headquarters be furnished with the following photographic reconnaissance:

(a) From 20 November, 1943 to D-4 days, weekly photographic reconnaissance of:

BACKHANDER	# 15
GREYHOUND	# 16
COCKNEY	# 14
TORTILLA	# 13
APPEASE	# 20
BARNYARD	
SANATOGEN	
NORTH POLE	
BLONDIE	# 17 A
TRACY - MOTOROLA	# 17 B

Numbers refer to Sixth Army Mission Number.

(b) Daily photographic reconnaissance from D-4 days, of:

BACKHANDER	# 15
GREYHOUND	# 16
COCKNEY - BRISSIERE	

Numbers refer to Sixth Army Mission Number.

(c) Tree top level obliques of beaches from "F" to "G" and STONEFACE - DAISYMAE to be taken on D-2 days.

2. It is further requested that two (2) copies of all photographs taken on missions in the Western end of ARABIC be furnished this headquarters.

W. H. RUPERTUS.

UNCLASSIFIED - - - - - - - - - - - - -

SECRET

APPENDIX "3"

to

ANNEX "A", OPERATION ORDER Number 1 - 43.

PASSWORDS

From D-day through D-plus 14th day inclusive.

1.
	D-day	GUADALCANAL
	D plus 1 day	TULAGI
	D plus 2 day	LUCKY STRIKE
	D plus 3 day	YELLOW
	D plus 4 day	HONOLULU
	D plus 5 day	LILLIAN
	D plus 6 day	PHILIPPINES
	D plus 7 day	LUNGA LAGOON
	D plus 8 day	SULTRY
	D plus 9 day	SLOWLY
	D plus 10 day	PARALLEL
	D plus 11 day	CELLULOID
	D plus 12 day	LOLLYPOP
	D plus 13 day	CLOTHESLINE
	D plus 14 day	DILL PICKLE

2.   The word DILL PICKLE will be a universal password to be used in case of emergency, such as overdue patrols, cut off parties, etc.

3.   These passwords are not to be released prior to D-day.

OFFICIAL :

E. J. BUCKLEY,
Lt.Col. USMC,
D-2.

APPENDIX "4"

to

ANNEX "A", OPERATION ORDER No. 1-43.

SUNRISE AND SUNSET TABLES

(December through February)

AUSTRALIAN EASTERN DAYLIGHT SAVINGS TIME

December	Sunrise	Sunset	January	Sunrise	Sunset
1	0644	1907	1	0656	1921
2	0644	1907	2	0656	1921
3	0645	1907	3	0657	1922
4	0645	1908	4	0658	1922
5	0645	1908	5	0659	1923
6	0646	1908	6	0659	1923
7	0646	1908	7	0659	1924
8	0646	1909	8	0700	1924
9	0646	1910	9	0700	1925
10	0647	1911	10	0701	1925
11	0647	1911	11	0702	1925
12	0648	1911	12	0702	1925
13	0648	1912	13	0702	1925
14	0648	1912	14	0703	1926
15	0649	1913	15	0703	1926
16	0649	1913	16	0704	1926
17	0650	1914	17	0704	1926
18	0650	1914	18	0705	1927
19	0651	1915	19	0705	1927
20	0651	1915	20	0706	1927
21	0652	1916	21	0707	1928
22	0652	1916	22	0707	1928
23	0652	1917	23	0708	1928
24	0652	1917	24	0708	1929
25	0653	1918	25	0709	1929
26	0653	1918	26	0709	1929
27	0654	1919	27	0710	1929
28	0654	1919	28	0710	1930
29	0655	1920	29	0710	1930
30	0655	1920	30	0710	1931
31	0655	1921	31	0710	1931

- -

-1-

S E C R E T   -2-

February	Sunrise	Sunset	February	Sunrise	Sunset
1	0710	1930	15	0713	1928
2	0711	1930	16	0714	1928
3	0711	1929	17	0714	1927
4	0711	1929	18	0714	1927
5	0711	1929	19	0714	1927
6	0711	1929	20	0714	1927
7	0712	1929	21	0714	1926
8	0712	1929	22	0714	1926
9	0712	1929	23	0714	1926
10	0713	1929	24	0714	1926
11	0713	1929	25	0714	1925
12	0713	1929	26	0714	1925
13	0713	1928	27	0714	1925
14	0713	1928	28	0714	1924

-2-

APPENDIX "5"

to

ANNEX "A", OPERATION ORDER No. 1-43

MOONPHASE TABLES

AUSTRALIAN DAYLIGHT SAVINGS TIME

December	Moonrise	Moonset	January	Moonrise	Moonset
1	1055	2239	1	1220	0007
2		2336	2	1314	
3	1154	2430	3	1406	0056
4	1249	0122	4	1457	0143
5	1343	0211	5	1548	0230
6	1435	0258	6	1639	0315
7	1526	0345	7	1730	0403
8	1616	0433	8	1821	0451
9	1708	0521	9	1912	0540
10	1759	0610	10	2002	0630
11	1851	0700	11	2050	0721
12	1944	0751	12	2138	0810
13	2034	0840	13	2222	0857
14	2123	0930	14	2304	0948
15	2211	1019	15	2345	1025
16	2256		16	0020	1113
17	2340	1106	17	0106	1158
18	0023	1151	18		1242
19	0104	1235	19	0147	1329
20	0145	1320	20	0240	1418
21	0227	1405	21	0317	1510
22	0311	1451	22	0407	1605
23	0359	1539	23	0501	1705
24	0448	1631	24	0600	1806
25	0543	1726	25	0702	1907
26	0641	1824	26	0805	2007
27	0742	1925	27	0908	2105
28	0843	2025	28	1007	2159
29	0945	2126	29	1104	2250
30	1045	2223	30	1200	2339
31	1143	2316	31	1252	0026

February	Moonrise	Moonset	February	Moonrise	Moonset
1	1344		15	2425	1124
2	1434	0113	16	0110	1211
3	1527	0201	17		1300
4	1615	0249	18	0157	1352
5	1706	0338	19	0248	1448
6	1752	0427	20	0343	1547
7	1847	0515	21	0442	1647
8	1934	0606	22	0543	1747
9	2018	0653	23	0645	1846
10	2101	0740	24	0747	1942
11	2143	0825	25	0847	2035
12	2223	0910	26	0943	2127
13	2303	0955	27	1040	2217
14	2344	1039	28	1135	2306
			29	1228	2456

-2-

ANNEX "T" TO OPERATION ORDER NO. 2-43, BACKHANDER FORCE

NAVAL GUNFIRE

00591
1990-5-80
160/33?

Headquarters Backhander Force
A.P.O. 320

November 14, 1943.   1000

MAPS: Gridded photo-map, ARABIC Series, 1:20,000, dated October
1943, BACKHANDER AIRDROMES, DAISYXAE, and RANDOLPH Sheets.

1. Naval Attack Force will execute shore gunfire as follows:

FSG	FSU	Mission	Target	Time	Rounds	Remarks
A	---	Deep Supporting	Installations in vicinity of airfield (16-24)	H-1 hour 30 Min to H-hour	700(8") 800(4.7")	This group composed of Australian ships
		Deep Supporting	Opportunity (vicinity of airfield)	H-hour until withdrawal	100(8") 200 (4.7")	
B	(1) NASHVILLE	Deep Supporting	1,2,& 5	H-1 hour to H-10 Min	750(6") 400(5")	
		Close Supporting	2	H-10 to H-4		
		Close Supporting	5	H-4 to H-hour		
B	(2) PHOENIX	Deep Supporting	3, & 4	H-1 hour to H-10 Min	750 (6") 400 (5")	
		Close Supporting	3	H-10 to H-4		
B	(3) 1 DD	Close Supporting	4	H-12 to H-2 300 (5")		

B (4) 1 DD	General Support	Opportunity (YELLOW Beaches to airdrome	H-1 hour 30 Min to withdrawal of FSG B	50% AA Common (Ca. 350)		
(5) 1 DD	Deep Supporting	25	H-50 to H-45	100 (5")	While inside reefs FSG C be	
	Close Supporting	5	H-8 to H⁄2	250 (5")	alert to engage targets of	
C (6) 1 DD	Deep Supporting	6	H-50 to H-47	75 (5")	opportunity in BORGEN BAY.	
	Close Supporting	1	H-10 to H-3	225 (5")	Leave Fire Support Area No.1 at H⁄15.	
D (7) 1 DD	Direct Support of FSCP No. 1	Opportunity	H-hour to H⁄4 hours	350 (5")	FSU No. 7 & 8 set watch at H-hour on primary	
D (8) 1 DD	Direct Support of FSCP No. 1	Opportunity	H-hour to H⁄4 hours	350 (5")	frequency of SFCP No. 1	
Hq Ship (CONYNGHAM)	Reserve Support	Opportunity	H-1 hour 30 Min to H⁄4 hours	350 (5")	Fire missions at discretion of CTF 76	

Rocket Ships

1 LCI	Close Supporting	BEACH YELLOW - 1	H-4	24 (rockets)	Rocket ships be prepared	
1 LCI	Close Supporting	BEACH YELLOW - 2	H-4	24 (rockets)	to engage targets of opportunity until first wave hits beach	
E (9) 1 DD	Deep Supporting	30	H-20 to H-15	125 (5")		

- 2 -

	Close Supporting	35	H-8 to H/2	200 (5")
	General Support	Oppor-tunity	H/2 Min to H/1 hour	
(10) SMITH	Deep Supporting	38	H-20 to H-15	75 (5")
	Close Supporting	36	H-10 to H-4	200 (5")
	Close Supporting	37	H-1 to H/2	75 (5")
	General Support	Oppor-tunity	H/2 Min to H/1 hour	

BY COMMAND OF MAJOR GENERAL RUPERTUS:

AMOR LeR. SIMS,
Colonel, U. S. Marine Corps,
Chief of Staff.

DISTRIBUTION: Same as Opn O No. 2-43

O F F I C I A L:

E. A. POLLOCK,
Colonel, USMC,
D-3.

ANNEX "B" TO OPERATION ORDER NO. 1-43, BACKHANDER FORCE

NAVAL GUNFIRE

00591
1990-5-80
160/332

Headquarters Backhander Force
A.P.O. 320

November 14, 1943.   1000

UNCLASSIFIED

MAPS: Gridded photo-maps, ARABIC Series, 1:20,000, dated
       October 1943, BACKHANDER AIRDROMES, DAISYMAE, and
       RANDOLPH Sheets.

1. Naval Attack Force will execute shore gunfire as follows:

FSG	FSU	Mission	Target	Time	Rounds	Remarks
A (2 CA's)	---	Deep Supporting	Install-ations in vicinity of air-field (16-24)	H-1 hour 45 Min to H-25 Min	700(8") 800(4.7")	This group composed of Austra-lian ships
		Deep Supporting	Targets of oppor-tunity in vicinity of air-field	H-hour to withdrawal of cruiser force	100(8") 200(4.7")	
B (1) NASHVILLE		Deep Supporting	1,2,& 5	H-1 hour 20 Min to H-28 Min	750(6") 400(5")	
		Close Supporting	2	H-28 to H-18		
		Close Supporting	5	H-1 to H-42		
B (2) PHOENIX		Deep Supporting	3, 4	H-1 hour 20 Min to H-28 Min	750(6") 400(5")	
		Close Supporting	3	H-28 to H-18		
B (3) 1 DD		Close Supporting	4	H-28 to H-18	250(5")	

UNCLASSIFIED   - 1 -

B (4) 1 DD	General Support	Opportunity (YELLOW BEACHES to air- drome	H-1 hour 20 Min to H-18 Min	50% AA Common Mk. 18 (ca.350)	
	General Support	Opportunity (YELLOW BEACHES to air- drome	H-hour to withdrawal of cruisers		
C (5) 1 DD	Deep Supporting	25	H-50 to H-45	100 (5")	While inside reefs, FSG "C" be alert to engage targets of opportunity in BORGEN BAY. Leave Fire Support Area No. 1 at H-15
	Close Supporting	5	H-25 to H-18	175 (5")	
	Close Supporting	5	H-1 to H/2	75 (5")	
C (6) 1 DD	Deep Supporting	6	H-50 to H-47	75 (5")	
	Close Supporting	1	H-25 to H-18	225 (5")	
D (7) 1 DD	Direct Support of SFCP No. 1	Opportunity	H-hour to H/4 hours	350 (5")	FSU No. 7 & No. 8 set watch at H-hour on primary fre- quency of SFCP No. 1
D (8) 1 DD	Direct Support of SFCP No. 1	Opportunity	H-hour to H/4 hours	350 (5")	
Hq. Ship (CONYNGHAM)	----	----	H-18	1 (Star Shell	Signal for "Cease Fir- ing" to all ships
Rocket Ships					
1 LCI	Close Supporting	BEACH YELLOW 1	H-2	24 (rockets)	Rocket ships be prepared to engage targets of opportunity until first wave hits beach
1 LCI	Close Supporting	BEACH YELLOW 2	H-2	24 (rockets)	

- 2 -

E	(9) REID	Counter Battery	30	H-25 to H-20	125 (5")
		Close Supporting	35	H-14 to H-8	125 (5")
		Close Supporting	35	H-1 to H/2	75 (5")
		General Support	Opportunity (GREEN BEACH to SAG SAG)	H/2 Min to H/1 hour	
E	(10) SMITH	Deep Supporting	38	H-25 to H-20	75 (5")
		Close Supporting	36	H-14 to H-8	200 (5")
		Close Supporting	37	H-1 to H/2	75 (5")
		General Support	Opportunity (GREEN BEACH to DORF POINT)	H/2 Min to H/1 hour	

BY COMMAND OF MAJOR GENERAL RUPERTUS:

AMOR LeR. SIMS,
Colonel U. S. Marine Corps,
Chief of Staff.

DISTRIBUTION: Same as Opn O No. 1-43

O F F I C I A L:

E. A. POLLOCK,
Colonel, USMC,
D-3.

ANNEX "C" TO OPERATION ORDER NO. 2-43, BACKHANDER FORCE

AIR SUPPORT PLAN

00591
1990-5-80
160/283

Headquarters Backhander Force
A.P.O. 320

November 14, 1943.   1000

Excerpts from Fifth Air Force Operation Plan.

1. **Fi Cover.-**

    (a) D-1 day.

        (1) Sufficient cover will be maintained to insure the safety of the convoy.

    (b) D-day.

        (1) One (1) Fi Sq Area cover from 0630 until 0700.
        (2) Three (3) Fi Sq Area cover from 0700 until 1400.
        (3) One (1) Fi Sq Convoy cover from 1400 until 1830.

    (c) D/days.

        (1) Area cover by at least one (1) flight of Fi will be maintained from 0700 until 1400 D/3 days.
        (2) After D/3 day Fi cover will be withdrawn unless friendly convoys are unloading.

2. **Atk Avn.-**

    (a) D-day.

        (1) One (1) Atk Gp will neutralize by bombing and strafing BEACHES YELLOW 1 and 2 from H minus seventeen (17) minutes until H minus two (2) minutes, or until landing boats are 500 yards from beach. One (1) Atk Sq of this Gp using W/P bombs, will strafe and smoke TARGET HILL to prevent enemy observed fire from these defenses.
        (2) One (1) Atk Sq will neutralize by bombing and strafing landing beach GREEN from H minus twelve (12) minutes until H minus two (2) minutes; if directed by the fighter director ship off GREEN BEACH, the time of ATK will be postponed up until 30 minutes and will cease at Atk time plus 10 minutes or when landing boats are 500 yards from beach.
        (3) Four (4) Sq of Atk Avn will Atk targets along the coast from DORF POINT N and E to the Adrm Area. Approximate time of this attack will be H plus one (1) hour and forty-five (45) minutes.

- 1 -

(b) D days.

    (1) Sufficient Atk Avn will be available for use as directed by Com Gen FATF, to enable the Backhander Force to expeditiously accomplish its mission.

3. Bomb Avn.-

  (a) D-day.

    (1) Two (2) Sq of H Bomb will bomb TARGET HILL from H minus forty-five (45) minutes to H minus twenty-five (25) minutes or TARGET RIDGE as an alternate target.

    (2) Three (3) Sq of H Bomb will bomb GREYHOUND Area from H minus forty-five (45) minutes to H minus twenty-five (25) minutes to destroy enemy mortar and automatic weapons positions in this Area, or HILL 660 as an alternate target.

    (3) Four (4) Sq of H Bomb will bomb TARGET RIDGE at approximately H plus one (1) hour and fifteen (15) minutes or NATAMO POINT Area as an alternate target.

  (b) D days.

    (1) Sufficient Bomb Avn will be available for use as directed by Com Gen FATF, to enable the Backhander Force to expeditiously accomplish its mission.

4. Air Alert.-

  (a) D-day.

    (1) One (1) Sq of Atk Avn will be on air alert from H Hour until H plus one (1) hour and thirty (30) minutes. Three (3) Sq of Atk Avn will be used with one (1) Sq over target for thirty (30) minutes. If no targets are called for by the Backhander Force alternate targets will be attacked as follows: 1st Sq - TARGET RIDGE, 2nd Sq - TARGET RIDGE, 3rd Sq - HILL 660.

  (b) D days.

    (1) Air Alert will not be provided after H plus one (1) hour and thirty (30) minutes unless directed by Com Gen FATF.

  - 2 -

5. <u>Ground Alert and Repeat Missions.-</u>

   (a) D-day.

      (1) Two (2) Sq of M Bomb will be on ground alert from
         H minus forty-five (45) minutes until H plus
         eight (8) hours and fifteen (15) minutes.

      (2) Four (4) Sq of Atk Avn will be prepared to go on
         Ground Alert status two (2) hours after return
         from strike missions.

      (3) Nine (9) Sq of H Bomb immediately upon landing will
         be refueled and re-armed and will conduct a second
         mission on D-day against targets selected, prior
         to D minus three (3) days, by the Backhander Force.

      (4) Four (4) Sq of Atk Avn immediately upon landing will
         refuel and rearm and will conduct a second mission
         on D-day against targets selected, prior to D minus
         three (3) days, by the Backhander Force.

      (5) Four (4) Sq of Atk Avn will be prepared to go on
         Ground Alert status two (2) hours after returning
         from strike missions against shipping targets of
         opportunity.

   (b) D/days.

      (1) Sufficient Ground Alert will be available for use,
         as directed by Com Gen FATF, to enable the Back-
         hander Force to expeditiously accomplish its
         mission.

BY COMMAND OF MAJOR GENERAL RUPERTUS:

AMOR LeR. SIMS,
Colonel, U. S. Marine Corps,
Chief of Staff.

<u>DISTRIBUTION</u>: Same as Opn O No. 2-43.

O F F I C I A L:

E. A. POLLOCK,
Colonel, USMC,
   D-3.

ANNEX "E" TO OPN O NO. 2-43

SIG COM

00591
1990-5-80
114/283

Headquarters Backhander Force
A.P.O. 320
November 14, 1943.   1000

MAPS: Special Map - ISLAND of ARABIC, 1:20,000, BACKHANDER
AIRDROMES, DAISYMAE, RANDOLPH, GOLDBERG, COCKNEY Sheets.

1. (a) (1) See Opn O No. 2-43.

    (2) The Enemy is known to have extensive Com installations
        including intercept, goniometric and jamming facilities
        on CARDIAC, ARABIC, DIPPER, and the northern portion
        of CENTRAL.

   (b) CP's and Ax of SIG COM:

	INITIAL	D-DAY
Task Force Hq(1st MarDiv)	LST 466	BEACH YELLOW - 2
Greyhound Gp (CT "C")	To be reported	BEACH YELLOW - 2
Stoneface Gp (LT 21)	REDHERRING	BEACH GREEN
AA Gp	To be reported	To be reported
Wild Duck Gp (CT "B")	REDHERRING	To be reported
Engr Gp	To be reported	To be reported
Res Gp (CT "A")	PEMMICAN	Report subsequent locations
Garrison Gp	PENUMBRA	

2. Installations and operation in accordance with 1st MarDiv SOI
   and SOPSIG 1 except as augmented herein.

3. (a) 1st Sig Co.-

    (1) Land Pers and combat equipment of Fwd Ech on BEACH
        YELLOW - 2 establish Com facilities to operate CP.
        On order Rr Ech land and assemble in 1st Sig Co
        Bivouac Area.

    (2) Establish following Sp Rad Nets immediately upon landing:

        (a) ESCALATOR (SX9) - Escalator Adv M/C (6CU) - Back-
            hander Force
            (4UD): 7705 kcs 0800L to 1900L, 4340 kcs 1900L to 0800L,
            2020 kcs standby (SCR-299).
        (b) ESCALATOR Adv M/C (Voice - "WILFRED") - Backhander
            Force
            (Voice "KODAK"); 4095 kcs (SCR -299).

- 1 -

UNCLASSIFIED

(c) CTF 76 (X3X) – Backhander Force (4UD): For frequencies see
    CTF 76 Com Plan. (Use SISM authenticators).

(3) Install direct To service between D-2 and AW plotting center.
(4) Assign 1 SCR-193 with operating pers from ADC Com Plat to
    STONEFACE Gp prior embarkation (For use in Force Comd Net).

(b) STONEFACE Gp operate in Force Comd Rad Net.

(c) CO, Co A, 99th Sig Bn on order install and maintain Fi
    Sector and Army Base Wire Net at BACKHANDER.

(d) 22d Rad & M/C Team 832d Sig Serv Co on order establish
    following Rad circuit:
    ESCALATOR (SX9) – BACKHANDER (4UD): 7305 kcs 0800L to 1900L,
    4425 kcs 1900L to 0800L; 2780 kcs standby.

(e) Force Res operate in Force Comd Rad Net unless in contact by
    Tp.

(f) Asst Div Comdr maintain listening watch on ESCALATOR circuits
    listed in paragraph 3 (a) (2) commencing at H-5 hours.

(g) Shore Party Com.

    (1) Beach YELLOW 1 and Beach YELLOW 2 – as prescribed in
        SOPSIG 1 less Ship – Shore Administrative net which will
        not be used.
    (2) Beach GREEN – as prescribed by Comdr STONEFACE Gp.
    (3) Task Force Sig O will provide three SCR-536 Radios for
        SP – SPC – BM local net on each beach.

(h) Naval Gunfire Nets: See CTF 76 Comm Plan.

(i) Arty – Spot Plane Net.

    Arty ground sta (Call word OREGON) – Spot plane (Call word
    ATLANTA) 4455 kcs primary, 4335 kcs 1st alternate, 4415 kcs
    2d alternate 4615 3d alternate. Use 2d alternate frequency
    (4415 kcs) initially. Use no authenticators.

(j) O-in-C Adv Ech Record Section be prepared to handle all Safe-
    hand Airplane Courier mail upon establishment of that service.

(x) (1) Lift Rad silence only as follows:

        (a) When directed by this Hq.
        (b) When this Force is attacked by the enemy and/or the
            element of surprise has been lost.
        (c) For radio operating on Voice ONLY with less than 15
            watts output, when leading wave crosses line of
            departure.

                            – 2 –

UNCLASSIFIED

(2) Codes and ciphers within this Force as prescribed in Codes and Ciphers Allowance Table, 1st MarDiv SOI; For communication outside of this Force, as prescribed in Item 10, ESCALATOR SOI.

(3) For authentication within this Force, use 1st MarDiv NO's 2 & 3, except with aircraft and ground stations of aircraft. Comdrs may prescribe systems for use within own unit.

(4) (a) For recognition signals from shore to ship and ship or shore to air use ACB Ø224 series initially. BACK-HANDER Task Force will be prepared to use Admiralty Key Memos when security conditions permit, at which time Task Force Comdr will inform all interested commands. Task Force Sig O will furnish Comdr Coastal Defense units and Senior Shore Party Comdr with daily extracts from effective Recognition Publications. STONEFACE Gp use ACB Ø224 only.

(b) For recognition between ground units use effective Recognition - Identification Signals as shown in First MarDiv SOI No. 2-43. Patrols of DIRECTOR Force are prepared to use these Recognition - Identification Signals when possibility of contact with BACKHANDER Force patrols exists.

(c) Force Intelligence officer is responsible for promulgation and distribution of daily pass words.

(5) Units without Air Support Parties atchd will pass requests for Air Support through Force Com Channels.

4. (a) Task Force and Div units submit requisitions for Sig Supplies to Task Force Sig O.

(b) Upon landing, Div Sig Sup and Rep Sec establish Sig Dump at 1st Sig Co Bivouac.

(c) Transportation of Div Sig Co is exempted from any vehicular pool established.

(d) Messenger vehicles carrying URGENT messages have priority on roads.

5. (a) Index No. 9-43 to SOI.

(b) In all communications between Army/Marine, Navy and Air Force Units, as well as when messages cross time zones, use GCT (zone suffix letter ZEBRA). In all other cases, use local daylight saving time, zone suffix letter LOVE. Always use zone suffix letter in the time groups, both in heading and texts of messages.

- 3 -

(c) Synchronize watches prior to debarkation.

UNCLASSIFIED   BY COMMAND OF MAJOR GENERAL RUPERTUS:

AMOR LeR. SIMS,
Colonel, U. S. Marine Corps,
Chief of Staff.

DISTRIBUTION: Same as Opn O plus Dist. "S".

O-F-F-I-C-I-A-L:

E. A. POLLOCK,
Colonel, USMC,
    D-3.

ANNEX "F" TO OPERATION ORDER NO. 2-43, BACKHANDER FORCE

AA ARTILLERY AND COAST DEFENSE

00591
1990-5-80
160/283

~~UNCLASSIFIED~~

Headquarters Backhander Force
A. P. O. 320

November 14, 1943.   1000

MAPS: Special Map - ISLAND of ARABIC, 1:20,000, BACKHANDER
AIRDROMES, DAISYMAE, RANDOLPH, GOLDBER, COCKNEY Sheets.
AA Artillery and Coast Defense Overlay, Opn Overlay.

TASK ORGANIZATION

(a) 12th Defense Bn   Col W. H. Harrison, USMC

(b) 3d Plat Btry A 1st Sp Wpns Bn (CT "C")   Lt L. L. Patrow, Comdg

(c) 4th Plat Btry A 1st Sp Wpns Bn (LT 21)   Lt L. M. Alford, Comdg

(d) 1st Plat Btry A 1st Sp Wpns Bn (CT "B") Lt D. G. Battista, Comdg

1. See Annex A Opn O No. 1-43. Aerial attack may be expected
enroute and particularly at the landing. All usual methods
of attack may be employed with emphasis on dive and low
level bombing at seaborne targets. Low strafing attacks
have been encountered during darkness.

2. The AA Gp augment and coordinate AA defense of landing
craft during overseas movement; land on BEACHES YELLOW - 1
and YELLOW - 2; establish AA and coast defense of beaches and
area occupied by Backhander Task Force; be prepared to displace forward upon seizure of Adrm area.

3. (a) 12th Defense Bn.-

    (1) Initial Phase - Overseas Movement:

        See Par 3(x)1.

    (2) Second Phase - Debarking and Establishing of Beachhead:
        (a) Provide AA and seacoast defense of BEACHES YELLOW
        1 & 2 from positions in the vicinity of those
        beaches, and the emplacement of one (1) 90mm Btry
        in the clearing (71.7 - 91.6).

    (3) Third Phase - Occupation of Adrm:
        (a) Displace (Slt and AA Wpns) upon occupation of
        the airfield in defense thereof. Maintain
        sufficient AA and seacoast defense of BEACHES
        YELLOW 1 & 2 pending the displacement of these

~~UNCLASSIFIED~~   - 1 -

landing areas to beaches within the Adrm perimeter. See Appendix 3 (**AA Art and Coast Defense Overlay**).

(b) Provide Long Range AWS by emplacement of SCR 270 within the Adrm perimeter.

(c) Establish Met station and make ballistic information available to all Art units of the Force.

(d) Prepare two (2) Slts to provide illumination of surface targets for seacoast Art.

(4) Final Phase - Consolidation of Defenses.

(a) Completion of wire Com net.
(b) Improve and fortify the positions of all Wpns and installations.
(c) Construct alternate and dummy positions.

(b) <u>3d Plat Btry A 1st Sp Wpns Bn</u>.-

(1) Initial Phase - Overseas Movement:
See Par 3(x)1.
(2) Second Phase - Debarking and Establishment of Beachhead:

Provide AA and seacoast defense of BEACHES YELLOW 1 & 2 from positions in the vicinity of these beaches. For position See Appendix 3 (AA Art and Coast Defense Overlay).

(3) Third Phase - Occupation of Adrm:

Upon order displace to positions within the Adrm perimeter and Adrm. For positions See Appendix 3 (AA Art and Coast Defense Overlay).

(c) <u>4th Plat Btry A 1st Sp Wpns Bn</u>.-

(1) Initial Phase - Overseas Movement:
See Par 3(x)1.
(2) Second Phase - Debarkation and Establishment of Beachhead:

Provide AA and seacoast defense of BEACH GREEN from positions in the vicinity of that beach.

(3) Third Phase - Atk:

Provide AA defense of troops and supplies of LT 21.

(d) <u>1st Plat Btry A 1st Sp Wpns Bn.</u>-

    (1) Initial Phase - Overseas Movement:
        See Par 3(x)1.

    (2) Second Phase - Debarking and Establishment of
        Beachhead:

        Provide AA and seacoast defense of BEACHES YELLOW
        1 & 2 from positions in the vicinity of these
        beaches. For positions See Appendix 3 (AA Art
        and Coast Defense Overlay).

    (3) Third Phase - Occupation of Adrm:

        Upon order displace to positions within the Adrm
        perimeter and Adrm. For positions See Appendix
        3 (AA Art and Coast Defense Overlay).

(x) (1) During Phase 1 (Overseas Movement) control of fire
        of all embarked AA units rests in the Comdr of the
        ship. All such units will augment the ships
        armament by the fire of individual arms, and the
        fire of automatic weapons emplaced on deck.

    (2) Requirements for various conditions of readiness
        are given in Appendix 1 (Condition of Readiness).
        Standard usage of these readiness conditions are
        indicated below:

        Condition 1 - During Red Alert.
        Condition 2 - During Yellow Alert.
        Condition 3 - Normal Night.
        Condition 4 - Normal Day.

    (3) The 12th Defense Bn will inform all AA units of the
        frequency of the 5th Fighter Sector Air Warning Net.
        Each AA unit embarked will request the ships captain
        to monitor such net and furnish continuous coverage
        thereof.

    (4) 12th Defense Bn will during second and subsequent
        phases monitor the 5th Fighter Sector Air Warning
        Net and furnish air warning service to ground and
        naval units of the Force until relieved of this
        responsibility by arrival of the Fighter Sub Sector
        Comdr.

    (5) AAAIS will be maintained by 12th Defense Bn through-
        out the operation.

    (6) During disembarkation naval AA weapons will be
        included in the AA defense thereof, especially
        against those aircraft targets approaching through
        the "Blind Spots" of the AA weapons emplaced on the
        beach.

(7) Automatic weapons will insure that their fire does not endanger friendly troops within their zone of fire.

(8) Automatic weapons will not fire at unseen targets.

(9) Except when endangering friendly aircraft, automatic weapons and small arms shall be directed against any identified enemy aircraft within range. Any aircraft committing an act hostile to our forces shall be considered enemy.

(10) The Seacoast Art O of the 12th Def Bn shall coordinate fire of all weapons used against seaborne targets.

(11) The CO 12th Def Bn will control and coordinate the fire of organic AA weapons of all units when employed in an AA role, and will use these weapons as a definite part of the fighter AA team under the general direction of the Fi Sub-Sector Comdr.

4. See Adm O No. 2-43.

5. AA Com.

    (a) See Appendix 2 (AA Hq Rad Net)

    (b) AA CP

        (1) First Phase – LST #

        (2) Second Phase – Vicinity of BEACH YELLOW 1 with alternate CP in vicinity of (70.5 – 95.1).

        (3) Third Phase – Vicinity of (85.1 – 95.1).

            BY COMMAND OF MAJOR GENERAL RUPERTUS:

                AMOR LeR. SIMS,
            Colonel, U. S. Marine Corps,
                Chief of Staff.

APPENDICES:
    1 – Condition of Readiness.
    2 – AA Headquarters Radio Net.
    3 – AA Artillery and Coast Defense Overlay.

DISTRIBUTION: Same as Opn O No. 2-43.

O-F-F-I-C-I-A-L:

E. A. POLLOCK,
Colonel, USMC,
   D-3.

APPENDIX 1 TO ANNEX "F" TO OPERATION ORDER NO. 1-43, BACKHANDER FORCE

CONDITION OF READINESS

00591
1990-5-80
160/283

Headquarters Backhander Force
A. P. O. 320
November 14, 1943.   1000

A. Condition ONE: All Pers manning battle stations, on the alert, and ready for instant action. This condition will normally be maintained only during critical periods and at such times as contact is imminent.

(1) Btry G (Slt)

(1') Daylight: Slt equipment to be under cover. Lookout positions manned.

(2') Darkness: All Pers manning battle stations, on the alert and ready for instant action.

Condition TWO: This is an alert condition (a modification of Condition ONE) from which all units will be required to go into action within one (1) minute. This will be the normal condition for critical periods (such as morning standby) even though no targets are reported. Pers not required for Com and lookouts may be resting but must be fully dressed, awake and at positions. At least two (2) men will be on the alert at every gun or fire control position.

C. Condition THREE: This is an alert condition from which half of the Wpns of all units will be required to go into action within one (1) minute and the remainder within five (5) minutes. All tactical Com and Sbs will be manned and one (1) officer will be present at each CP on call. Regular watches will be maintained in the Bn. CP. OP's will be manned. The crews of half the guns will be at their guns but only two (2) men need be awake at these guns. This will be the normal night condition and in daylight when the Bn is in an alert status but no targets have been picked up.

(1) 90mm Gp:

90mm Guns:

Two (2) guns manned and three (3) men on the director (two (2) of whom will be on the alert), three (3) men on heightfinder and one (1) power plant operator, will be in the vicinity of each instrument.

- 1 -

SCR 268's:

Full crew asleep in vicinity of radar, two (2) men awake and alert.

Slt Btry:

Two (2) men at each control station, one (1) man at each Slt, remainder of men resting in vicinity of battle stations as directed by Unit Comdr.

(2) **Sp Wpn Gp:**

40mm Guns:

Gun Sec of each gun in vicinity of the gun position with two (2) men on the alert.

20mm:

Two (2) men alert for each two (2) guns (of guns sited in pairs) on the gun having a Tp, and at least one (1) man sleeping in each gun position. Remainder of gun crews in vicinity of guns.

(3) **Bn CP:**

CP and Msg Cen manned. One (1) officer on watch. All tactical Tp Com manned as necessary. MT dispatcher on watch and one-half (½) of MT force immediately available for duty. Met station manned as directed by Bn Met O.

D. **Condition FOUR:** This is a condition from which half of the Wpns of all units will be required to go into action within five (5) minutes and the remainder within twenty (20) minutes. Part of the men may remain in vicinity of positions. In general under Condition FOUR, CP's, OP's and Tp Com will be maintained as in Condition THREE, except that either an officer or staff NCO will be at unit CP's at all times. This is the normal daylight condition.

(1) **Sp Wpn Gp:**

40mm, 20mm:

At least half of the Wpns of each class will be prepared to fire within five (5) minutes. One (1) man on the alert at each Wpn.

(2) Bn CP:

Same as Condition THREE.

BY COMMAND OF MAJOR GENERAL RUPERTUS:

AMOR LeR. SIMS,
Colonel, U. S. Marine Corps,
Chief of Staff.

DISTRIBUTION: Same as Opn O No. 1-43.

O-F-F-I-C-I-A-L:

E. A. POLLOCK,
Colonel, USMC,
    D-3.

APPENDIX 2 TO ANNEX "F" TO OPERATION ORDER NO.1-43, BACKHANDER FORCE

AA HQ RAD NET

00591
1990-5-80
160/283

Headquarters Backhander Force
A. P. O. 320

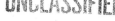

November 14, 1943.   1000

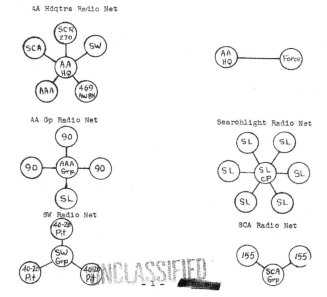

AA Hdqtrs Radio Net

AA Gp Radio Net

Searchlight Radio Net

SW Radio Net

SCA Radio Net

- 1 -

1 Radio at SCR 270 in Fighter Sub-sector Telling Net.
1 Radio (TBW) available for external communication.

BY COMMAND OF MAJOR GENERAL RUPERTUS:

AMOR LeR. SIMS,
Colonel, U. S. Marine Corps,
Chief of Staff.

DISTRIBUTION: Same as Opn O No. 1-43.

O-F-F-I-C-I-A-L:

E. A. POLLOCK,
Colonel, USMC,
D-3.

ANNEX "G" TO OPN O NO. 1-43 BACKHANDER FORCE

ENGINEER

UNCLASSIFIED

Headquarters Backhander Force
A. P. O. 320
November 14, 1943.   1000

MAPS: Special Map - ISLAND of ARABIC, 1:20,000, BACKHANDER
AIRDROMES, DAISYMAE, RANDOLPH, GOLDBERG, COCKNEY
sheets. Annex D (Opn Overlay)

TASK ORGANIZATION

(a) 17th Mar Gp   Col H. E. Rosecrans, USMC.
    H&S Co
    1st Bn (less Cos A, B, & C)
    3d Bn

(b) Base Engr Gp   Col L. G. Yoder, USA.

    Comd Gp
    864th Engr Avn Bn
    1913th Engr Avn Bn
    Surv Plat, 69th Engr Topo Co

(c) Sup Gp   1st Lt. D. Torgenson, USA.

    One Plat 453d Engr Dep Co

1. See Opn O No. 1-43, Backhander Task Force.
2. The Task Force Engr Units will assist in the landing,
   Adv, and capture of objective of the Task Force, and
   will construct an Adrm and Base Facilities.
3. (a) (1) 17th Mar Gp - land on D plus 1 at BEACHES YELLOW
           1 & 2, and be prepared to support the tactical
           Opn furnishing:

           (a) Water Supply
           (b) Construction, repair, and maintenance of routes
               of Com, and landing facilities at the beaches.
           (c) Such other construction as directed.

       (2) Detached units revert to 17th Marines Group upon order.

   (b) Base Engr G-.- upon landing, be prepared to undertake
       construction in the following priorities:

       (1) That essential to support of tactical operation.
       (2) Airfield Construction:

- 1 -   UNCLASSIFIED

(a) Repair existing strips to accommodate troop-
        carrying planes, in accordance with specifi-
        cations to be furnished.
    (b) Construct a strip for one (1) Fi Gp.
    (c) Such other construction as directed.

    (3) Dock and other landing facilities.
    (4) Sup roads, for dispersion.
    (5) Shelter, covered storage, and other Base Facilities.
    (6) Obtain vertical and horizontal control, prepare
        to pographical map of area, establish control points
        for antiaircraft and field artillery.

(c) Sup Gp.— upon landing, maintain and issue Engr Sup as
    directed by Task Force Engr Sup Officer.

(x) (1) Land an Adv Ech of the Base Engr Gp with the 17th
        Marines Gp on D plus 1, prepared to conduct
        extensive Rcn for detailed information of Adrm.
    (2) Tr labor will be furnished for contruction when
        consistent with the tactical situation.
    (3) Native labor will be controlled by the Task Force
        Comdr, to be used on construction to the maximum,
        under the supervision of ANGAU.
    (4) Use of Engr Trs for construction of defensive works,
        including Cam, will be limited to highly specialized
        construction and supervision.

4. (a) See Adm O No. 2-43.
   (b) All construction materials moved to the area of operations will
       be turned into the Task Force Engr Dp for use in the manner
       directed by the Task Force Comdr.
   (c) Issue Sup according to priorities set up by the Task
       Force Comdr.
   (d) Map Sup will be a function of the Task Force Int O.

5. (a) See Annex E (Sig Com)
   (b) CP's;
       LST # _____ to be reported.
       Report location ashore.

                   BY COMMAND OF MAJOR GENERAL RUPERTUS:

                         AMOR LeR. SIMS,
                Colonel, U. S. Marine Corps,
                      Chief of Staff.

DISTRIBUTION: Same as Opn O No. 1-43.

O-F-F-I-C-I-A-L:

E. A. POLLOCK,
Colonel, USMC,
   D-3.

ANNEX "H" TO OPERATION ORDER NO. 2-43, BACKHANDER FORCE

FORCE ARTILLERY

00591
1990-5-80
160/283

Headquarters Backhander Force
A. P. O. 320

November 14, 1943. 1000

MAP: (1) Same as Force Opn O No. 2-43. Appendix A (Overlay of Fires).

1. See Opn O No. 2-43.

2. Art units of Greyhound Gp to be prepared to mass fires in all sectors outside beachhead; support Atk and be prepared to mass fires in Z of action of CT "B". Art unit of Stoneface Gp will assist in preventing enemy withdrawal to SW and enemy Adv from SW.

3. (a) 1st Bn 11th Mar will land on BEACH YELLOW - 2 in support of defense of eastern sector of perimeter.

    (1) Normal Z - Land approaches to Beachhead Area from SE.
    (2) Contingent Z - Land approaches to Beachhead Area from SW.
    (3) Position Area - See Appendix 1 (Overlay of Fires).

  (b) 4th Bn 11th Mar will land on BEACH YELLOW - 1 in direct support of CT "B".

    (1) Normal Z - Z of action CT "B".
    (2) Contingent Z - Land approach to Beachhead Area from SE.
    (3) Position Area - See Appendix 1 (Overlay of Fires).

  (c) 2d Bn 11th Mar will land on BEACH YELLOW - 1 in general support.

    (1) Rendezvous Area - See Appendix 1 (Overlay of Fires).

  (d) H Btry 3rd Bn 11th Mar will land on BEACH GREEN in direct support of Stoneface Gp.

    (1) Normal Z - as ordered by CO of Stoneface Gp.
    (2) Contingent Z - as ordered by CO of Stoneface Gp.
    (3) Position Area - as ordered by CO of Stoneface Gp.

  (x) (1) Minimum Range lines 200 yards in front of own lines.
    (2) Distant Range lines: Maximum effective range of Bns.
    (3) Gp Base Point, Check Points - See Appendix 1 (Overlay of Fires).
    (4) Registration will be conducted as soon as positions are occupied - Report completion of registration and check point registration on to Gp CO.

- 1 -

(5) Bns maintain level of one (1) u/f at Btry position — remainder in Bn Dps.
(6) Ln: 1st Bn 11th Mar with CT "C".
4th Bn 11th Mar with CT "B".
4th Bn 11th Mar with 1st Bn 11th Mar.
(7) 4th Bn 11th Mar will provide Met data every four (4) hours for Art Gp.

Art units of Greyhound Gp will revert to control of Art Gp under command LtCol R. B. Luckey upon landing.
(8) Control of Stoneface Gp Art remains with Stoneface Gp CO.

4. See Adm O No. 2-43.

5. (a) Sig Com – See Annex E to Force Opn O No. 2-43.
(b) Bns lay direct lines to Art Gp CO.
Command Net – Gp Rad to Bns.
(c) Gp CP at Div CP.
Bn CP's to be reported.

BY COMMAND OF MAJOR GENERAL RUPERTUS:

AMOR LeR. SIMS,
Colonel, U. S. Marine Corps,
Chief of Staff.

APPENDIX:
1 – Overlay of Fires.

DISTRIBUTION: Same as Force Opn O No. 2-43.

O-F-F-I-C-I-A-L:

E. A. POLLOCK,
Colonel, USMC,
D-3.

ANNEX "K" TO OPERATION ORDER NO. 1-43, BACKHANDER FORCE

LIST OF CODE NAMES

00591
1990-5-80
160/283

Headquarters Backhander Force
A.P.O. 320

November 14, 1943.   1000

UNCLASSIFIED

CODE NAMES	GEOGRAPHICAL NAMES
AMOEBA	GOODENOUGH ISLAND
ARABIC	NEW BRITAIN
BACKHANDER	CAPE GLOUCESTER
BARNYARD	ROOKE ISLAND
COCKNEY	SAG SAG
CORNFIELD	ITNI RIVER
DAISYMAE	DORF POINT
DIMINISH	FINSCHHAFEN
DIRECTOR	ARAWE
DISCUS	GILNIT
ESCALATOR	NEW BRITAIN TASK FORCE
GOLDBERG	MT. LANGLA
GREYHOUND	BORGEN BAY
LETTERBOX	DOBODURA
PEMMICAN	MILNE BAY
PENUMBRA	ORO BAY
RANDOLPH	SILIMATI POINT
REDHERRING	LANGEMAK BAY
SANATOGEN	LONG ISLAND

BY COMMAND OF MAJOR GENERAL RUPERTUS:

AMOR LeR. SIMS,
Colonel, U. S. Marine Corps,
Chief of Staff.

DISTRIBUTION: Same as Opn O No. 1-43

O-F-F-I-C-I-A-L:

E. A. POLLOCK,
Colonel, USMC,
D-3.

UNCLASSIFIED

ANNEX "I" OPERATION ORDER NO. 2-43, CKHANDER FORCE

LANDING SCHEDULE

00591
1990-5-80
160/283

Headquarters Bachkander Force
A.P.O 320

November 14, 1943.   1000

"D" DAY					
BEACH YELLOW - 1			BEACH YELLOW - 2		
Time	No of Ships	Ship Type	Time	No of Ships	Ship Type
H-Hour	6 (LCVP's)	APD	H-Hour	6 (LCVP's)	APD
H/5 Min	6 (LCVP's)	APD	H/5 Min	6 (LCVP's)	APD
H/10 Min	4 (LCVP's)	APD	H/10 Min	4 (LCVP's)	APD
H/15 Min	4 (LCVP's)	APD	H/15 Min	4 (LCVP's)	APD
H/20 Min	3	LCI	H/20 Min	3	LCI
H/30 Min	3 (CT "B")	LCI	H/30 Min	3	LCI
			H/40 Min	2	LCI
H/50 Min	3 (1 for CTB)	LST	H/50 Min	4	LST
1400	3 (CT "B")	LST	1400	4 (2 for CTB)	LST
"D" PLUS 1 DAY					
0730	2	LST	0730	3	LST
1400	2	LST	1400	3	LST

"D" DAY		
BEACH GREEN		
Time	No of Ships	Ship Type
H-Hour	4	LCM
H/5 Min	4	LCM
H/10 Min	4	LCM
H/15 Min	2	LCM
H/25 Min	3	LCI
H/35 Min	3	LCT
H/45 Min	3	LCT
H/1:45 Min	3	LCT
H/3:45 Min	3	LCT

BY COMMAND OF MAJOR GENERAL RUPERTUS:

AMOR LeR. SIMS,
Colonel, U. S. Marine Corps,
Chief of Staff.

DISTRIBUTION: Same as Opn O No. 2-43

O-F-F-I-C-I-A-L:

E. A. POLLOCK,
Colonel, USMC,
D-3.

SECRET

00591
1990-25
144/246.

Headquarters, Backhander Force,
APO 320
14 November 1943.   1000

ADMINISTRATIVE ORDER) - To accompany Opn O No. 1-43.
No. 2-43

Maps: Special Map - ISLAND of ARABIC, 1:20,000, BACKHANDER
        AIRDHOMES, DAISYMAE, RANDOLPH, GOLDBERG, COCKNEY
        sheets.   Annex D (Opn Overlay)

1. SUPPLY.

    a. Labor.

        (1) BACKHANDER force will:

            (a) Furnish troop labor to load all ships moving
                 the TF to BACKHANDER.
            (b) Unload supply ships and cargo trucks used for
                 mobile loading.

        (2) Upon departure of BACKHANDER TF units, ESCALATOR
             will furnish troop labor at USASOS bases for load-
             ing Amphibious Craft.
        (3) All units will leave necessary service personnel
             in Staging Areas to protect and insure the forward-
             ing of respective property to BACKHANDER.
        (4) Native labor supervised by ANGAU will be employed
             in the BACKHANDER Area under control D-4.

    b. Bases.

        PENUMBRA - Supplementary Base PEMMICAN.
        Equipment and supplies peculiar to Marine Corps - AMOEBA.

    c. Levels.

        (1) Assault units on movement to objective.

            (a) 503d Prcht Inf Regt. As prescribed by CO,
                 503d Prcht Inf Regt and approved by Comdr
                 BACKHANDER TF.

            (b) Remainder of BACKHANDER TF.

                 Class I - IV., - 20 days. (This includes 503d
                 Prcht Regt).
                 Rations:

                        5 Days - Type C.
                        5 Days - Type D.

UNCLASSIFIED

- 1 -

5 Days - Type K.
5 Days - Type B. (Amphibiously packed).
Class V, 3 U/F.
Class V, 2 U/F (Additional for 503d Prcht Regt.)
(See Annex B for loading).

(2) Supporting garrison units on movement to objective.
Class I - IV, incl., - 30 days.
Rations:

10 Days - Type C or K.
5 Days - Type D.
15 Days - Type B. (Amphibiously packed).
Class V, (AA) 5 U/F.
Class V, (Except AA) 3 U/F.

(3) (a) Insofar as practicable, BACKHANDER TF Comdr will
provide such information as will enable ESCALATOR
to maintain prescribed levels of supplies.

(b) ESCALATOR will build up and maintain levels of
supply forward of USASOS Bases as follows:

On AMOEBA for forces staged thereon:

Class I - IV, incl., - 30 days.
Class V - (Except AA), - 3 U/F.
Class V - (AA) - 5 U/F.

In the BACKHANDER Area for forces therein:

Class I - IV, incl., - 30 days.
Class V, (Except AA) - 6 U/F.
Class V, (AA) - 10 U/F.

d. Routing of Requisitions:

All requisitions originating within the BACKHANDER TF
after departure from Staging Area will be submitted to
the appropriate Supply O (QM, Engr, Ord, etc.), of the
BACKHANDER TF. Only requisitions originated by TF
Supply Officers will be forwarded to Hqts, ALAMO Force,
APO 712, Alamo Liaison Grp APO 928 or to Alamo Liaison
Grp APO 503 in accordance with instructions to be issued
by ESCALATOR Special Staff Officers concerned, to the
corresponding Supply Officers of BACKHANDER TF. These
requisitions will be submitted to the appropriate
representative, ALAMO Liaison Grps APO 928 or APO 503 or
direct to the designated USASOS Base via ship or safehand
air messenger, in accordance with instructions issued by
the appropriate special staff section, ALAMO Force.

- 2 -

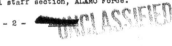

e. <u>Re-Supply</u>.

    (1) Class V. 3 U/F all weapons will be dispatched so as to arrive in the BACKHANDER Area on the afternoon of D-Day. (This includes 3 U/F for 503d Prcht Inf Regt). Thereafter, requirements to replace expenditures and build to the prescribed level will be forwarded by scheduled Ech of supply ships (See Annex B).

    (2) Re-Supply of rations will be automatic to include Army gratuitous issue of tabacco, candy and toilet goods.

    (3) Daily telegrams will not be required.

    (4) Emergency requisitions only may be transmitted by radio.

f. <u>Dumps</u>.

    Dumps will be established in accordance with par 10, Div G O 79 SOP for Supply and Evacuation during Landing Operations. The BACKHANDER MTO will operate the fuel dumps.

g. <u>Water</u>.

    (1) All cans and water trailers of assault units to be filled prior to embarkation.

    (2) CT C will carry water for 503d Prcht Regt (2 gals per men). Water containers from 503d Prcht Regt will be utilized. All extra three hundred (300) gal water trailers at PENUMBRA will be carried (filled) by the Assault Force to augment this supply.

    (3) Supply to be from local sources as soon as possible.

    (4) All water from sources ashore should be chlorinated. Local sources of water supply will not be used until approved by a Med O.

h. <u>Medical</u>.

    See Annex C to BACKHANDER Adm O 2-43.

i. <u>Uniform and Equipment</u>:

    (1) Marine Corps Units:

- 3 -

(a) Grps 1 to 9 incl as prescribed in 1st Mar Div G O 78, SOP for Embarkation, except that under Grp 2 Utility Clothes will be carried in lieu of summer service.

(b) Grps 10 and 11 as specified above.

(c) Grp 12 not to exceed 1/3 of authorized replenishment for each item embarked except under "clothing" which will be limited to 30 days replenishments for utility suits, cotton drawers, socks and shoes only. These items will be sent in with re-supply ships.

(d) Grp 13 none.

2) Army Units.

(a) Army Unit Comdrs will be responsible for restricting their equipment to applicable T/Es or TBAs (and such additional equipment as authorized by ESCALATOR). Take no tentage initially, except paulins, hospital tentage and communications tents. Equipment left behind will be moved by supply ships. Take no cots or camp furniture initially.

(b)
1' Uniform – Fatigue clothes, field shoes, leggings and helmets.

2' Individual Equipment – Take all.

3' Baggage – Enlisted: Blanket, extra socks, underwear, fatigue suit and shoes.
Commissioned: Small bedding roll, barracks bag or hand bag.

2. EVACUATION.

a. Casualties.

See Annex C to BACKHANDER Adm O 2-43.

b. Burial.

See Annex A to BACKHANDER Adm O 2-43.

c. Salvage.

- 4 -

(1) As soon as the situation warrants all units will thoroughly perform salvage operations in their respective areas for all items of equipment (Allied and Enemy). These items will be placed in a dump and an inventory report made to the BACK-HANDER Salvage O.

(2) The BACKHANDER TF Med O will designate a Salvage O to collect all weapons and individual equipment from casualties being evacuated. This equipment will be turned over to the BACKHANDER Salvage O.

(3) The equipment not usable in the BACKHANDER Area will be returned to USASOS Bases in CENTRAL by the BACKHANDER Salvage O. All usable equipment will be released to the BACKHANDER QM.

Captured Materials.

(1) All captured enemy Ord material will be turned over to BACKHANDER Salvage O. TF Intelligence O will designate an officer to inspect and segregate items required to be shipped to USASOS Bases.

(2) Unit Comdrs are responsible for safe-guarding and promptly reporting captured enemy material to D-4. Captured enemy material is a vital source of supply for our own troops and all personnel will be instructed prior to embarkation to seize all enemy materials intact. Extreme caution should be exercised however to avoid discharging booby traps.

e. Prisoners of War.

(1) Task Grp Comdrs will deliver prisoners to the TF Intelligence O who will be responsible for the safe-guarding and evacuation of prisoners to the PW enclosure established by the Shore Party. See Annex A to BACKHANDER TF Adm O 2-43.

3. TRAFFIC.

a. Landing of Supplies and Equipment.

(1) Landing and storage of supplies and equipment will be under direction of Shore Party Comdr.

(2) Unloading will be accomplished as rapidly as possible. Time allowed for unloading LSTs will not exceed 3 hrs.

- 5 -

(3) Upon delivery of supplies and equipment to respective dumps TF QM will assume control.

b. Circulation and Control.

    (1) By subordinate units within their assigned areas. This Hqs will designate principal supply routes through subordinate areas.

    (2) Traffic control in Beach area by Shore Party.

    (3) Marking of routes and preparation of circulation maps will be accomplished under the direction of the TF Engr at the earliest practicable time.

    (4) All vehicle lights to be blacked out after sunset.

Maintenance.

    (1) Routes will be maintained initially by Engr units Atchd to CT C, thereafter by TF Engr under the supervision of the TF Engr O.

d. Road priority will be as follows:

    (1) Staff and Messenger Vehicles.

    (2) Prime Movers and Am carrying vehicles.

    (3) Wire laying vehicles.

    (4) Ration and water carrying vehicles.

    (5) Fuel and Oil carrying vehicles.

    (6) Ambulances.

4. TRANSPORT.

a. Beaches.

    (1) Shore Party Comdr will supervise and coordinate the unloading; direction of units to assigned bivouacs, supplies to dumps and vehicles to parking areas upon arrival at BACKHANDER.

b. Transport.

    (1) Unit transport loaded to capacity will be embarked in accordance with Task Grp Embarkation Plan.

- 6 -

(2) Additional trucks, mobile loaded will be provided
for transportation of supplies from LSTs to dumps -
trucks to be returned on LSTs.

(3) MT and tractors not required for tactical purposes
during early stages of operation will operate under
Shore Party Comdr for transportation of bulk stores
to dumps.

(4) CT Comdrs will furnish necessary transportation to
atchd Grave Registration Sections until transportation
reverts to TF control.

5. PERSONNEL.

See Annex A to BACKHANDER TF Adm O 2-43.

6. MISCELLANEOUS.

   a. Shore Parties.

      (1) LtCol. Robert G. Ballance, USMCR, is designated
Shore Party Comdr.

      (2) 2d Bn 17th Mar reinforced by two replacement Cos
will comprise the Shore Party.

      (3) Comdr 7th Fleet will provide a Naval Beach Party.

      (4) Shore Party SOP 1st Mar Div will be followed except
as modified by Shore Party Comdr.

      (5) On order Shore Party will pass to TF control.

   b. Periodic Reports.

      (1) The BACKHANDER QM, MTO and Comdrs of all organizations
and separate units in the BACKHANDER Area will
submit daily as of 1800L a G-4 Periodic Report.
These reports will follow Form 18, page 118 FM
101-5 omitting par 4 and original only will be
forwarded. Periodic Reports will pertain only to
units or parts thereof who are in the BACKHANDER
Area and will include the following information:

         (a) Location of Adm Troops and installations.
After initial report, only changes will be
reported.

         (b) 1' Class I - Total balanced rations on hand
by type in terms of days of supply.

- 7 -

2' Class II, III, IV and V - Items in which critical shortages exist.

(c) Any matters of importance pertaining to motor, water and/or air transportation.

(d) Condition of roads. General statement of condition, thereafter important changes only.

(e) Captured material. List and give disposition.

(f) Any activities and/or information of particular importance.

(g) The BACKHANDER TF Med O will submit daily at the above specified time a report of the status of evacuation to include number of casualties evacuated during the preceding 24 hrs and number awaiting evacuation.

c. Rear Echelon.

   (1) AMOEBA.

   (2) Dets at PENUMBRA and PEMMICAN.

d. Other Adm Details.

   No change.

BY COMMAND OF MAJOR GENERAL RUPERTUS:

AMOR LeR. SIMS,
Colonel, U. S. Marine Corps,
Chief of Staff.

ANNEXES:

A - Personnel.
B - Special Assignment and Loading Instructions.
C - Medical.
D - Ordnance Plan.
E - Chemical Plan.
F - Engineer Supply.

DISTRIBUTION: Special.

O-F-F-I-C-I-A-L:

W. S. FELLERS,
Colonel, USMC,
D-4.

Annex A to Administrative Order No. 2-43, Backhander Force.

PERSONNEL

(00591)
1990-25
401/329

Headquarters, Backhander Force,
APO 320.
14 November, 1943, 1000.

1. INTERNAL ADMINISTRATION.

The internal administration of organizations of this TF including attached units of the U. S. Army will in no way be affected by directions issued by the CG, Backhander TF. Additional reports as prescribed by this Hq or Hq, Army Section attached to BACKHANDER TF will be submitted on direction.

2. REPORTS.

(a) G-1 Periodic Reports as directed in Div Circular 113-43 will be submitted daily to D-1 BACKHANDER TF by all organizations under operational control of the CG, BACKHANDER TF.

(b) Casualty Reports. Procedure for reporting of Marine Corps casualties is outlined in Div Adm Circular 25-43. U. S. Army casualties will be reported as prescribed by Sixth Army Casualty Reporting Manual, 1Oct43, amended by Change No. 1, 3Nov43. These reports will be submitted to Army Section, Backhander TF, APO 320.

(c) Routine Reports. Personnel records, reports, and routine correspondence peculiar to Army or Navy will be processed through their respective administrative channels.

3. CASUALS.

Marine Corps casuals in rear areas will be returned directly to their organization via first available transportation when practicable, otherwise they will be sent to the Casual Co at AMOEBA. Army casuals will be handled by the CO, Advanced Base A.

4. RELATIONS WITH CIVIL GOVERNMENT.

Angau representatives will be responsible for the control of all natives and for the operation of any civil government in our theatre of operations.

-1-

(00591)

~~SECRET~~

Annex to Adm O
No. 2-43.

5. MAIL.

(a) Postal Unit APO 320 will accompany this TF to provide mail service.

(b) Marine Corps personnel will be serviced through the Fleet Post Office at PEMMICAN.

(c) Group Commanders will provide all mail units with suitable shelter for safeguarding and processing of all mail.

(d) Outgoing mail will be deposited in any Army or Navy Post Office for despatch through proper channels.

(e) Official Mail for CG, Backhander, TF will be addressed: Commanding General, U. S. Forces, APO 320. Official mail for units of this TF will be addressed in care of APO 320.

(f) Army units will retain their permanent APO numbers for routine or personal mail.

(g) Hq, ALAMO Force at AMOEBA is APO 712, ALAMO Liaison GP at PEMMICAN is APO 928 and ALAMO Liaison GP at PENUMBRA is APO 503.

6. STRAGGLERS.

Group Commanders will be responsible for strict straggler control within their command.

7. PRISONERS OF WAR.

(a) Prisoners of war captured by TF groups will be tagged with WD, PMG Form No. 1. Prisoner of War Tag ("No Tag - No Food"). These blank tags will be filled out by the unit effecting the capture. The tag will show the date, the hour, the place of capture, and the force making the capture (USA, USMC).

(b) Prisoners of War will be allowed to retain personal effects after they have been inspected by Intelligence Officers.

(c) The Military Police are responsible for the escorting, guard and security of prisoners of war when released to them by the Intelligence Officer. They will keep complete records on each prisoner as directed by the CG,

-2-

(00591)
~~SECRET~~
~~Annex to Adm O~~
No. 2-43.

Backhander TF. The CG, Backhander TF will be responsible
for the evacuation of prisoners of war to advanced
Base A or B, or to Prisoner of War Enclosure at AMOEBA.

8. SOUVENIRS.

Troops will not be permitted to retain articles found on
the battlefield or on the person of the enemy. They may,
however, attach tags giving their name and organization
to articles found. When such articles have served their
purpose for military information and identification they
may be returned to the individual.

9. BURIALS AND CEMETERIES.

(a) The dead will not normally be buried at sea, but
ashore.

(b) Should the military situation prevent this, the
longitude and latitude of burial at sea shall be re-
corded and logged and the information forwarded to GRS,
U. S. Forces, APO 928, Unit One.

(c) If death occurs aboard an evacuation ship, or at
an evacuation hospital, the GR unit in that area will
forward a copy of the GR Form No. 1 to U. S. Forces,
APO 928, Unit One.

(d) Burials are under the direction of the One Section
of each Combat Group. A GRS is attached to each group
to perform all duties in connection with burials in
established cemeteries or on the field of battle when
necessary. Burials on the field of battle will, when
circumstances permit be reburied in regular established
cemeteries. The procedure of burials and disposition
of personal effects of Marine Corps personnel is outlined in Adm Circular 28-43, Division Surgeon's Adm
Order 4-43 and Div Circular 186-43.

(e) Instructions given in TM 10-630 GR will be followed when practical.

(f) In combat sectors each cemetery will be named giving
the geographical location and a number. Each cemetery
established in the same geographical location will be
numbered serially (i.e., U. S. Armed Forces Cemetery,
SANANANDO No. 1, NG). Report of burials will be made
to CG, BACKHANDER TF on "Report of Interment" QMC Form
No. 1 - GRS in triplicate, accompanied by tooth chart
if fingerprints cannot be obtained.

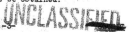

(00591)

~~SECRET~~

Annex to Adm O
No. 2-43.

10. DISPOSITION OF ENEMY DEAD.

(a)   Enemy dead will be buried in the same manner as
American dead, when practicable. In order to secure
reciprocal treatment it is required that units obtain
full reports on enemy dead when possible, using the same
procedure as outlined in 9 (f) above. Effects found
on enemy dead will be collected, listed, and together
with the list placed in a bag or secure package with
tag bearing the same serial number as on the grave of
the enemy dead and then sent to the Intelligence Officer.
These effects will then be sent to Hq, Alamo Force,
APO 712.

BY COMMAND OF MAJOR GENERAL RUPERTUS:

AMOR LeR. SIMS,
Colonel, U. S. Marine Corps,
Chief of Staff.

DISTRIBUTION: Same as Adm O 2-43.

O-F-F-I-C-I-A-L:

W. S. FELLERS,
Colonel, USMC,
  D - 4.

-4-

UNCLASSIFIED

Annex B to Administrative Order No. 2-43, Backhander Force.

SPECIAL ASSIGNMENTS AND LOADING INSTRUCTIONS

00591
1990-25
144/246

Headquarters, Backhander Force,
APO 320
14 November 1943.   1000.

1.   a.   LtCol. Robert H. McDowell, USMC, is hereby designated
          BACKHANDER Forwarding Officer at PENUMBRA.

     b.   LtCol. James M. Clark, USMC, is hereby designated as
          BACKHANDER Regulating Officer at PENUMBRA.

     c.   LtCol Earl E. Holmes, USMCR, is hereby designated as
          BACKHANDER Transport Quartermaster at PENUMBRA.

2.   Duties assigned the above officers will consist principally
     in supervision of movement of material, equipment and personnel
     from the PENUMBRA Staging Area to the Combat Zone in accord-
     ance with designated priorities in BACKHANDER TF Opn O 1-43.

3.   The BACKHANDER Forwarding O will organize the Forwarding Depot
     at PENUMBRA to assure the movement of essential material, or
     critical items to the Combat Zone; these articles will initi-
     ally consist of ammunition, rations, clothing and maintenance
     equipment of an organizational nature. Requirements must be
     conveyed to the BACKHANDER Regulating O in sufficient time to
     permit a priority loading. Once established, priorities will
     not be changed except on authority of the BACKHANDER Regulat-
     ing O.

4.   The BACKHANDER Regulating O will organize the Port of Embark-
     ation and will control the movement of materials and personnel
     in accordance with established priorities. He is authorized to
     call upon all units for working parties essential to effect
     the rapid and efficient loading of all vessels moving into the
     Combat Zone. He will check all vessels during and after load-
     ing to insure that only essential items of combat equipment
     and supplies accompany the troops initially.

5.   The BACKHANDER TQM will prepare all loads for execution,
     arrange for spotting of same at designated loading points
     and comply with the loading instructions listed below. He
     will provide the ship with a complete list of personnel and
     impediments aboard for delivery to the Shore Party Comdr at
     BACKHANDER. Effect loading of assigned vessel insofar as
     practicable in accordance with SOP for this Div.

6.   a.   All organizational vehicles will be loaded to capacity
          and borrowed Army trucks will be used, when possible, to
          augment mobile loading.

-1-

S-E-C-R-E-T

b. The echelon of six (6) LSTs arriving at BACKHANDER on the morning of D-Day, from PENUMBRA, will carry ten (10) days supplies, Class I - IV, incl and 3 U/F for all units aboard.

c. The echelon of two (2) LSTs arriving at BACKHANDER, from PENUMBRA, on the afternoon of D-Day will carry four (4) 40mm guns of 12th Def Bn, remaining personnel of CT C, Det TF Hqrts, Det Signal Co, Det Serv Bn, Div Band, Det 263d Ord MM Co, Det ESB, 622d Ord AM Co ten (10) days supplies, Class I - IV incl for CT C, 200 drums diesel fuel for ESB, ten (10) days Class I - IV incl and 3 U/F for units aboard, and one (1) U/F for CT C.

d. The echelon of five (5) LSTs arriving at BACKHANDER, from PENUMBRA, on the morning of D plus 1 will carry the remaining AA units of 12th Def Bn, E Med Co, Base Engr Det and one gun section 155mm of 12th Def Bn. This echelon will also carry twenty (20) days supplies, Class I - IV, incl and 3 U/F for units aboard (except AA) 5 U/F AA, 2 U/F for CT C and 1 U/F for CT B (less one LT).

e. The echelon of five (5) LSTs arriving at BACKHANDER, from PENUMBRA, on the afternoon of D plus one Day will carry the 17th Marines. This echelon will carry twenty (20) days supplies, Class I - IV incl and 3 U/F for units aboard, one (1) U/F for CT B (less 1 LT) and 200 drums diesel fuel for ESB.

f. The LST arriving at BACKHANDER, from REDHERRING, on the morning of D-Day will carry one LT (less dets) of CT B. This LT will carry ten (10) days supplies, Class I - IV incl and 3 U/F.

g. The five (5) LSTs arriving at BACKHANDER, from REDHERRING, on the afternoon of D-Day will carry CT B (less dets). This echelon will carry fifteen (15) days supplies Class I-IV incl and four (4) U/F for units aboard, five (5) days supplies, Class I - IV incl and one (1) U/F for the LT (less dets) in par. 6 f. above.

h. Landing Team 21 will carry twenty (20) days supplies and six (6) U/F initially.

i. The following officers will prepare the loading plans and coordinate the loading of LST echelons leaving PENUMBRA:

        par 6 b above - CO, 7th Marines.
        par 6 c above - CO, 12th Def Bn detail an officer
                      from 12 Def Bn.
        par 6 d above - CO, 12th Def Bn.
        par 6 e above - CO, 17th Marines.

j. The CO, 17th Marines (Engineer) will provide each of the

UNCLASSIFIED

-2-

six (6) LSTs in the first Ech with suitable pieces of lumber for emergency extension ramps. This lumber to be retained by the Shore Party for use in unloading succeeding Echs.

k. All available space in succeeding shipping of organizations will be utilized to carry ammunition, rations, and supplies to units at BACKHANDER.

7. a. All Army BACKHANDER Units staged at PENUMBRA, Div Ord Section, Div Commissary Section and Div Med Section, will detail an officer and required clerks to BACKHANDER Regulating O for purpose of Administration and Forwarding of Property.

b. The above personnel will revert to the control of respective organizations upon completion of their movements to BACKHANDER.

c. The following BACKHANDER Units will be utilized at PENUMBRA initially for designated tasks:

622d Ord AM Co (less det) - Operate Ord dumps.
1 Co, 543d QM Serv Bn - Assist the BACKHANDER QM in handling cargo.
1913th Engineer Aviation Bn - Working parties.
Detachment ANGAU - Working Parties.
263d Ord MM Co - Operate as directed by BACKHANDER Ord O.

BY COMMAND OF MAJOR GENERAL RUPERTUS:

AMOR LeR. SIMS,
Colonel, U. S. Marine Corps,
Chief of Staff.

DISTRIBUTION: Same as for Adm O 2-43.

O-F-F-I-C-I-A-L:

W. S. FELLERS,
Colonel, USMC,
D-4.

-3-

Annex C to Administ... tive Order No. 2-43, Backha... er Force.

MEDICAL

00591
1990-25
144/286

Headquarters, Backhander Force,
APO 320.
14 November, 1943.   1000.

UNCLASSIFIED

1. ORGANIZATION.

a. Navy Med Units.

Co A 1st Med Bn Atchd CT A.
Co B 1st Med Bn (less 1 Surg Team) Atchd CT B.
Co C 1st Med Bn Atchd CT C.
Co D 1st Med Bn Atchd CT B.
Co E 1st Med Bn Atchd CT C upon landing.
Surg Team Co B 1st Med Bn Atchd LT 21.
Med Dets (1 O-Corpsman from 7th Fleet) Atchd to each LST.

b. Army Med Units.

30th Evac Hosp.
58th Evac Hosp.
Co A (Coll) 135th Med Regt.
Co B (Coll) 135th Med Regt.
Co C (Clr) 135th Med Regt.
Army Surg Teams (4 Med Os, 25 enl from ALAMO Force) Atchd
to 1 LST in each Ech of 6.
21st Med Sup Plat (Avn).

c. Army Malaria Control Units.

5th Malaria Control Unit.
26th Malaria Control Unit.

2. EMBARKATION AND LANDING

a. Medical units embark as directed by Opn O 1-43, BACKHANDER
TF.

b. Upon landing Medical units carry out normal duties.

c. Co C 1st Med Bn with Co E Atchd be prepared to pass control
TF Med O on order.

d. Army Med units pass to control TF Med O upon landing.

e. Navy Med Det embarked each LST render medical care to
casualties enroute and evacuees.

f. Army Surg Team embarked LSTs assist Navy Det in care of
casualties.

g. Malaria control units perform normal duties under direction
TF Med O.

UNCLASSIFIED

-1-

S-E-C-R-E-T

3. EVACUATION.

   a. Enroute.

      By returning LSTs or other vessels with Med Units embarked.

   b. After landing.

     (1) From BACKHANDER and STONEFACE areas by returning ships to AMOEBA, PENUMBRA, PEMMICAN or REDHERRING.

     (2) Evac by air of most serious casualties when situation permits.

     (3) TF Med O responsible for evacuation of all casualties.

   c. Collecting Stations.

      Location and time of opening to be prescribed by Task Grp Comdrs.

   d. Clearing Station.

      As prescribed by Shore Party Comdr.

   e. Casualties.

     (1) Serious casualties in BACKHANDER area requiring hospitalization in excess of 15 days will be evacuate through Shore Party Clearing Station to LSTs containing Army Surg Teams. Serious casualties in STONEFACE area will be evacuated by APDs. First APD on night of D plus 1 Day, others on call.

     (2) Minor casualties requiring hospitalization not in excess of 30 days will not be evacuated if number of beds and tactical situation warrants.

     (3) Automatic exchange of stretchers and blankets between units in line of evacuation.

   f. Tags.

      Emergency Medical tags (Form 526) completed by Med Pers will be atchd to each evacuee, disposition to be made as follows:

        One retained at destination; one returned to unit from which evacuated, filled in to include date, time and place of arrival.

S-E-C-R-E-T

g. Reports.

    (1) The TF Med O is responsible for the submission of daily reports of all evacuees to the TF, D-1 Sec for inclusion in the D-1 periodic report. This report to include: Name, Rank, Serial Number, Organization, Diagnosis, Date of Evacuation, Carrier and Destination.

    (2) The Naval Med O Atchd to each LST, report in duplicate all casualties evacuated or that occur on board. This report containing, Name in Full, Rank Serial Number, Organization, Diagnosis, Date and Location of Debarkation to be forwarded through the Shore Party Comdr to the BACKHANDER TF Med O.

4. PRISONERS.

Unit Med Os provide such medical attention as practicable to enemy casualties. Care should be exercised to avoid acts of violence by recalcitrant wounded Japanese.

5. DISPOSAL OF THE DEAD.

See Adm O 2-43, Backhander TF.

6. EQUIPMENT AND SUPPLIES.

a. Equipment.

Organic equipment only will be carried initially by Med units. The embarkation of organic and supplementary equipment will be governed by space available for shipping.

b. Uniform and Personal Equipment.

As prescribed in Adm O 2-43, BACKHANDER TF.

c. Supplies.

    (1) Initial – In accordance with prescribed Tables of Allowances.

    (2) Resupply – 21st Med Sup Plat (Avn) will provide resupply of all Med Units after landing.

    (3) Emergency supplies by airplane drop where necessary.

7. WATER.

See Adm O 2-43, BACKHANDER TF.

8. SALT.

Salt tablets will be provided by unit Med Os for all personnel.

-3-

9. <u>ATABRINE</u>

All personnel will be given 0.1 gram atabrine daily under the direct supervision of an officer.

10. <u>WASTE DISPOSAL</u>.

a. Burn or bury all garbage and refuse.

b. All units dig straddle trenches, urinals and garbage pits as soon as tactical situation permits.

c. All Med Os under direction of Unit Comdrs will strictly enforce field sanitation.

d. Particular attention will be paid to washing and rinsing of individual mess gear.

11. <u>MEDICAL COMMAND</u>.

a. <u>TF Med O</u>.

Comdr E. B. Keck (MC) USN, is designated at BACKHANDER TF Med O.

b. <u>Location</u>.

(1) Afloat - LST.
(2) Ashore - BACKHANDER TF CP.

BY COMMAND OF MAJOR GENERAL RUPERTUS:

AMOR LeR. SIMS,
Colonel, U. S. Marine Corps,
Chief of Staff.

DISTRIBUTION: Same as Adm O 2-43.

O-F-F-I-C-I-A-L:

W. S. FELLERS,
Colonel, USMC,
D-4.

-4-

Annex D to Administrative Order No. 2-43, Backhander Force.

ORDNANCE PLAN

00591
1990-25
144/246.

Headquarters, Backhander Force,
APO 320
November 14, 1943.

UNCLASSIFIED

Enclosure: (A) - Ammunition Status Report (Form).
(B) - Ammunition Identification Code.

1. The Ordnance Officer, ESCALATOR, will:

   a. Supervise all Ord service for BACKHANDER TF forward of USASOS Bases in CENTRAL.

   b. Coordinate thru USASOS Agencies to insure stockage of all necessary Ord supplies at USASOS Bases A and B (PEMMICAN and PENUMBRA, respectively).

2. All correspondence and reports forwarded to ALAMO pertaining to Ord will be marked: "ATTN: Ordnance Officer". Requisitions for Ord supplies within authorized allowances will be submitted by the TF Ord O direct to designated USASOS Supply Bases. An information copy of such requisitions will be furnished ALAMO Ord O. Requisitions for supplies in excess of authorized allowances will be submitted to ALAMO Ord O.

3. ATCHD UNITS.

   263d Ord MM Co.
   622d Ord AM Co. (less det 1 O, 10 EM).

4. PLAN OF SERVICE.

   a. During Staging.

      The 263d Ord MM Co, assisted by USASOS Ord installations at PENUMBRA, will provide service for units staging at PENUMBRA, supporting garrison units staged at places other than PENUMBRA will be furnished Ord Service by ALAMO Ord Units or USASOS Ord installations located in the staging areas concerned. The stocks of Class II Ord supplies in hands of BACKHANDER TF units will not be used during staging. Parts and supplies necessary for maintenance during staging will be supplied by USASOS Ord Depots except for units at AMOEBA, which will be supplied by the Ord Depot, ALAMO Base.

UNCLASSIFIED   -1-

b. **During Assault and after Occupation.**

   (1) A detachment of the 263d Ord MM Co will accompany the assault units and perform such maintenance as is within its capabilities. The remainder of the company will move to the objective area with the supporting garrison units of the TF. The Company will take with it 30 days of Class II Ord supplies for the entire BACKHANDER TF and will establish and operate maintenance shops and Class II Supply Depots under direction of BACKHANDER TF Ord O.

   (2) The 622d Ord AM Co will accompany the third Ech of LSTs to BACKHANDER. This company will establish and operate ammunition depots as directed by TF Ord O.

5. **Supply, Initial.**

  a. **Class II.**

   (1) Units will carry with them the organizational sets of spare parts prescribed in the BNLs pertinent to the major items of Ord in their possession.

   (2) The 263d Ord MM Co will carry 30 days of supply for maintenance of all major items of Ord in the BACKHANDER TF.

  b. **Class V.**

  See Adm O 2-43.

6. **Resupply.**

  a. **Class II.**

  Without action on part of BACKHANDER TF, 15 days of supply of Class II supplies will be shipped to BACKHANDER on first available supply ships. This "automatic" shipment is to replace supplies which it is estimated will be consumed before the BACKHANDER TF can submit first resupply requisitions and to compensate for time - lag in filling such requisitions. Thereafter, resupply of Class II supplies will be as follows: Units will replenish organizational spare parts and obtain replacements for unserviceable items from BACKHANDER TF Ord Depot. Parts, supplies and major items required to maintain levels prescribed for the TF will be furnished by requisition on designated USASOS Supply Bases. Ordinarily, requisitions will be submitted twice monthly. However, parts necessary to remove equipment from deadline will be requisitioned twice weekly. In cases

-2-

of extreme emergency, requisitions may be submitted by
radio, at the time the emergency arises.

b. Class V.

Supply to units in objective areas will be thru the TF
Ammunition Depot. Re-supply to maintain prescribed
stock levels will be furnished by requisition on designated USASOS Bases. Copy of requisitions will be furnished
ALAMO Ord O.

7. Reports.

a. A radio report of ammunition expenditures will be submitted to CG, ESCALATOR, daily by the TF Ord O.

b. A report of status of ammunition, giving the information
shown below will be submitted to CG, ESCALATOR, on the
10th, 20th and last day of each month by the BACKHANDER
TF Ord O. Ammunition on hand last report. Ammunition
received since last report. Ammunition expended since
last report. Balance on hand. Number of weapons, except
replacement reserves, on hand. Ammunition will be reported
by AIC code only.

c. All units in the BACKHANDER Area will submit to D-4 as
of 1800 Love, daily an ammunition report as outlined in
enclosure (A) using the AIC code in enclosure (B). The
TF Ord O will have access to this report for any desired
information.

8. Maintenance and Inspections.

a. Vehicles and weapons will be carefully protected against
possible immersion in salt water. As soon as possible
after landing, water proofing material will be removed
and vehicles and weapons washed in fresh water and carefully lubricated.

b. Vehicles and weapons will be inspected daily and kept in
the best possible condition.

c. Competent mechanics and stocks of major items, repair
parts and cleaning and preserving materials are available
in the 263d Ord MM Co.

S-E-C-R-E-T

    d. Unserviceable equipment which cannot be promptly repaired locally, will be evacuated to USASOS Depots by returning supply ships.

BY COMMAND OF MAJOR GENERAL RUPERTUS:

AMOR LeR. SIMS,

Colonel, U. S. Marine Corps,

Chief of Staff.

DISTRIBUTION: Same as for Adm O 2-43.

O-F-F-I-C-I-A-L

W. S. FELLERS,
Colonel, USMC,
   D-4.

UNCLASSIFIED

-4-

AMMUNITION STATUS REPORT

UNIT: _____ LOCATION: _____

FROM: _____ TO: _____
　　　　(Hour and Date)　　　　　　　(Hour and Date)

Code No. AIC	AMMUNITION NOMENCLATURE	ON HAND LAST REPORT	RECEIVED	EXPENDED	BALANCE ON HAND	WEAPONS ON HAND No	TYPE

ENCLOSURE "A"

AMMUNITION IDENTIFICATION CODE

FOR 155-MM GUNS, M1917-17A1-18M1

CODE:

NO.	A.I.C.	ITEM
1	P1EAA	SHELL, HE, M101, unfuzed.
2	P1FCA	SHELL, HE, Mk. III, unfuzed.
3	P1FAA	SHELL, HE, Mk. IIIA1, unfuzed.
4	P1ERA	SHELL, gas, HS, M104, unfuzed.
5	P1FHA	SHELL, gas, HS, Mk. VII, unfuzed.
6	P1FIA	SHELL, gas, HS, Mk. VIIA1, unfuzed.
7	P1EFA	SHELL, smoke, FS, M104, unfuzed.
8	P1FQA	SHELL, smoke, FS, Mk. VII, unfuzed.
9	P1FRA	SHELL, smoke, FS, Mk. VIIA1, unfuzed.
10	P1ECA	SHELL, smoke, WP, M104, unfuzed.
11	P1FKA	SHELL, smoke, WP, Mk. VII, unfuzed.
12	P1FEA	SHELL, smoke, WP, Mk. VIIA1, unfuzed.
13	R2AGA	SHRAPNEL, Mk. I, fuzed.
14	P1EDA	PROJECTILE, AP, M112, w/BDF, M60.
15	P1EYA	PROJECTILE, AP, M112B1, w/BDF, M60.

PROPELLING CHARGES FOR 155-MM GUNS, M1917-17A1-18M1

25	P2FAC	CHARGE, propelling.
26	P2FCC	CHARGE, propelling, NH powder.

FOR 20MM AUTOMATIC GUN, Mk. IV (OERLIKON)

30	P5BCA	SHELL, HE-T, Mk. III.
31	P5BBA	SHELL, HE-T, Mk. IV.
32	P5BAA	SHELL, HE, Mk. III.
33	P5BEA	SHELL, BL&P, Mk. IV.
34	P5BDA	SHELL, HE, Mk. III, M21.

FOR 37-MM AUTOMATIC GUN, M1A2 (ANTIAIRCRAFT).

40	P5EAB	SHELL, HE, M54, w/PDF, M56.
41	P5EIA	SHOT, APC, M59, w/Tracer.
42	P5EKA	SHOT, AP, M74, w/Tracer.
43	P5ERB	SHELL, practice, M55A1, w/dummy Fuze, M50.

FOR 40MM AUTOMATIC GUN, M1.

45	P5HGA	SHELL, HE, Mk. I.
46	P5HAA	SHELL, HE, Mk. II, w/Fuze, percussion, D.A., No. 251.
47	P5HDA	SHELL, HE, Mk. III.
48	P5HCA	SHELL, HE, Mk. II, w/PDF, M64, or M64A1.

ENCLOSURE "B"

49	P5HEA	SHELL. HE, Mk, III, w/Fuze, percussion, D.A., No. 251.
50	P5HBA	SHOT, AP, M81, w/Tracer.
51	P5HYX	CARTRIDGE, drill (AUST).
52	P5HXX	SHELL, HE, w/Fuze, No. 251 (FOREIGN MANUFACTURE).
53	P5HFA	SHELL, HE, Mk. II, w/Fuze, Mk. 27 (NAVY)

FOR "3" AA GUNS (MOBILE)

55	P5NNA	SHELL, HE, M42, w/TMF, M43 (all mods.).
56	P5NSA	SHELL, HE, M42A1, w/ TMF, M43, (all mods.).
57	P5NIA	PROJECTILE, APC, M62, w/BDF, M66, cr M66A1.

FOR "3" AA GUNS (MOBILE)

58	P5NHA	PROJECTILE, APC, M62, w/Tracer.
59	P5NUA	SHOT, AP, M79, w/Tracer.
60	P5NMA	SHRAPNEL, Mk. I.

FOR 90-MM AA GUN, M1.

80	P5SBA	SHELL, HE, M71, w/TMF, M43, (all mods.).
81	P5SCA	SHOT, AP, M77, W/Tracer.
82	P5SHA	PROJECTILE, APC, M82, w/BDF, M68.
83	P8CJA	CARTRIDGE, drill, M12.
84	P8CJX	CARTRIDGE, drill (INERT).
85	P8LKX	BASE, drill cartridge, M12.
86	P5SGA	SHELL, HE, M71, w/PDF, M48.

FOR 37-MM FUNS, M3 AND M3A1 (AT) AND M5 AND M6 (T)

100	R1GHB	CANISTER, M2?.
101	R1GBA	SHELL, HE, M63, w/BDF, M58.
102	R1GFB	SHOT, AP, M74, w/Tracer.
103	R1GIB	SHOT, APC, M51,w/Tracer.
105	R1GGB	SHOT, TP, M51, w/Tracer.
106	R1GDA	SHOT, TP, M51A1, w/Tracer.
107	R6ZAB	CARTRIDGE, drill, M13.

FOR 75-MM GUNS, M1897-16-17.

110	R1LDA	SHELL, HE, M48, w/PDF, M48 (normal).
111	R1RAA	SHELL, HE, M48, w/PDF. M48A1 (normal).
112	R1LGA	SHELL, HE, M48, w/PDF, M54 (normal).
113	R1LEA	SHELL, HE, M48, w/PDF, M48 (reduced).
114	R1RBA	SHELL, HE, M48, w/PDF, M48A1 (reduced).
115	R1LHA	SHELL, HE, M48, w/PDF, M54 (reduced).
116	R1LCA	SHELL, HE, M48, w/PDF, M48 (super).
117	R1RCA	SHELL, HE, M48, w/PDF, M48A1 (super).
118	R1LFA	SHELL, HE, M48, w/PDF, M54 (super).
119	R1LBA	SHELL, HE, Mk. I, unfuzed (reduced).

120	R1LAA	SHELL, HE, Mk. I, unfuzed (normal).
121	R1LNA	PROJECTILE, APC, M61, w/BDF, M66 or M66A1 (super).
122	R1L1A	PROJECTILE, APC, M61, w/Tracer (super).
123	R1LJA	SHOT, AP, M72, w/Tracer (super).
124	R1LLA	SHELL, gas, HS, Mk. II, unfuzed (normal).
125	R1LPB	SHELL, smoke, WP, Mk. II (normal).
126	R1LVA	SHRAPNEL, Mk. I, fuzed.
127	R6ZAC	CARTRIDGE, drill, M7.
128	R6YAC	ROUND, inert, 75-mm gun.
129	R6HDX	BASE, drill cartridge, M7.

UNCLASSIFIED

FOR 75-MM HOWITZERS M1 AND M1A1.

135	R1MMA	SHELL, HE-AT, M66, w/BDF, M62.
136	R1MAA	SHELL, HE, M41A1, w/PDF, M48.
137	R1MHA	SHELL, HE, M41A1, w/PDF, M48A1.
138	R1MEA	SHELL, HE, M41 A1, w/PDF, M54.
139	R1MCA	SHELL, HE, M48, w/ PDF, M48.
140	R1MLA	SHELL, HE M48, w/PDF, M48A1.
141	R1MDA	SHELL, HE, M48, w/PDF, M54.
142	R1MJA	SHELL, gas, HS, M64, w/PDF, M57.
143	R1MIA	SHELL, smoke, WP, M64, w/PDF, M57.
144	R6ZAE	CARTRIDGE, drill, M2A2.
145	R6HCX	BASE, drill cartridge, M2A1 or M2A2.

FOR 105-MM HOWITZER, M2 AND M2A1.

150	R1QEA	SHELL, HE-AT, M67, w/BDF, M62.
151	R1QBB	SHELL, HE M1, w/PDF, M48.
152	R1QDA	SHELL, HE, M1, w/PDF, M48A1.
153	R1QCB	SHELL, HE M1, w/PDF, M54.
154	R1QIB	SHELL, gas, HS, M60, w/PDF, M57.
155	R1QJB	SHELL, smoke, WP, M60, w/PDF, M57.
156	R5GAA	AMMUNITION, blank.
157	R6CIA	CARTRIDGE, drill, M14.
158	R6HEX	BASE, drill cartridge, M14.
159	R6FHX	FUZE, dummy, M59, for M14 cartridges.

FOR 105-MM HOWITZER, M3,(A.B.)

161	R1SDA	SHELL, HE,M1, w/PDF, M48, f/105-mm How., M3(A.B.).
162	R1SCA	SHELL, HE,M1, w/PDF, M54, f/105-mm How., M3(A.B.).

FOR 155-mm HOWITZERS, M1917-17A1-18.

165	R2LBB	CHARGE, propelling, M1 (green bag).
166	R2LCA	CHARGE, propelling, M1A1 (green bag).
167	R2LDA	CHARGE, propelling, M2 (white bag).
168	R2ADA	SHELL, HE, M102, unfuzed.
169	R2AAA	SHELL, HE, Mk. I, unfuzed.
170	R2ABA	SHELL, HE, Mk. LA1, unfuzed.

　　　　　AMMUNITION IDENTIFICATION CODE

171	R2ACA	SHELL, HE, Mk. IV, unfuzed.
172	R2APA	SHELL, gas, HS, M105, unfuzed.
173	R2AKA	SHELL, gas, HS, Mk. II, unfuzed.
174	R2AIA	SHELL, gas, HS, Mk. IIA1, unfuzed.
175	R2AQA	SHELL, smoke, WP, M105, unfuzed.
176	R2ANA	SHELL, smoke, WP, Mk. II, unfuzed.
177	R2AJA	SHELL, smoke, WP, Mk. IIA1, unfuzed.
178	R2AWA	SHELL, smoke, FS, Mk. IIA1, unfuzed.
179	R2ARX	SHELL, smoke, HC, B.E., M115, w/PDF, 54.
180	R2CWA	GROMMET, rope.
181	R2ASA	SHELL, gas, HS, Mk. IIA1, Mod. 1, unfuzed.

FOR 155-MM HOWITZER, M1.

185	R2MAA	CHARGE, propelling, M3 (green bag).
186	R2MBA	CHARGE, propelling, M4 (white bag).
187	R2BAA	SHELL, HE, M107, unfuzed.
188	R2BCA	SHELL, gas, HS, M110, unfuzed.
189	R2BEA	SHELL, smoke, FS, M110, unfuzed.
190	R2BDA	SHELL, smoke, WP, M110, unfuzed.
191	R2BFX	SHELL, smoke, HC, B.E., M116, w/PDF, M54.

FUZES, POINT DETONATING AND MECHANICAL FOR FIELD ARTY WPNS.

195	R3BEA	FUZE, PD, M46, f/unmodified Mk. series shells.
196	R3BFA	FUZE, PD, M47, f/unmodified Mk. series shells.
197	R3BHA	FUZE, PD, M51, f/M and modified Mk. series shells.
198	R3BSA	FUZE, PD, M51A1, f/M and modified Mk. series shells.
199	R3BJA	FUZE, PD, M55, f/M and modified Mk. series shells.
200	R3BTA	FUZE, PD, M55A1, f/M and modified Mk. series shells.
201	R3EAX	FUZE, time, mechanical, M67, f/155-mm, M1, How., He shell.
204	R6FOX	FUZE, inert, P.D., M48.
205	R6FLX	FUZE, inert, P.D., M54.

FUZES, MECHANICAL, FOR AA SHELLS.

202	P7ICA	FUZE, time, mechanical, M43A2.
203	R3EXA	ADAPTER, f/M43, mechanical time fuzes.

PRIMERS.

207	R3DCA	PRIMER, percussion, 21-grain, Mk. IIA, f/155-mm.
208	R3DBA	PRIMER, percussion, 21-grain Mk. IIA1, f/155-mm.

FOR 60-MM MORTARS, M1 AND M2.

209	R4VFA	CARTRIDGES, ignition, M5A1, complete w/Fin.
210	R4VBX	CARTRIDGE, ignition, M4.
211	R4CAA	SHELL, HE, M49A2, w/PDF, M52, (w/M5A1 ignition cartridge).
212	R4CDA	SHELL, illuminating, M83, w/FUZE, time, fixed, M65.
213	R4CEA	SHELL, practice, M50A1, w/PDF, M52.
214	R4CFA	SHELL, practice, M50A2, w/PDF, M52.
215	R4CAX	SHELL, HE, M49A2, w/PDF, M52 (w/M4 or M5 ignition cartridge).

AMMUNITION IDENTIFICATION CODE

| 216 | R4GBA | SHELL, HE, M49A1, w/PDF, M52. |

FOR "3" AND 81-MM MORTARS.

218	R4VCX	CARTRIDGE, ignition, M3.
219	R4FCA	SHELL, HE, M43A1, w/PDF, M52.
220	R4FWA	SHELL, HE, M43 w/PDF, M52.
221	R4FLA	SHELL, HE, M56, w/PDF, M53.
222	R4FPA	SHELL, smoke, WP, M57, w/PDF, M52.
223	R4MAA	SHELL, HE, 3" Mortar.
224	R4FGA	SHELL, practice. M43A1 w/PDF, M52.

MINES AND DEMOLITION MATERIAL.

227	R7AIA	MINE, AT, HE, M1A x/Fuze, M1A2.
228	R7ABA	MINE, antitank, M1 w/Fuze M1A1.
229	R7AAA	MINE, antitank, HE, M1, W/O Fuze.
230	R7CAB	FUZE, mine, antitank, HE, M1A1.
231	R7CBA	BOOSTER, f/M1A1 Fuze.

233	R7AYX	MINE, contact. AT, Mk. II (AUST).
234	R7AXX	MINE, contact, AT, Mk. IV (AUST).
235	R7EPA	TORPEDO, bangalore, M1, w/accessories.
236	R7EAA	EXPLOSIVE, TNT, $\frac{1}{2}$-lb.
237	R7ECA	EXPLOSIVE, nitrostarch, $\frac{1}{2}$-lb.
238	R7ECB	EXPLOSIVE, nitrostarch, 1-lb.
239	R7EOX	GELIGNITE, Nobel, AN "60".

GRENADES HAND.

240	S4GBA	GRENADE, hand, frag, Mk. II, w/igniting fuze, M10A2.
241	S4GAA	GRENADE, hand, frag, Mk. II, w/igniting fuze, M10A1.
242	S4GDA	GRENADE, hand, frag, Mk. II, w/igniting fuze, M10.
243	S4SBA	FUZE, igniting, M10A2, f/Mk. II grenade.
244	S4KAA	GRENADE, hand, offensive, Mk. IIIA1, unfuzed.
245	S4SAA	FUZE, detonating M6A2, f/Mk. IIIA1 grenade.
246	S4GCX	GRENADE, hand, frag., Mk. I, No. 36M (AUST).
247	S4GYX	IGNITER, set, 4 Sec. delay, f/Mk. I, No. 36M, grenade.
248	S4KYX	GRENADE, hand offensive, No 69. Mk. I (AUST).
249	S4KXX	FUZE, detonating, ASA, No. 46, f/No. 69, Mk.I, gren(AUST)
250	S4JCA	GRENADE, hand, CN, M7.
251	S4JAA	GRENADE, hand, CN-DM M6.
252	S4SEA	FUZE, percussion, f/chem. grenade.
253	S4LAA	GRENADE, hand, smoke, HC, M8.
254	S4GEA	GRENADE, hand, incendiary, M14.
255	S4MAA	GRENADE, hand, training, Mk. IA1.

257	S4SDX	FUZE, for petrol grenade, (PAT HANNA).
258	S4HAX	IGNITER, for Molotov Cocktail.
259	S4IAX	SWITCH, booby trap, (AUST).
260	S4SYX	FUZE, detonating, M6A3, f/Mk. IIIA1 grenade.

SECRET   AMMUNITION IDENTIFICATION CODE.

GRENADE, RIFLE.

```
265  S4NAA    GRENADE, rifle, HE. M9.
266  S4NBA    GRENADE, AT, M9A1.
267  S4NGA    GRENADE, rifle, practice, M11A2.
268  S4NDA    FIN, assy. rifle practice grenade, M11A2.
269  S4NEA    OGIVE, assy. rifle, practice grenade, M11A2.
270  S4NFA    GRENADE, AT, practice, M11A1.
271  S4QCX    FIN, assy., AT, practice grenade, M11A1.
272  S4NCA    GRENADE, AT., practice, M11.
273  S4QAX    FIN, assy., f/M11 practice grenade.
274  S4NEA    GRENADE, AT, practice, M13.
275  S4QBX    FIN, assy., f/M13 practice grenade.
276  S4PAA    CARTRIDGE, rifle grenade, cal. .30. M3.
277  S4RCA    KIT, AT, grenade, M9A1, f/cal. .30, M1903, and M1903-
              A1 rifles.
278  S4RAA    KIT, HE, rifle, grenade, M9, f/cal. .30, M1903, and
              M1903A1, rifles.
279  S4QYX    ADAPTER, grenade, projection. M1.
280  S4NYX    GRENADE, rifle, impact, fragmentation, M17 or T2.
```

GROUND PYROTECHNICS.

```
285  S5HAA    LIGHT, signal, Very, green star, Mk. II.
286  S5HGA    LIGHT, signal, Very, green, Mk, II.
287  S5HBA    LIGHT, signal, Very, red star, Mk. II.
288  S5HCA    LIGHT, signal, Very, red, Mk. II.
289  S5HDA    LIGHT, signal, Very, white star, Mk. II.
290  S5HEA    LIGHT, signal, Very, white, Mk. II.

295  S5RTA    SIGNAL, ground, white star, parachute, M5A1.
296  S5RUA    SIGNAL, ground. red chain, parachute, M7.
297  S5RFA    SIGNAL, ground, white star, parachute, M17.
298  S5REA    SIGNAL, ground, white star, cluster, M18.
299  S5RDA    SIGNAL, ground, green star, parachute, M19.
300  S5RGA    SIGNAL, GROUND, green star, cluster, M20.
301  S5RBA    SIGNAL, ground, amber star, parachute, M21.
302  S5RAA    SIGNAL, ground, amber star, cluster, M22.
303  S5RHA    SIGNAL, ground, high burst ranging, M27.
304  S5RJX    SIGNAL, ground, range indicating, parachute, M47.
305  S5IYX    KITE, rocket (BRITISH)
```

FOR 2.36" AT ROCKET LAUNCHER. M1.

```
308  S9AAA    ROCKET, AT, 2.36", M6.
309  S9ABA    ROCKET, practice, 2.36", M7.
```

FOR 3.25" AA TARGET ROCKET PROJECTOR. M1.

```
312  S9BNA    ROCKET, target, AA, 3.25", M2.
```

-6-

AMMUNITION IDENTIFICATION CODE.

SMALL ARMS AMMUNITION.

```
313   T1CQX    CARTRIDGE, carbine, cal. .30, M1 (3000 rds. wax liner)
314   T1AYX    CARTRIDGE, ball, cal. .22, extra long rifle.
315   T1AAA    CARTRIDGE, ball, cal. .22, long rifle.
316   T1ABA    CARTRIDGE, ball, cal. .22, short.
317   T1CAD    CARTRIDGE, carbine, cal. .30, M1.
318   T1CAX    CARTRIDGE, carbine, cal. .30, M1.
319   T1UAA    CARTRIDGE, blank, cal. .30 (f/bolt action rifles only)
320   T1EGC    CARTRIDGE, ball, cal. .30 (in 5rd clips).
321   T1EDC    CARTRIDGE, AP, cal. .30 (in 5rd clips).
322   T1EKB    CARTRIDGE, incend., cal. .30 (in 5rd clips).
323   T1EPC    CARTRIDGE, tracer, cal. .30 (in 5rd clips).
324   T1EGD    CARTRIDGE, ball, cal. .30 (in 8rd clips).
325   T1EDB    CARTRIDGE, AP, cal. .30 (in 8rd clips).
326   T1EKC    CARTRIDGE, incend., cal. .30 (in 8rd clips).
327   T1IPB    CARTRIDGE, tracer, cal. .30 (in 8rd clips).
328   T1EGE    CARTRIDGE, B&T, cal. .30 (4-1) (in web belt).
329   T1EHB    CARTRIDGE, B&T, cal. .30 (9-1) (in web belt).
330   T1EDD    CARTRIDGE, AP & T, cal. .30 (4-1) (in web belt).
331   T1EEC    CARTRIDGE, AP & T, cal. .30 (9-1) (in web belt).
332   T1EGX    CARTRIDGE, ball, cal., .30 (in ctns).
333   T1EDG    CARTRIDGE, AP, cal., .30 (in ctns).
334   T1EKX    CARTRIDGE, incend., cal. .30 (in ctns).
335   T1EPX    CARTRIDGE, tracer, cal. .30 (in ctns).

337   T1WAA    LINK, metallic belt, cal. .30, M1.
338   T1WBA    LINK, metallic belt, cal. .30, M2.
339   T1WXA    LINK  metallic belt, cal. .30, M1, cadmium plated.
340   T1EGF    CARTRIDGE, B&T, cal. .30 (4-1) (in met. belt).
341   T1EDF    CARTRIDGE, AP & T, cal. .30 (4-1) (in met. belt).
342   T1EDM    CARTRIDGE, AP & T, cal. .30 (9-1) (in met. belt).
343   T1EDI    CARTRIDGE, AP I & T, cal. .30 (5-3-2) (in Met. belt).
344   T1EEF    CARTRIDGE, AP I & T, cal. .30 (2-2-1) (in met. belt).
345   T1EZX    CARTRIDGE, AP I & T, cal. .30 (1-1-1).
346   T1EGW    CARTRIDGE, B&T, cal. .30 (one 250-rd web belt per box).
347   T1UAB    CARTRIDGE, bland, cal. .30 (for use in rifles and auto-
                matic wpna).
348   T1WGX    BANDOLEER, f/5rd clips, (empty).
349   T1WHX    BANDOLEER, f/8rd clips, (empty).
350   T1WFA    CLIP, cartridge, 5rd (empty).
351   T1WEA    CLIP, cartridge, 8rd (empty).
352   T1EYX    CARTRIDGE, ball, cal. .303 (AUST).
353   T1EXX    CARTRIDGE, tracer, cal. .303 (AUST).
360   T1IGB    CARTRIDGE, ball, cal. .50 (in ctns).
361   T1IBX    CARTRIDGE, AP, cal. .to (in ctns).
362   T1IKA    CARTRIDGE, incend., cal. .50 (in ctns).
363   T1IPB    CARTRIDGE,, tracer, cal. .50 (in ctns).
365   T1WCA    LINK, metallic belt, cal. .50, M1.
366   T1EDA    LINK, metallic belt, cal. .50, M2.
367   T1WYA    LINK, metallic belt, cal. .50, M1, cadmium plated.
368   T1IED    CARTRIDGE, B&T, cal. .50 (4-1) (in met. belt).
```

AMMUNITION IDENTIFICATION CODE

369	T1IFF	CARTRIDGE, B, AP & T, cal..50 (5-3-2).
370	T1IFE	CARTRIDGE, B, AP & T, cal..50 (2-2-1).
371	T1IGE	CARTRIDGE, AP & T, cal..50 (4-1).
372	T1IGI	CARTRIDGE, AP & T, cal..50 (9-1).
373	T1IGH	CARTRIDGE, AP & T, cal..50 (2-1).
374	T1IOG	CARTRIDGE, AP I & T, cal..50 (2-2-1
375	T1IGF	CARTRIDGE, AP I & T, cal..50 (2-2-1
376	T1IXX	CARTRIDGE, AP I & T, cal..50 (1-1-1).

380	T2AAA	CARTRIDGE, ball cal..45 (2,000rds. met. liner).
381	T2APA	CARTRIDGE, tracer, cal..45.
382	T2UAA	CARTRIDGE, blank, cal..45.
383	T2AAD	CARTRIDGE, ball, cal..45 (1,800 rds. wax liner).
384	T2AAX	CARTRIDGE, ball, cal..45 (1,800 rds. met. liner).
385	T2DAX	CARTRIDGE, ball, cal..38.
386	T2CAX	CARTRIDGE, ball, cal..38 (jacketed)(AUST).
387	T2BAA	CARTRIDGE, ball, cal..38, special (plated).
388	T2YXX	CARTRIDGE, ball, cal..32 (7.65-mm)(jacketed).
389	T2YWX	CARTRIDGE, ball, 9-mm (AUST).

SHOTGUN AMMUNITION.

390	T3AAA	SHELL, shotgun, 12 gauge, brass, loaded w/smokeless powder, and No. 00 buckshot.
391	T3ADA	SHELL, shotgun 12 gauge, paper, loaded w/smokeless powder and No. 00 buckshot.
392	T3AEA	SHELL, shotgun, 12 gauge, paper, loaded w/smokeless powder and No. 7½ c.s.
393	T3AYX	SHELL, shotgun,12 gauge, No. 4 shot (AUST).
394	T3AWX	SHELL, shotgun, 12 gauge, No. 6 shot (AUST).

400	T5CAA	CLIP, cartridge, cal..45, for revolver.
401	T5EAX	BELT, ammunition, cal..30, M1917 (250-rd.).

ANTIPERSONNEL DEVICES.

411	R7AWX	DEVICE, firing, M1, release type.
412	R7AVX	DEVICE, firing, M1, delay type.
413	R7AUX	DEVICE, firing, M1, pressure type.
414	R7ATX	DEVICE, firing, M1, pull type.
415	R7AEA	MINE, antipersonnel, M3 w/accessories.
416	R7AKA	MINE, antipersonnel, M2A1, w/accessories.

PYROTECHNIC CARTRIDGES.

921	S5BCA	FLARE, AC., parachute, M9.
922	S5BYA	SIGNAL, AC, white star, parachute, M10.
923	S5LAA	SIGNAL, AC, red star, parachute, M11.
924	S5LBA	SIGNAL, AC, red star, cluster, M14.
925	S5LCA	SIGNAL, AC, white star, blinker, parachute, M15

```
926  85LDA    SIGNAL, AC, green star, blinker, parachute, M16.

928  85NDA    SIGNAL, AC, double star, red-red, AN-M28.
929  85NFA    SIGNAL, AC, double star, yellow-yellow, AN-M29.
930  85NAA    SIGNAL, AC, double star, green-green, AN-M30.
931  85NEA    SIGNAL, AC, double star, red-yellow, AN-M31.
932  85NCA    SIGNAL, AC, double star, red-green, AN-M32.
933  85NBA    SIGNAL, AC, double star, green-yellow, AN-M33.
934  85NHA    SIGNAL, AC, single star, red. AN-M34.
935  85NLA    SIGNAL, AC, single star, yellow, AN-M35.
936  85NGA    SIGNAL, AC, single star, green AN-M36.
937  85PDA    SIGNAL, AC, double star, red-red, AN-M37.
938  85PFA    SIGNAL, AC, double star, yellow-yellow, AN-M38.
939  85PAA    SIGNAL, AC, double star, green-green, AN-M39.
940  85PEA    SIGNAL, AC, double star, red-yellow, AN-M40.
941  85PCA    SIGNAL, AC, double star, red-green, AN-M41.
942  85PBA    SIGNAL, AC, double star, green-yellow, AN-M42.
943  85PHA    SIGNAL, AC, single star, red, AN-M43.
944  85PIA    SIGNAL, AC, single star, yellow, AN-M44.
945  85PGA    SIGNAL, AC, single star, green, AN-M45.
```

Annex E to Administrative Order No. 2-43, Backhander Force.

CHEMICAL PLAN

00591
1990-25
144/246

Headquarters Backhander Force,
APO 320,
14 November 1943.   1000.

UNCLASSIFIED

1. GENERAL.

    a. There are no indications of immediate probability of enemy initiation of chemical warfare, though enemy gas discipline appears to have improved.

    b. The Cml O, ESCALATOR, will supervise and insure the delivery of CWS supplies from USASOS Bases to the BACK-HANDER TF.

    c. All correspondence, requisitions and reports pertaining to Cml Warfare, forwarded to ALAMO will be marked "ATTN: Chemical Officer".

2. ATCHD CWS UNITS.

    a. One O and 20 EM are atchd to BACKHANDER for supply and maintenance.

    b. The echelon of Cml Warfare Service next in rear of the BACKHANDER TF is under the control of USASOS. All correspondence with USASOS regarding CWS will be routed through Hqts, ESCALATOR.

3. SUPPLY.

    a. Class II and IV.

        (1) The CWS detachments atchd to the TF will receive all CWS supplies and establish supply points as directed by the BACKHANDER Cml O.

        (2) The training gas mask (waterproofed) and one tube of ointment will be carried by each individual. Ten D/S (4%) of gas masks and 3 D/S (10%) of protective ointment will be carried in unit supply by each unit on movement to BACKHANDER. All other protective equipment and supplies (individual, organizational and maintenance) will be turned in to depots at staging areas to be replaced in stock. In case of emergency, or as soon as suitable storage facilities have been provided, such supplies will be forwarded to BACKHANDER on call of this Hqts.

UNCLASSIFIED

-1-

374

(3) After the prescribed levels of supply have been reached, requisitions to maintain that level will be submitted in quadruplicate by TF Cml O, direct to Depot A or B in accordance with instructions to be issued by CG, ESCALATOR.

b. Class V.

(1) Supply of flame thrower fillings and chemical munitions to units of the TF will be through the CWS detachment under direction of the TF Cml O. Prescribed levels of flame thrower fillings for the BACKHANDER Area are as follows:

Nitrogen and hydrogen - 6 U/F.
Liquid fuel (gasoline and oil mixture) - 3 U/F.
Thickened fuel (gasoline and NaPalm) - 3 U/F.

(2) Resupply will be based on reports required by par(3)(b) below, and upon emergency requisitions.

(3) Reports.

(a) Initial.

The TF Cml O will submit to Hqts, ESCALATOR, immediately after establishment of Cml Am dumps, a report of initial stockage of flame thrower fillings and chemical munitions.

(b) Weekly.

A weekly status report of Cml munitions and flame thrower fillings will be submitted by BACKHANDER TF Cml O, as of 1200 each Saturday, so as to reach Hqts, ESCALATOR by next available transportation. This report will show:

Amount on hand last report.
Amount received since last report.
Amount expended since last report.
Balance on hand.

(4) MAINTENANCE.

a. Repair will be by the attached CWS detachment. Unserviceable equipment will be replaced.

b. Unserviceable equipment which cannot be repaired promt-

UNCLASSIFIED   -2-

S-E-C-R-E-T

ly by the CWS detachment will be evacuated to USASOS Bases by returning supply ships.

BY COMMAND OF MAJOR GENERAL RUPERTUS:

AMOR LeR. SIMS,
Colonel, U. S. Marine Corps,
Chief of Staff.

DISTRIBUTION: Same as for Adm O 2-43.

O-F-F-I-C-I-A-L:

W. S. FELLERS,
Colonel, USMC,
   D-4.

UNCLASSIFIED

-3-

Annex F to Administrative Order No. 2-43, Backhander Task Force;

ENGINEER SUPPLY

00591
1990-25
144/246

 UNCLASSIFIED

Headquarters, Backhander Force,
APO 320
14 November, 1943.   1000L.

1. **ENGINEER EQUIPMENT AND SUPPLIES.**

   a. All units will be fully equipped as authorized by applicable TBAs or T/Es while in staging areas.

   b. Equipment authorized in excess of TBA or T/E and certain Class IV supplies will be shipped to each CT in staging areas.

   c. Initially there will be no automatic issue of items of Engr supply to ESOs of the BACKHANDER TF.

   d. Class IV supplies for construction by BACKHANDER TF will be issued on call after D plus 5, and will be used exclusively for construction authorized by the TF Engr O.

   e. All construction authority will be in accordance with construction policy issued by ALAMO Force, dated 10 November, 1943, previously furnished.

   f. Requirements for Engr supplies of all classes will be anticipated by the BACKHANDER Supply O to minimize the use of emergency requisitions and to assure the maintenance of proper stocks. For items within TBA, requisitions will be submitted to Engr O, ALAMO Liaison Grp, APO 928.

   g. Spare parts for Engr construction equipment will be stocked at USASOS intermediate base, PEMMICAN.

   h. Shortage of spare parts and tires for Engr Construction equipment precludes units acquiring large stock of parts. TF Engr O will closely supervise requisitioning of spare parts and tires.

-1-

UNCLASSIFIED

i. All requisitions for items over and above authorized allowances will be submitted to, ALAMO Engr O.

BY COMMAND OF MAJOR GENERAL RUPERTUS:

AMOR LeR. SIMS,
Colonel, U. S. Marine Corps,
Chief of Staff.

DISTRIBUTION: Same as for Adm O 2-43.

O-F-F-I-C-I-A-L:

W. S. FELLERS,
Colonel, USMC,
    D-4.

UNCLASSIFIED   -2-

ANNEX H

First Marine Division Station List.
1 January, 1944.

Headquarters, First Marine Division,
Fleet Marine Force,
C/o Fleet Post Office, San Francisco, Calif.

1 January, 1944.

NAME	RANK	DUTIES	Left US

COMMANDING GENERAL

NAME	RANK	DUTY	Left US
RUPERTUS, William Henry	MajGen	DivComdr	22Jun42
SIMS, Amor LeRoy	Col.	Chief of Staff	7Apr42
MC LEOD, William Joseph	Capt.	Aide to CG	20Jun42
PETRAS, Theodore Argyres	Capt.	Aide & Pilot for CG	18May42

EXECUTIVE STAFF.
D-1 Section

MYERS, Elmer Walter	Maj	Asst CofS, D-1.	7Jun42
SPURLOCK, Woodson	Capt(VS-FCA)	Civil Affairs O.	8Jul43

D-2 Section

BUCKLEY, Edmond John	LtCol.	Asst CofS, D-2	22Jun42
EVANS, Richard Allen	Maj.	Asst D-2	22Jun42
MORAN, Sherwood Ford	Maj.	Asst D-2, JapIntp.	16May42
BURCHAM, Levi Turner	Capt.	Asst D-2, AerPhotoIntp	19Oct42
FOLEY, Jerome John	Capt.	Asst D-2, AerPhotoIntp	19Oct42
GREGG, Gene Edwin	Capt(VS-L)	Asst D-2, JapIntp.	18Apr43
BRADEEER, John David	1stLt.	Asst D-2, IntO	16May42
PEACHY, Frederic	1stLt.	Asst D-2, IntO.	*22Jun42
PRADO, Miguel Angelo	1stLt.	Asst D-2, IntO.	8Jan43
SCHILLER, John Charles, Jr.	1stLt.	Asst D-2, IntO.	*22Jun42
COE, Murray B.	2dLt(VS-L)	Asst D-2, JapIntp.	
FOOTE, Harry T.	2dLt(VS-L)	Asst D-2, JapIntp.	
GREENWOOD, Richard T.	2dLt(VS-L)	Asst D-2, JapIntp.	
HACKETT, Roger F.	2dLt(VS-L)	Asst D-2, JapIntp.	
HASBROUCK, John DeP	2dLt(VS-L)	Asst D-2, JapIntp.	
KAASA, Thomas H., Jr.	2dLt(VS-L)	Asst D-2, JapIntp.	
CARPENTER, Arthus E., Jr.	Lt(jg)A-V(S)	Asst D-2, temp att.	
SPRAGUE, John S.	Lt(jg)A-S(S)	Asst D-2, temp att.	
MATHER, John V.	Maj(A.I.F.)	Asst D-2, temp att.	
PITT, Mark J.F.A.	Lt(ANGAU)	Asst D-2, temp att.	
WIEDEMANN, William G.C.	Sub-Lt(RANVR)	Asst D-2, temp att.	

D-3 Section

POLLOCK, Edwin Allen	Col.	Asst CofS, D-3.	22Jun42
BUSE, Henry William, Jr.	LtCol.	Asst D-3	22Jun42
KOLP, Hal Richard	Maj.	DivAirLiaisonO.	30Sep43
WILT, Robert Dudley	Capt.	Asst D-3	22Jun42
BUELL, Charles Melvin	1stLt(EDO)	Asst D-3	22Jun42

- 1 -

D-4 Section

FELLERS, William Stanley	Col.	Asst CofS, D-4		30 Jun42
CLARK, James Matthew	LtCol.	Asst D-4		22 Jun42
GOBER, George Freeman	Maj.	Asst D-4		22 Jun42
HUFF, John Vardis	1stLt.	Asst D-4		*22 Jun42

ASSISTANT DIVISION COMMANDER SECTION

SHEPHERD, Lemuel Cornick, Jr.	BrigGen	ADC		Jan43
HANNEKEN, Herman Henry	Col.	CofS to ADC		8 Apr42
DAY, John Sidney	Maj.	ADC-3		8 Apr42
CRAWFORD, Robert Thompson	Capt.	ADC-4		20 May42
BENDA, Michael Daniel	1stLt.	Aide to ADC		9 Jan43
FISHEL, Sydney Joseph	WO	ADC-2		*22 Jun42
WEED, Alton Carswell	WO	Adj. to ADC.		*22 Jun42
WILLIAMS, Joseph Arthur	WO.	Asst ADC-4		*10 May42

Liaison At GHQ

BOWEN, Robert Oliver	LtCol.	Temp d fr D-2 Sect.		20 May42
FULLER, Donald Walker	LtCol.	Temp d fr D-3 Sect.		20 May42

SPECIAL STAFF
Adjutant Section

LINCH, John Edinger	LtCol.	DivAdj.		19 Jun42
CHRISTIE, James Julies	Maj.	OIC DicRecordSect		22 Jun42
EVANS, William Deveomon	Capt.	Asst to OIC RecordSec		10 Jun42
CLINGAN, Charles Edward, Jr.	Capt(VS-PC)	DivMailO.		28 Aug43
COX, Lester Dilwyn	1stLt.	AsstDivAdj.		18 May42

Legal Section

STICKNEY, William Wallace	LtCol.	DivLawO		14 Jun42
HARTNETT, Andrew Curtin John	Capt.	AsstDivLawO		22 Jun42

Medical Section

LOGUE, Joseph Bruce	Capt(MC)	DivSurg		8 Jul43
FARWELL, Howard Marsden	LtComdr(DC)	DivDent.		18 Apr43
STOVALL, Ernest Ray	Lt(jg)(HC)	AdmAsst To DivSurg		22 Feb43
BROWN, Leonard	Lt (jg)(MC)	AdmAsst, DivSurgOff.		22 Feb43

Malaria Control Section

BOZARTH, Clyde Lesile	Comdr(MC)	DivMalariaControlO		23 Jun43
O'CONNELL, Hugh Vincent	LtComdr(MC)	AsstMaraliaControlO		5 Jun43
CARLEO, Louis James	Ens(HC)	AsstMalariaControlO		5 Jun43
KRAUSE, James Barber	Ens(HC)	AsstMarlaiaControlO		5 Jun43

Chaplain Section

MANSFIELD, Colonel Henry	Comdr(ChC)	DivChaplain		19 Apr43

- 2 -

Paymaster Section

SHAW, Alexander Duncan	LtCol.	DivPM	10Apr42
GREENING, Eugene Edward	1stLt.	DivPayOffice.	10Apr42
GADDIS, Earl Ivan	CWO	DivPayOffice.	10Apr42
SHAMBAUGH, Levi "J"	WO	DivPayOffice.	*22Jun42

Quartermaster Section

COFFMAN, Raymond Paul	Col.	DivQM.	22Jun42
MATHENY, Gallais "E"	LtCol.	QM SplTrs(REch)	22Jun42
MC DOWELL, Robert Haden	LtCol.	AsstDivQM.	22Jun42

Communication Section

HALL, Robert	Maj.	DivSigO.	19May42

Public Relations Section

HOUGH, Francis Olney	Capt.	DivPubReIO	8Sep43
BRUSILOFF, Leon	Maj.	DivBandO.	22Jun42
NICHOLAS, Henry Thompson	Maj.	DivRecreationO.	20May42
GREEAR, William Brown, Jr.	WO	AsstDivBandO.	*22Jun42
WALKER, Howard Irwin	WO	AsstDivRecreationO.	*22Jun42

Photo-litho, Mapping & Reproduction Section

JONES, Edmund Leroy	Comdr.	OIC	11Mar43
KAPIN, Herbert Russell	Capt.	Asst to OIC	5Jun43
KELSEY, Richmond Irwin	Capt.	OIC Mapping unit.	20Jan43
GIBBON, Theodore Edward	WO.	ReproductionO.	*15Oct42

Photographic Section

CARTER, Arthus Stanley	1stLt.	OIC.	5Mar43

Transport Quartermaster Section

HOLMES, Earl Edward	LtCol.	DivTQM.	9Jun42
MUNSON, Malcolm Arthur	1stLt.	Asst to DivTQM.	8Jan43
GOODSELL, Gordon Hoopes	2dLt.	Asst to DivTQM.	5Jun43

Audit Section

MC PHERSON, Fred Garland	Capt(VS-AAU)	DivAuditor)	6Mar43
CARTWRIGHT, Myron Roser	1stLt.	AsstDivAuditor.	5Jun43

DIVISION HEADQUARTERS BATTALION

WORTHINGTON, Frank Russell	LtCol.	BnComdr;DivProvo Marshal;HqComdt.	23Jun43
SMITH, Asa Jessup	LtCol.	Bn-X;CO HqCo.	20May42
ROBB, Preston Herbert	1stLt.	BnQM;BnSalvageO.	22Jun42
ROZYZKI, Jerome Joseph	1stLt.	Bn-2;BnPslO.	22Jun42
NEWELL, Thomas Edmund	LtComdr(MC)	BnSurg.	6Aug42
NEMECEK, Edward Joseph	Lt(DC)	BnDenO.	23Aug42

Headquarters Company

MATTHEWS, George Bernard	Capt.	CoO	22Jun42
SCHAILL, William Emmet	Capt.	CoO.	15Apr42
PORTER, Carlton Harvey	1stLt.	ChemO.	9Jan43
MURPHY, Robert Francis	2dLt	Co-Pilot for CG.	*18May42

First Signal Company

WISMER, Ralph Merrill	Maj.	CO.	5Apr42
GRIFFITH, Joseph Hoyt	Capt.	Co-X.	5Apr42
FINLEY, Edward Davis, Jr.	Capt.	CoO.	19May42
STEIN, John Beecher	Capt.	CoO.	22Jun42
BAKER, Frank Sloan, Jr.	1stLt.	CoO.	8Jan43
COYLE, Dennis Peter	1stLt.	CoO.	22Jun43
NEWMAN, Charles Sanford	1stLt.	CoO.	22Jun42
SEARTH, Tony Joseph	1stLt.	CoO.	*22Jun42
HATCH, Frederick Francis, Jr.	2dLt(CP)	CoO.	
HAYS, Johnson Carlisle, Jr.	2dLt.	CoO.	22Jun42
TURNER, George Harrell	2dLt.	CoO.	22Jun42
WALKINGTON, Floyd Wassan	2dLt.	CoO.	*15Oct42
BRUNER, William	CWO.	CoO.	22Jun42
STEWART, Westley Hiram	WO.	CoO.	22Jun42
ISAACSEN, Elmer Emil, Sr.	CWO.	DivSigQM.	22Jun42
MC ADAMS, John	WO.(CP)	OIC SigRepairSection.	*20May42

First Military Police Company

BROOKS, Clyde Albert	Capt.	CO.	22Jun42
DOHERTY, Albert John	Capt.	CoO.	18May42
WARVEL, John Earley	1stLt.	CoO.	7Jan43
YOST, Robert Carl	2dLt.	CoO.	13Apr42
CONNER, Carl Columbus	WO	CoO.	*20May42
FAIRLEY, Willis	WO.	CoO.	*22Jun42
MC LENDON, Luther Alexander	WO.	CoO.	*22Jun42
MONTGOMERY, James Russell	WO.	CoO.	*18May42
WITTEN, Olen Dellus	WO.	CoO.	*22Jun42
DAVIS, Walter Baker	WO.	CoO.	*20May42

- 4 -

Casual Company

SHIELDS, Henry Donald	Maj.	CO.	5Jun43
GUSTAFSON, John Henry	Maj.	CO, ResCo.	23Oct43
ANDERSON, Walter Dumas	Capt.	Liaison at APO#924	19Jul42
BRACE, Burnace Frederick	Capt.	CoAdj.	22Jun42
DAVIES, John Harding	Capt.	ResCo.	20May42
GRADY, Thomas Treutler	Capt.	CoO.	18May42
MOLLOY, Robert Armstrong	Capt.	CoO.	29Jun42
MOORE, Edward Joseph, Jr.	Capt.	ResCo.	20May42
NAYLOR, James Herbert	Capt.	Liaison at APO#711.	18May42
RIDER, Charles Franklin	Capt.	Liaison at APO#711.	19May42
ROBINSON, Franklin Clement	Capt.	CoO.	5Jun43
SWINSTON, George, Jr.	Capt.	CoO.	22Jun42
LEAKE, George Murray	1stLt.	CoO.	16May42
ROHRER, Richard Eugene	1stLt.	ResCo.	23Oct43
STEWART, James Ernest, Jr.	1stLt.	ResCo.	23Oct43
BELON, Marc Gede	WO.	CoO.	*20May42
BOGA, Theodore Nick	WO.	CoO.	*20May42
METZGER, Butler, Jr.	WO.	CoO.	*20Jun42
PERROTIS, Peter Charles	WO.	PslO.	*18May42
RASNICK, Hiram	WO.	CoO.	*20May42

FIRST SPECIAL WEAPONS BATTALION
H&S Battery

DAVIS, Raymond Gilbert	Maj.	BnComdr; DivAAO.	22Jun42
LEONARD, John Paul, Jr.	Maj.	Bn-X; Div AT O.	22Jun42
BEATTY, Joe Page	Capt.	CO H&SCo; BnAdj.	22Jun42
KOLLER, Charles Hartmann	Capt.	Bn-4	22Jun42
SCANTLING, Frederick Holland	Capt.	Bn-3	22Jun42
GAHALA, Anthony Michael	1stLt.	BnLiaisonO.	* 2Dec42
KEITH, Albert Howard	1stLt.	BnMTransO.	22Jun42
WAGNER, Joseph Philip	1stLt.	Bn-2	2Dec42
WANDELE, Frank Emmett	1stLt.	BnComO.	19May42
HAVICAN, John Edward	WO.	BnChemO.	*22Jun42
SCHNEIDER, Mathias William	WO.	BnPslO; AsstBnAdj	*22Jun42
WILSON, Burl	WO.	BnOrdO.	*22Jun42
HUNLEY, Henry Cleveland, Jr.	LtComdr(MC)	BnSurg.	22Jun42
MILICI, John Joseph	Lt(MC)	AsstBnSurg.	22Jun42

"A" Battery

PARRY, Sherman William	Capt.	CO.	22Jun42
HANSON, Richard Curtis	Capt.	Btry-X	22Jun42
ALFORD, Lee Marcellus, Jr.	1stLt.	BtryO.	12Mar43
DI GIAMBATTISTA, Vincent	1stLt.	BtryO.	6Jan43
HONSBRUCH, Merlyn Henry	1stLt.	BtryO.	5Jun43
MC CAFFERY, Charles Joseph	1stLt.	BtryO.	12Jun43
PATROW, Lelon Laverne	1stLt.	BtryO.	12Jun43
VAN CAMPEN, John Gerritt	1stLt.	BtryO.	6Jan43
STEWART, Cornelius Wittington	WO.	BtryO.	*22Jun42

"B" Battery

MENTZINGER, Robert	Capt.	CO.	20Jun42
FORD, Francis Ignatius, Jr.	1stLt.	Btry-X	5Mar43
BROWN, David Tucker, Jr.	1stLt.	BtryO.	7Jan43
GROSHON, Robert Milton	1stLt.	BtryO.	7Jan43
NASSEF, Vincent Joseph	2dLt.	BtryO.	*22Jun42
GREGAN, Lawrence Joseph	WO.	BtryO.	*22Jun42

"C" Battery

UNCLASSIFIED

CUNNINGHAM, Edward Joseph	Capt.	CO.	22Jun42
BELL, Arthus William	Capt.	Btry-X	22Jun42
KINDRED, Lawrence Eugene	1stLt.	BtryO.	7Jan43
MC DONALD, John Lyon	1stLt.	BtryO.	7Jan43
MUELLER, Raymond Walter	2dLt.	BtryO.	5Jun43

"D" Battery

DICKINSON, William Julian	Capt.	CO.	22Jun42
MACLURE, David Paul, Jr.	1stLt.	BtryO.	*22Jun42
LOWE, Jack Adair	1stLt.	BtryO.	22Jun42
MAIN, Robert Gordon	1stLt.	BtryO.	7Jan43
O'DONNELL, John Joseph	1stLt.	BtryO.	7Jan43
KERR, William Stewart	WO.	BtryO.	*22Jun42

FIRST TANK BATTALION
H&S Company

MEINTS, Charles Griffith	LtCol.	BnComdr.	22Jun42
HALL, Rowland Lowe	Maj.	Bn-X; Bn-3	10Apr42
MORGAN, Thomas Gracey	Maj.	Bn-4	22Jun42
BUCK, Lyle Ellis	1stLt.	BnComO.	7Jun42
HEATH, John Edgar	1stLt.	CO H&SCo; Bn-2;BnAdj	*19May42
SWANN, Moody Blaxton	1stLt.	AsstBnComO.	10Apr43
TRIPPE, Samuel Marion	1stLt.	BnMaintO; BnMTransO.	10Apr43
WILSON, Elbert Woodrow	2dLt.	Asst Bn-4.	
SUNDHAUSEN, Theodore Herman	CWO.	Sk hosp.	*22Jun42
CROUSEN, Joe Winn	WO.	BnMunO; BnGasO.	*22Jun42
TREADWELL, Arthur Elroy	WO.	BnPslO; AsstBnAdj.	*10Apr43
SMITH, Edward Barney	LtComdr(MC)	BnMedO.	22Jun42
MC GANNON, Robert Ferdinand	Lt(jg)(DC)	BnDentO.	1Jul43

"A" Company

ROBINSON, Donald James	Maj.	CO.	22Jun42
MURPHY, John McEagan	Capt.	Co-X.	10Apr42
KELLY, Richard Baker	1stLt.	CoO.	8Jan43
MARKHAM, Charles Albert	1stLt.	CoO.	*19May42
WENZEL, Edmund Joseph	1stLt.	CoO.	22Jun42
HOGAN, John Vincent, Jr.	2dLt.	CoO.	
ROBINSON, John Talghman	2dLt.	CoO.	23Oct43

UNCLASSIFIED

"B" Company

ROFF, Edward Girard, Jr.	Capt.	CO.	22Jun42
BRANT, Robert Elgin	1stLt.	CoO.	*17May42
CAPPELETTO, Nicholas	1stLt.	CoO.	*10May42
HAYDEN, Ernest Arthur, Jr.	1stLt.	CoO.	15May42
WILBANKS, John Henry	1stLt.	CoO.	10Jun42
MILLER, Albert Arthur, Jr.	2dLt.	CoO.	5Jun43

"C" Company UNCLASSIFIED

FOWLER, Edward William	Capt.	CO.	19Jul42
CHASE, Lester Thomas	1stLt.	CoO.	5Jun43
DE SANDIS, Michael Joseph	1stLt.	CoO.	22Jun42
PIKE, Ernest Adolph	1stLt.	CoO.	22Jun42
SCARBOROUGH, John Marshall	1stLt.	CoO.	*19May42
MORGAN, Joe Pope	2dLt.	CoO.	

"D" Company (Scout)

O'MAHONEY, Thomas James	Capt.	CO.	22Jun42
DAVIS, Herbert Llewellyn	1stLt.	CoO.	*22Jun42
HENDLEY, John Meyer	1stLt.	CoO.	22Jun42
JERUE, George Edward	1stLt.	CoO.	8Jan43
TAYLOR, Howard Richard, Jr.	1stLt.	CoO.	8Jan43

FIRST SERVICE BATTALION
Hq. Company

DOYLE, Edward Frank	LtCol.	BnComdr.	22Jun42
TRIEBEL, James Glein	Capt.	Actg Bn-X; BnPolO.	12Mar43
MITCHELL, Joseph	Capt.	CO HqCo; Bn-1	16May42
BUCKLE, James Edward	1stLt.	Temp/d/w CasCo.	22Jun42
FOSTER, Joseph Robert	1stLt.	BnQM.	8Apr42
WANDT, Henry William	1stLt.	DivDO.	16May42
JONES, Thomas Henry	2dLt.	Asst to DivQM.	*22Jun42
BENZ, James Frank, Jr.	WO	BnPslO.	*22Jun42
LOHR, Phillips Eugene	Lt(MC)	BnMedO.	13Mar43

Service and Supply Company

BARNES, Robert John	Capt.	CO.	20May42
ATKINSON, Joseph Ellis	Capt.	DivChemO.	22Jun42
CAVIN, Wade Leonard	Capt.	DivExchO.	22Jun42
ALBEE, Robert Emerson	1stLt.	OIC GravesRegSect.	18Feb45
BARNES, Robert David	1stLt.	AsstExchO.	* 1Dec42
CORCORAN, George Herbert	1stLt.	DivAccountableO.	22Jun42
CORINOFF, Mark Malcolm	1stLt.	CoO.	18Feb45
GOLDBLATT, Julius Eli	1stLt.	Salvage O.	18May42
MC NEILL, Vinson Andrew	1stLt.	DivCommissaryO.	22Jun42
PETERSON, Herbert Ralph	1stLt.	CoAdj.	8Jan43
TESKO, Stanley	2dLt.	ChemO.	*22Jun42
ELSWICK, Isom Hugh	WO	AsstDivCommissaryO.	22Jun42
HANCOCK, Travis Myrtin	WO	AsstGravesRegO.	20Jun42
LENDO, Henry John	WO	AsstOICSer&SupSect.	*22Jun42
TROJAN, David Joseph	WO.	OIC Ser&SupSect.	22Jun42

- 7 -

Ordnance Company

OLSEN, Peter Irving	Capt.	CO; DivOrdO.	22Jun42
AMBROSE, Philip Spencer	Capt.	OoO.	15Oct42
CURRY, Charles Allen	1stLt.	CoO.	15Oct42
GIBSON, David Caldwell	1stLt.	CoO.	30Oct42
KNOLL, Frank Philip	1stLt.	CoO.	1Dec42
MILLER, David Robert	1stLt.	CoO.	8Jan43
POPE, Mark Arthur	CWO.		22Jun42
LUCHT, Robert William	WO.		8Apr42
MOORE, Andrew Clay	WO.	CoO.	
ROSSMAN, Harry	WO.	CoO.	22Jun42

FIRST MOTOR TRANSPORT BATTALION
H&S Company

BOYER, Kimber Hicks	Maj.	BnComdr.	14Jun42
DELANEY, James Armstrong, Jr.	Capt.	Bn-X.	9Apr42
BYRD, William Hayden	Capt.	BnQM.	8Jun42
HARRINGTON, Joseph Leonard	Capt.	Bn-3; BnAdj.	10May42
NICOLAS, Alfred Martin	Capt.	CoO.	19Jul42
WERTMAN, Howard Everett	Capt.	CO H&SCo.	14May42
CALHOON, Harold Marquis	1stLt.	CoO.	*20May42
DEBISKI, Mike	1stLt.	RepairO.	14Jun42
EDWARDS, Grammer Grant	1stLt.	BnMaintO.	20May42
SEHL, Edwin Jacob	1stLt.	BnPslO.	7Jan43
MILLER, Wayne "W"	2dLt.	CoO.	5Jun43
ROBERTSON, Eugene Clyde	2dLt.	CoO.	23Oct43
GOTTSCHALK, George John	WO.	Salvage O.	* 9Apr42
PURCELL, William Francis	WO.	Asst to BnQM.	*20May42
BOLAND, John Dempsie	Lt(MC)	BnMedO.	21Jun42

"A" Company

BACHHUBER, Robert Richard	Capt.	CO.	19Jul42
CRUTCHFIELD, James Henry	Capt.	CoO.	20Jun42
BROWNE, Frank Walworth	1stLt.	CoO.	7Jan43
GRYBOSH, Enoch Joseph	1stLt.	CoO.	*20May42
BRUNDAGE, Zebulon Pendleon	CWO.	CoO.	*20May42

"B" Company

MC BROON, Robert Bogardus	Capt.	CO.	20Jun42
JORDAN, Foy Ellis	1stLt.	CoO.	15May42
CUSHING, Joseph Paul	2dLt.	CoO.	*15May42
OVERTON, Robert Wagster	2dLt.	CoO.	*20May42
CRAFT, Henry Erastus	WO.	CoO.	"10Apr42
SMITH, Marion Edward	WO.	CoO.	*10Apr42

"C" Company

DE BELL, George John	Capt.	CO.	15May42
DOGGETT, Loy Lee	1stLt.	CoO.	6Apr42
GAUSE, Lowell Leland	1stLt.	CoO.	3Dec42
GREENSPAN, Walter Mortimer	1stLt.	CoO.	7Jan43
MC COOL, Thed Dell	WO.	CoO.	*10May42

- 8 -

FIRST AMPHIBIAN TRACTOR BA. ALION
H&S Company

```
COOPER, Francis Howland          Maj.        BnComdr.                        10Jun42
REUTLINGER, Albert Fontaine      Capt.       Bn-X; Bn-3.                     10Jun42
MAXON, Glenn DeVere              Capt.       Bn-4.                           10Jun42
PETERSON, John Monroe            1stLt.      BnMaint&TransO.                 10Jun42
BRYAN, William Elbert, Jr.       2dLt.       BnMessO, BnPolO.               *18May42
CLOSSON, Robert Edward Lee       WO.         BnAdj.                         *10Jun42
GALLOWAY, James Barrentine       WO.         BnPslO.                        *10Jun42
PURVIS, Thomas Waldon            WO.         BnComO.                        * 8Apr42
SAWYER, George Portwood, Jr.     WO.         Asst Bn-4; Salvage O.*10Jun42
NAY, Newell                      Lt(MC)      BnSurg.                         1Sep42
```

"A" Company

```
BOLER, Thomas Huston             Capt.       CO.                             10Jun42
HARMAN, Harold Franklin          1stLt.      CoO.                            23Oct43
KITCHIN, Robert Neal             1stLt.      CoO.                            10May42
LEE, Harry Owen                  1stLt.      CoO.                             7Jan43
PHILLIPS, Paul                   1stLt.      CoO.                             7Jan43
```

"B" Company

```
FITZGERALD, John Ignatius, Jr.Capt.          CO.                             10Jun42
BAILIE, James Glover             1stLt.      Co-X.                          *10Jun42
RLATTI, William Harold           1stLt.      CoO.                             7Jan43
JOHNSON, Woodrow Wilson          2dLt.       CoO.                            10Jun42
STROHKIRCH, Paul Douglas         2dLt.(MT)   CoO.                           *10Jun42
```

"C" Company

```
NOONAN, Arthur James             Capt.       CC.                             10Jun42
BRYANT, Norman Holmes            1stLt.      Actg Co-X.                     *10Jun42
PARKER, Tom Solomon              1stLt.      CoO.                             7Jan43
RICE, Keith Michael              1stLt.      CoO.                            10May42
BANKS, John Stoute, Jr.          2dLt.       CoO.                            10Jun42
EMMONS, Ned Mohollen             2dLt.(MT)   CoO.                           *16Jun42
```

FIRST MEDICAL BATTALION
H&S Company

```
KECK, Everett Blaine             Comdr(MC)   BnComdr; AsstDivSurg.22Jun42
WALLIN, Stanley Paul             Comdr(MC)   Bn-X;CO H&SCo.                  15Jul42
BOSSE, Frank                     ChPharm.    AdmAsst.                        25Jan43
MC BEE, Lance Thomas             2dLt.       BnQM.                           22Jun42
```

"A" Company

```
LYNCH, George William            LtComdr(MC) CO.                             20May42
GOLDSMITH, Alfred Sloane         LtComdr(MC) Co-X.                           20May42
AGREST, Francis Amerigo          LtComdr(MC) CoO.                            14May42
GROHOWSKI, Alphonsus             LtComdr(MC) CoO.                            20May42
BURNS, Robert Peirce             Lt(DC)      CoO.                            18Apr43
DEUELL, William Dillard          Lt(DC)      CoO.                            20May42
ROBERTS, Charles Thomas          Lt(DC)      CoO.                             1Aug43
EHEMANN, Nicholas, Jr.           Pharm.      AdmAsst.
```

- 9 -

"B" Company

HOOGERHYDE, Jack	LtComdr(MC)	CO.	1Sep42
BOWEN, Frederick Hardy	Lt)MC)	Co-X.	21Jun42
BUDGE, Edwin Stratford, Jr.	Lt(MC)	CoO.	18Apr43
HARTGE, Frank Joseph	Lt(DC)	CoO.	18Apr43
WOZNIAK, Frank Siegfried	Lt(DC)	CoO.	18Apr43
BURKETT, Vernon Warren	Pharm.	AdmAsst.	17Feb43

"C" Company

HUNTER, James Theron	LtComrd(MC)	CO.	20Oct42
STEIN, Ephraim	LtComdr(MC)	Co-X.	10Apr42
EMMERSON, James Harvey	Lt(DC)	CoO.	15Oct42
FISHBACK, Charles Franklin	Lt(MC)	CoO.	25Jun43
KIMBALL, Cyril VanWyck	Lt(MC)	CoO.	10Apr42
MAC LEAN, Grant Alexander	Lt(DC)	CoO.	18Apr43
TYROLER, Frederic Nathan	Lt(MC)	CoO.	1Sep42
BEAN, Joshua "S"	Pharm.	AdmAsst	20Feb43
GILL, George, Joseph	Pharm.	AdmAsst	

"D" Company

NEFF, William Everett, Jr.	LtComdr(MC)	CO.	10Apr42
SCHLOSBERG, Stanley Soffin	LtComdr(MC)	Co-X.	10Apr42
GOWDY, Franklin Kamm	Lt(MC)	CoO.	25Jun43
MEAD, Meredith Hunt	Lt(DC)	CoO.	18Apr43
SMITH, Seymour Purdon	Lt(MC)	CoO.	6Nov42
BLOOM, Harvey James	Lt(jg)(DC)	CoO.	25Jun43
RHOADS, Glenson	Pharm.	AdmAsst	29Jul43

"E" Company

JOHNSON, Robert Benjamin	LtComdr(MC)	CO.	15Oct42
CLAUD, Phillips Lester	LtComdr(MC)	Co-X.	16May42
FORMAN, Joseph Bernard	LtComdr(MC)	CoO.	22Jun42
FOELL, Guy Hodges	Lt(DC)	CoO.	12Mar43
LEE, Theodore Hume	Lt(MC)	CoO.	22Jun42
MOORMAN, Vixtor Reuben	Lt(MC)	CoO.	22Jun42
CARPENTER, Seth James	Pharm.	AdmAsst.	14Feb43

FIRST MARINES
H&S Company

WHALING, William John	Col.	R-Comdr.	22Jun42
HARRIS, Harold Douglas	LtCol.	R-X.	4Jul42
EAGAN, Francis Thomas	Maj.	R-4.	22Jun42
HEMING, Henry Liebmann	Maj.	RPM.	22Jun42
ROCKMORE, Martin Frank	Maj.	R-3.	22Jun42
WARD, William Cleveland, Jr.	Maj.	R-ComO.	22Jun42
CODREA, George	Capt.	CO H&SCo.	22Jun42
HOLT, Martin Ellsworth	Capt.	RecreationO.	22Jun42
HUNT, George Pinney	Capt.	R-2.	22Jun42
SCHANZLE, Richard Francis	Capt.	Asst R-2.	22Jun42
STRATTON, George Marshall	Capt.	LiaisonO.	22Jun42

- 10 -

H&S Company (Cont'd)

TODD, John Sprague	Capt.	Mun&OrdO.	22Jun42
WAGNER, James Arthur	Capt.	BnPslO.	22Jun42
WILLIAMS, John Lee	Capt.	CoO.	22Jun42
WILLIAMSON, James Nummally	Capt.	Asst R-4.	22Jun42
HULL, Robert Harold, Jr.	1stLt.	Asst R-1.	22Jun42
BURKE, Paul Everett	1stLt.	AsstComO.	8Jan43
YOUNG, James Kenneth	1stLt.	R-1	*22Jun42
BAILEY, Jerman Lewis	1stLt.	Asst R-4.	22Jun42
MADEY, Joseph Henry	1stLt.	R-PayOffice.	22Jun42
CARR, Daniel Thomas, Jr.	2dLt.	Asst R-2.	25Jun43
WATTS, William Bryant, Jr.	2dLt.	Asst R-2.	*20Jun42
LOWRANCE, Floyd William	WO.	R-PolO.	*22Jun42
ORR, Emmett Walter	WO.	OrdO.	*22Jun42
MALONE, Titus	WO.	Asst R-4.	*22Jun42
DUPLAIN, Raymond Joseph	WO.	R-PayOffice.	*22Jun42
NASIN, Edward Rudolph	WO.	R-PayOffice.	*22Jun42
NAPP, Emil Edward	LtComdr(MC)	R-Surg.	22Jun42
HANSON, Harry Albert	LtComdr(MC)	Asst R-Surg.	22Jun42
OLTON, Robert Matthew	LtComdr(ChC)	R-Chap.	22Jun42
MORGAN, Kenneth LeRoy	Lt(DC)	R-Dent.	23Aug42
FLAHERTY, John Edward	Capt.	Awtg assignment	20May42
GUION, Charles Frederick	2dLt.	Awtg assignment	
HEBARD, George Richardson, Jr.	2dLt.	Awtg assignment	23Oct43
STRINGFIELD, Thomas	Lt(MC)	Awtg assignment	

Weapons Company

THOMASES, Robert	Capt.	CO.	22Jun42
HORTON, James Wright	Capt.	Co-X.	22Jun42
KARTEN, Milton Wilson	Capt.	CoO.	22Jun42
MC CAUL, Thomas Marion Jr.	1stLt.	CoO.	12Mar43
MC PARTLIN, Charles Edward,Jr.	1stLt.	CoO.	22Jun42
MEREDITH, Raymond	1stLt.	CoO.	15Mar43
MINER, John Robert	1stLt.	CoO.	8Jan43
MITCHELL, James Farrell, Jr.	1stLt.	CoO.	*22Jun42
MAZUREK, Norman	WO.	CoO.	*22Jun42

First Battalion
Hq. Company

REAVES, Robert	LtCol.	BnComdr.	22Jun42
HUDGINS, Louis Eugene, Jr.	Maj.	Bn-X.	22Jun42
BROOKS, Joseph Howard, Jr.	Capt.	Bn-4.	11May43
DAWES, George Moncrief	Capt.	CO HqCo.	22Jun42
MACKIN, Charles Philip	Capt.	BnMassO.	22Jun42
MC CLELLAND, Robert Kinter	Capt.	Bn-3.	13Apr42
RENTZ, John Nevin	Capt.	LiaisonO.	22Jun42
EDWARDS, Fred Thomas	1stLt.	ComO.	*22Jun42
FLYNN, Raymond Charles	1stLt.	BnPslO.	22Jun42
NEGUS, Raymond Anthony	1stLt.	Bn-2.	*22Jun42
THOMPSON, Herbert William, Jr.	1stLt.	BnGasO.	7Jan43
FRISBIE, Robert Lowell	WO.	AsstBn-4; MT&MunO.	22Jun42
HILLMAN, Robert Wright	Lt(MC)	BnSurg.	22Jun42
BUDENZ, Charles George	Lt(MC)	AsstBnSurg.	21Nov43

- 11 -

"A" Company

JENNINGS, Harold Fred	Capt.	CO.	22Jun42
ROGERS, James Michael	Capt.	Co-X.	22Jun42
HANSEN, Neil Martin	1stLt.	CoO.	13Mar43
PERKINSON, Tom Gramling	1stLt.	CoO.	5Mar43
POE, Richard Aulta	1stLt.	CoO.	7Jan43
RILEY, Charles Joseph	2dLt.	CoO.	*22Jun42
STANFIELD, James Clay	2dLt.	CoO.	*22Jun42

"B" Company

LESICK, John Richard	Capt.	CO.	22Jun42
BUSHELL, Joseph Francis	Capt.	Co-X.	22Jun42
BOLLACK, Theodore Shafer	1stLt.	CoO.	22Jun42
CURRIER, James Richard	1stLt.	CoO.	23Jun43
PETRUZZELLI, Victor Francis	1stLt.	CoO.	7Jan43
SIMMONS, Edward Lincoln	2dLt.	CoO.	4Jun43

"C" Company

STEVENSON, Nikolai Stanoyevich	Capt.	CO.	22Jun42
FOWLER, Robert Beals	Capt.	Co-X.	22Jun42
AHEARN, Maurice Francis, Jr.	1stLt.	CoO.	22Jun42
LONGBOTHAM, Weldon Monroe	1stLt.	CoO.	5Jun43
RACH, Albert Jacob	1stLt.	CoO.	20Oct43
SHAFFNER, Walter "F"	1stLt.	CoO.	12Mar43

"D" Company

GREGORY, Noel Clinton	Capt.	CO.	13Apr42
POPE, Everett Parker	Capt.	Co-X.	22Jun42
HILLARD, Henry Thurston	Capt.	CoO.	22Jun42
LAWRENCE, James Fugate, Jr.	Capt.	CoO.	22Jun42
SPEAKS, John Thomas	Capt.	CoO.	22Jun42
RINEER, Francis David	1stLt.	CoO.	23Oct43
HUTCHINS, Bernard Henry	2dLt.	CoO.	*22Jun42
YERXA, Fendall Winston	2dLt.	CoO.	25Jun43
ORLOWSKI, Joseph James	WO.	CoO.	*22Jun42

Second Battalion
Hq. Company

MASTERS, James Marvin, Sr.	LtCol.	BnComdr.	31Jan41
BRUSH, Charles Harris, Jr.	Maj.	Bn-X.	22Jun42
JACHYM, John James	Capt.	Asst R-3.	22Jun42
LARSON, Arthur William	Capt.	Bn-3.	22Jun42
MORIARTY, James Aloyisús, Jr.	Capt.	Bn-1; CO HqCo.	22Jun42
MURPHY, William Arthur	Capt.	BnPalO.	22Jun42
WHEATON, Don Carlenos, Jr.	Capt.	BnGasO.	22Jun42
CAPRARO, Michael Carl	1stLt.	Bn-2.	*22Jun42
CASSIDY, Joseph Raymond	1stLt.	LiaisonO.	8Jan43
ZOLLER, Roy	1stLt.	Asst Bn-4, TQM.	12Mar43
MC ILLWAIN, Noble	WO.	BnComO.	*22Jun42
GOLDSTEIN, Robert	Lt(MC)	BnMedO.	22Jun42
SEE, William Bernard	Lt(MC)	AsstBnMedO.	1Sep42
GALLAGHER, Frederick Augustine	Lt(MC)	BnChap.	21Oct42

"E" Company

STOVER, Dean Edwin	Capt.	CO.	22Jun42
KOINER, Fay Krauth, Jr.	1stLt.	CoO.	8Jan43
SCHMITT, Robert Warren	1stLt.	CoO.	8Jan43
STONER, William Lawrence	1stLt.	CoO.	5Jun43
LADWIG, Loran Robert	2dLt.	CoO.	5Jun43
RUSSO, Romolo Nicholas	2dLt.	CoO.	23Oct43

"F" Company

WALLACE, Roy William, Jr.	Capt.	CO.	22Jun42
RIAN, Stephen David, Jr.	Capt.	Co-X.	22Jun42
PAULK, Ellis Tyler, Jr.	Capt.	CoO.	22Jun42
BAKER, Bernard John	1stLt.	CoO.	*22Jun42
FOURNIER, Joseph Adelard Lionel	1stLt.	CoO.	25Jun43
MOREHEAD, Robert Andy	1stLt.	CoO.	* 9Mar42
VALA, John Bartholomew	2dLt.	CoO.	5Jun43
O'DONNELL, James Edmond	2dLt.	CoO.	23Oct43

"G" Company

JORDAN, James Luther, Jr.	Capt.	CO.	22Jun42
MAPLES, Gordon	1stLt.	Co-X.	22Jun42
POPLE, John Franklin	1stLt.	CoO.	22Jun42
DIDIER, Charles Peele	2dLt.	CoO.	23Jun43
PAULOS, Jim James	2dLt.	CoO.	5Jun43
ZUERCHER, Joseph Clement	2dLt.	CoO.	5Jun43
DECKER, John Albert	2dLt.	CoO.	23Oct43

"H" Company

FAWLEY, James Linwood	Capt.	CO.	20May42
WILSON, Robert Imlay	Capt.	Co-X.	22Jun42
ROBBINS, Val Jeane Francis	2dLt.	CoO.	23Oct43
BENNETT, Talmadge Wesley	1stLt.	CoO.	*22Jun42
BENSON, Carl Harold	1stLt.	CoO.	22Jun42
BURKE, Walter Eugene	1stLt.	CoO.	8Jan43
ROBBERSON, Ray Jack	WO.	CoO.	*22Jun42

Third Battalion
Hq. Company

HANKINS, Joseph Francis	Lt.Col.	BnComdr.	22Jan42
MC NULTY, William	Maj.	Bn-X.	22Jun42
BARRY, Thomas Hubert	Capt.	BnLiaisonO.	22Jun42
EDMONDSON, Russell Brown	Capt.	Bn-4.	22Jun42
GAGE, Gerald William	Capt.	BnPalO.	22Jun42
GIERHART, George Berry	Capt.	Bn-3.	22Jun42
HECKMAN, John Earl	1stLt.	OrdO; Asst Bn-3.	22Jun42
HILL Jake Benton	1stLt.	BnComO.	22Jun42
O'RORKE, Andrew William Jr.	1stLt.	Bn-1; CO HqCo.	22Jun42
ROEDER, George Albert, Jr.	1stLt.	Asst Bn-4.	8Jan43
ROSS, Paul Edward	1stLt.	Bn-2.	8Jan43
WELCH, James Robert	1stLt.	BnGasO.	8Jan43
KEYSERLING, Ben Herbert	Lt(MC)	BnMedO.	22Jun42
BENNETT, Lawrence Lesile	Lt(jg)(ChC)	BnChap.	7Aug42
OLSHAUSEN, Kenneth W.	Lt(jg)(MC)	AsstBnMedO.	23Oct43

- 13 -

"I" Company

CONRON, Carl Edward, Jr.	Capt.	CO.	6Jan43
WRIGHT, William Wilson	Capt.	Co-X.	22Jun42
ALESSANDRONI, Joseph, Jr.	1stLt.	CoO.	7Jan43
HORWATH, William John	1stLt.	CoO.	22Jun42
TAYLOR, Dennis Moore	1stLt.	CoO.	22Jun42
ZIEGLER, Harry Leonard, Jr.	1stLt.	CoO.	7Jan43
JUNKIN, James Ashby	2dLt.	CoO.	3Jun43

"K" Company

TERZI, Joseph Anthony	Capt.	KIA 26Dec43	22Jun42
WILHEIT, Philip Arthur	Capt.	KIA 26Dec43	22Jun42
BARRETT, Lee	1stLt.	CoO.	2Mar43
DUNCAN, Hoyt "C", Jr.	1stLt.	CoO.	22Jun42
RATTER, Scott Thomas, Jr.	1stLt.	CoO.	2Dec42
SELLERS, William Oliver	2dLt.	CoO.	5Jun43
STRAMEL, Raymond George	2dLt.	CoO.	23Oct43

"L" Company

SLAY, Ronald Joseph	Capt.	CO.	22Jun42
FITZHUGH, William DeHart III	Capt.	Co-X.	22Jun42
MINERVINI, Alfred Paul	Capt.	CoO.	22Jun42
CLAFFEY, Edward Francis	1stLt.	CoO.	*22Jun42
GROSS, Seymour Arnold	1stLt.	CoO.	19Feb43
UTTER, Richard Joseph	1stLt.	CoO.	*22Jun42

"M" Company

SIMPSON, Frank Hartwell	Capt.	CO.	22Jun42
QUINN, Edmond John	Capt.	Co-X.	22Jun42
CURRIE, James Daniel	1stLt.	CoO.	23Oct43
HAGGERTY, James Jerome	1stLt.	CoO.	7Jan43
HOPKINS, Carl Emory	1stLt.	CoO.	*22Jun42
YOUNG, William Arthur, Jr.	1stLt.	CoO.	5Mar43
CAFFERTY, Francis Joseph	2dLt.	CoO.	*22Jun42
PIERCY, Samuel Ephrim	WO.	CoO.	*22Jun42

FIFTH MARINES
H&S Company

SELDEN, John Taylor	Col.	R-Comdr.	14Oct42
ENRIGHT, William Keith	LtCol.	R-X.	22Jun42
GAYLE, Gordon Donald	Maj.	R-3.	20May42
MURRAY, Clay McNitt	Maj.	Asst R-3.	20May42
ADAMS, Henry Jackson, Jr.	Capt.	R-2.	12Apr42
COTE, Jerrold Oscar	Capt.	R-SupO.	20May42
DILL, Alan Francis	Capt.	R-1.	20May42
DONOGHUE, James Vincent	Capt.	R-LiaisonO.	20May42
NOONAN, Robert William	Capt.	R-ComO.	22Jun42
OTTERSON, Donald Brian	Capt.	Asst R-3.	20May42
PEPPARD, Donald Arthur	Capt.	CO H&SCo; R-GasO.	22Jun42
RICHARDS, Guy	Capt.	Asst R-2.	12Sep42

- 14 -

H&S Company (Cont'd)

SMITH, Thea Aubrey	Capt.	RPM.	7Jan43
WILLIAMS, William Louis	Capt.	R-4.	20May42
FIRM, Robert Bastress	1stLt.	Asst R-2.	*20May42
HEMPELMAN, Edward Charles	1stLt.	R-ExchO.	20May42
LUDVIGSON, James Darwin	1stLt.	R-MunO.	20May42
MAFFEO, Henry Anthony	1stLt.	Asst to RQM.	3Dec42
RIDGWAY, John Robert	1stLt.	Asst ComO.	22Jun42
STANKUS, John Stanley	1stLt.	Asst R-2.	*20May42
WILSON, John Hamilton	1stLt.	R-MTransO.	16May42
WOLTRING, Leo Theodore	CWO.	Asst R-1; R-PslO.	20May42
EILAND, James "C"	WO.	RCO.	*20May42
GIBBS, William Evert	WO.	R-PayOffice.	*20May42
HART, Cranford John	WO.	Asst to RQM.	*20May42
LAURACH, Richard Carlton	WO.	Asst to RQM.	*20May42
SASSER, Ruthledge Stanley	WO.	R-PayOffice.	*20May42
FORSYTHE, Richard Munroe	LtComdr(MC)	R-Surg.	20May42
GODBEY, John Randolph	Lt(MC)	Asst R-Surg.	20May42
PAGE, Joe Pacshal	Lt(DC)	R-Dent	8Jan42
BAECKER, Marvin P.	Lt(jg)(MC)	Awtg assignment.	
HIGGINS, Laurie W.	Lt(jg)(MC)	Awtg assignment.	

Weapons Company

DILLARD, Robert Hiram	Capt.	CO.	20May42
STRADLEY, Wilson	Capt.	Co-X.	20May42
NEAL, Judge Tallie, Jr.	Capt.	CoO.	20May42
AULT, Peter Nathan	1stLt.	CoO.	*20May42
HARLEY, Lloyd Drain, Jr.	1stLt.	CoO.	*20May42
PADGEN, Nicholas Charles	1stLt.	CoO.	7Jan43
THIBADEAU, Andrew Francis	1stLt.	CoO.	7Jan43
SULLIVAN, George Logan, Jr.	2dLt.	CoO.	25Jun43
BLOCK, Jacob Ingwert	WO.	CoO.	*20May42

First Battalion
Hq. Company

BARBA, William Herbert	Maj.	BnComdr.	20May42
CONNOR, Harry Sargent	Maj.	Bn-X.	20May42
BACON, Franklin Camp	Capt.	Bn-2.	20May42
GATELY, John Joseph	Capt.	Bn-4.	20May42
HANLEY, James Joseph, Jr.	Capt.	Bn-1; CO HqCo.	20May42
MC ILHENNY, Walter Stauffer	Capt.	Bn-2.	20May42
ELVINGS, Kells	1stLt.	BnGasO.	12Mar43
HAAS, Otto Frederick, Jr.	1stLt.	BnLiaisonO.	20May42
HUNSICKER, William Henry	1stLt.	Asst Bn-4.	5Jan43
IZBICKI, Anthony Francis	WO.	BnComO.	*20May42
KINTZING, William Baugher	Lt(MC)	BnMedO.	8Apr42
WADSWORTH, Elmer Eugene	Lt(MC)	AsstBnSurg.	23Aug42
EGGERT, Charles Melvin	Lt(jg)(ChC)	BnChap.	14Jul43

"A" Company

NELLSON, Richard Freeman	Capt.	CO.	20May42
MAHER, John Bernard	Capt.	Co-X.	1May42
JOHNSON, Thomas Haynes	1stLt.	CoO.	7Jan43
LARSEN, Ray Oliver	1stLt.	CoO.	25Jan43
WILLIAMS, John Edward, Jr.	1stLt.	CoO.	3Dec42
COX, David Marion	2dLt.	CoO.	25Jun43

"B" Company

HOLLAND, John Wisdom	Capt.	CO.	20May42
GUYER, George Henry, Jr.	1stLt.	Co-X.	20May42
RIVERS, William Joseph	1stLt.	CoO.	3Dec42
VAUGHT, Perle William	1stLt.	CoO.	5Jan43
NEWTON, William Burton, Jr.	1stLt.	CoO.	5Jun43
WIDSETH, Joseph Helmer	2dLt.	CoO.	25Jun43

"C" Company

MC LAUGHLIN, John Nicholas	Capt.	CO.	20Jun42
LIEBERMANN, Francis Stephen	1stLt.	Co-X.	20Jun42
LANGE, Walter Eugene	1stLt.	CoC.	25Jan43
KOHR, Dwight Archie	2dLt.	CoO.	23Oct43
SLACK, James William	2dLt.	CoO.	25Jun43
WILSON, Walter Raymond	2dLt.	CoO.	25Jun43

"D" Company

BOROUGH, Randal Burns	Capt.	CO.	20May42
RAPHAEL, Maurice	Capt.	Co-X.	20May42
BABBIN, Harold "H"	Capt.	CoO.	20May42
TREDUP, James Donald	Capt.	CoO.	20May42
LOONEY, William Aloysius	1stLt.	CoC.	5Jun43
TOMA, Charles, Jr.	1stLt.	CoO.	*20May42
WILLIAMS, James Berch	1stLt.	CoO.	*20May42
GARNER, Owen Wesley	2dLt.	CoO.	23Oct43
ROUH, Carlton Robert	2dLt.	CoC.	*20May42
MORTENSEN, Stanley Watson	WO.	CoO.	*20May42

Second Battalion
Hq. Company

WALT, Lewis William	LtCol.	BnComdr	17Apr42
BAKER, Charles Roland	Maj.	Bn-X.	20May42
BUZARD, Robert Edmund	Capt.	BnLiaisonO.	20May42
CROWN, John Albert	Capt.	Bn-1; CO HqCo.	20May42
CUENIN, Walter Henry	Capt.	Bn-3.	20May42
LYNCH, William Dean	Capt.	BnLiaisonO.	20May42
BEVAN, Burdette Francis	1stLt.	Bn-4.	8Jan43
METZ, Robert John	1stLt.	Bn-2.	*20Jun42
STEENDOM, Harold Jacob	1stLt.	BnComO.	*20May42
CARRIGAN, Edward Seelye	WO.	BnPslO.	*20May42
CLANCY, Edward John	Lt(MC)	BnMedO.	23Aug42
SHORE, Phillip Linus, Jr.	Lt(ChC)	BnChap.	12Jun43

- 16 -

"E" Company

BRYAN, Edward Ward	Capt.	CO.	20May42
BABASHANIAN, John Gabriel	Capt.	Co-X.	20May42
BAKER, John Mackay	1stLt.	CoO.	*14Oct42
MARTIN, Fred William	1stLt.	CoO.	*20May42
SLYE, George Henry	2dLt.	CoO.	*20May42
NELSON, Oscar Elwin	CWO.	CoO.	20Oct42

"F" Company

LAWTON, Leonard Gadi	Capt.	CO.	20Jun42
WING, Robert William	1stLt.	Co-X.	*20May42
MALLORY, Donald Lamb	1stLt.	CoO.	*20May42
RUST, Edward Sumner	1stLt.	CoO.	*20May42
STANKUS, Henry Walter	1stLt.	CoO.	*20May42
BARRETT, John Francis	2dLt.	CoO.	23Oct43

"G" Company

CALDER, Gordon Samuel	Capt.	CO.	20May42
BROWN, Thomas McGiffen	1stLt.	Co-X.	20May42
BREEN, Richard Rowley	1stLt.	CoO.	12Mar43
HUNTOON, Jack Edward	1stLt.	CoO.	*20May42
SCATENA, Ilo "J"	2dLt.	CoO.	5Jun43
RAILEY, Layton Wever	2dLt.	CoO.	5Jan43

"H" Company

RICHMOND, Harold Thomas Almond	Maj.	CO.	20May42
DOYLE, John Bernard, Jr.	Capt.	Co-X.	20May42
BOWLING, Joseph Harry	1stLt.	CoO.	8Jan43
BROUGHER, William Augusta	1stLt.	CoO.	12Mar43
JONES, Clovis Morgan	1stLt.	CoO.	23Oct43
MC CONNELL, George Lewis	1stLt.	CoO.	*20May42
MEWMAN, James Miller	1stLt.	CoO.	*20May42
STANLEY, Thomas Joseph	1stLt.	CoO.	8Jan43
TAYLOR, William Alexander	1stLt.	CoO.	8Jan43

Third Battalion
Hq. Company

MC DOUGAL, David Stockton	LtCol.	BnComdr.	10Apr42
SKOCZYLAS, Joseph Sylvester	Maj.	Bn-X.	20May42
BAKER, Jason Bruce	Capt.	BnGas&PolO.	20May42
MC ILVAINE, Rex Gibson	Capt.	BnLiaisonO.	20Jun42
SMITH, George Watson	Capt.	Bn-3.	20May42
FORCE, Vernon Edward	1stLt.	Bn-2.	12Mar43
O'NEILL, Thomas Edwin	1stLt.	Bn-4.	*20May42
SMITH, Robert Prime	1stLt.	Asst Bn-4.	
JONES, Edward Allison	2dLt.	Bn-1; BnPslO.	*12Mar43
SULLIVAN, Eugene Joseph, Jr.	2dLt.	BnLiaisonO.	25Jun43
HYDRICK, Lawrence Jasper	WO.	BnComO.	*20May42
MORRIS, Ivor Hugh, Jr.	Lt(MC)	BnMedO.	3Nov42
SOVIK, Ansgar Edward	Lt(ChC)	BnChap.	22Jun42

"I" Company

WELLS, Erskine Watkins	Capt.	CO.	20May42
NEVILLE, Robert Breen	Capt.	Co-X.	20May42
DAVIS, Hugh Mayo	1stLt.	CoO.	*20May42
PEARCE, William Reeves	1stLt.	CoO.	28Feb43
FREDENBERGER, John Adam	2dLt.	CoO.	5Jun43
SHARROCK, Forest Kirk, Jr.	2dLt.	CoO.	23Oct43

"K" Company

HALDANE, Andrew Allison	Capt.	CO.	20May42
CHISICK, Andrew	1stLt.	Co-X.	*20May42
DYKSTRA, Daniel	1stLt.	CoO.	12Mar43
RECKUS, William Francis	1stLt.	CoO.	*20May42
MC MAHON, Eugene James	2dLt.	CoO.	23Oct43
TOELLE, Lowell Raymond	2dLt.	CoO.	25Jun43

"L" Company

GUFFIN, Thomas Frederick, Jr.	Capt.	CO.	20May42
FLYNN, William	1stLt.	Co-X.	1Dec42
METZGER, Robert David	1stLt.	CoO.	6Jan43
NUGENT, Paul Russell	1stLt.	CoO,	5Jun43
SENGEWALD, Richard Herman	1stLt.	CoO.	25Jun43
LYNCH, James Patrick	2dLt.	CoO.	23Oct43

"M" Company

MC AULIFFE, Charles Patrick, Jr.	Capt.	CO.	9May42
GOODMAN, Howard Kenneth	Capt.	Co-X.	20May42
BISHOP, Joseph Francis, Jr.	Capt.	CoO.	20May42
ATKINS, Elisha	1stLt.	CoO.	28Feb43
O'LAUGHLIN, James Patrick	1stLt.	CoO.	3Dec42
COAN, Edmund Joseph	2dLt.	CoO.	25Jun43
KAISER, Eugene Chester	2dLt.	CoO.	25Jun43
LARSON, Olaus Wendell	2dLt.	CoO.	5Jan43

SEVENTH MARINES
H&S Company

FRISBIE, Julian Neil	Col.	R-Comdr.	22Jun42
PULLER, Lewis Burwell	LtCol.	R-X.	10Apr42
CROSS, Claude Byram	Maj.	TF-TQM.	10Apr42
STREIT, Victor Henry	Maj.	R-3.	10Apr42
GAVITT, William Marshall	Capt.	CoO.	10Apr42
IRVING, Edward Burroughs	Capt.	RPM.	13Jan43
MUSSELWHITE, Rora Tanner, Jr.	Capt.	R-ComO.	22Jun42
REED, Marion Stafford	Capt.	R-4.	13Apr42
SASSER, Joseph Ralph	Capt.	CO H&SCo.	10Apr42
AUBUCHON, John Joseph	1stLt.	Asst R-3.	8Jan43
FARRELL, Francis Thomas	1stLt.	R-2.	25Aug42
GUNSALUS, Robert Clarence	1stLt.	R-PayOffice.	10Apr42
ROBERTS, Roy Clifford	1stLt.	R-MumO.	*10Apr42
SHEPPARD, Frank Clayton	1stLt.	R-1.	*10Apr42

H&S Company (Cont'd)

REINKE, Sidney Carl	2dLt.	Asst R-2.	5Jun43
JONES, Paul Robert	2dLt.	Ass to RQM.	25Jun43
WILKINSON, Russell Milton	2dLt.	Asst R-2.	5Jun43
SHAW, Frank Richard	CWO.	Asst R-1; R-PslO.	10Apr42
NIEDER, Joseph Peter	WO.	Asst R-4.	*13Apr42
SMITH, Joseph Peter	WO.	Asst to RQM.	*10Apr42
SHELDON, Frank Phelps	WO.	R-PayOffice.	*10Apr42
TOWERS, Walter Randolph	WO.	R-PayOffice.	*22Jun42
MARTENS, Vernon Edward	LtComdr(MC)	R-Surg.	22Jun42
MEACHUM, Lonnie William	Lt(ChC)	R-Chap.	18Apr43
MISSMAN, Byrnes Ely	Lt(DC)	R-Dent.	28Dec42
CONERTY, Thomas Ignatius	Lt(ChC)	Asst R-Chap.	11Feb43
VENNO, Maurice William	Lt(jg)(ChC)	Asst R-Cahp.	14May43
OWENSBY, Thomas Claude	2dLt.	Awtg assignment	23Oct43
THOMAS, Milford John	2dLt.	Awtg assignment	23Oct43
WAGNER, William James	2dLt.	Awtg assignment	*22Jun42

Weapons Company

BUCKLEY, Joseph Edward	Capt.	CO.	10Apr42
POWERS, David Irick	Capt.	CoO.	10Apr42
WALLACE, Richard Haynes	Capt.	CoO.	10Apr42
BUNGER, Walton Henry, Jr.	1stLt.	CoO.	3Nov42
FLAKE, Keigler Eugene	1stLt.	CoO.	*10Apr42
TAMUCCI, Camillo Anthony	1stLt.	CoO.	*10Apr42
TRAHAN, Francis Balliveau	1stLt.	CoO.	10Apr42
WOODIN, Ray Palmer, Jr.	1stLt.	CoO.	3Nov42
MAZZEI, Louis Paul	WO.	CoO.	*10Apr42

First Battalion
Hq. Company

WEBER, John Edmund	LtCol.	BnComdr.	13Apr42
WORDEN, Waite Warren	Maj.	Bn-X.	16May42
DE VENOGE, Vincent Paul	Capt.	CoO.	13Apr42
MARTIN, Lloyd Wesley	Capt.	Bn-4.	10Apr42
MIGLIORE, Leonard Anthony	Capt.	CO HqCo.	10Apr42
PARISH, Preston Seiter	Capt.	Bn-3.	10Apr42
EDWARDS, Jerry	1stLt.	LiaisonO.	1Nov42
HIGGINS, Victor Hugo	1stLt.	Asst Bn-1; BnPslO.	*10Apr42
MC ILLWAIN, James William	1stLt.	Bn-2.	*10Dec40
SCHERR, Robert Arthur	1stLt.	Bn-1.	10Nov42
DOW, Warren Leonard	WO.	R-ComO.	*22Jun42
STOCKER, George Earl Francis	Lt(MC)	BnMedO.	19Jul42
HAMILTON, Eugene Green	Lt(MC)	AsstBnMedO.	6Nov42
BALLARD, Volney B.	Lt(jg)(MC)	AsstBnMedO.	

"A" Company

MOORE, Marshall Washburn	Capt.	CO.	10Apr42
BENTLEY, Walter Frank	1stLt.	Co-X.	1Nov42
FITSTHOMAS, Edward Arthur	1stLt.	CoO.	*10Apr42
KNIGHT, Ralph Edward, Jr.	1stLt.	CoO.	1Nov42
VAGOUN, Edward	1stLt.	CoO.	8Jan43
LYONS, Lee Edward	2dLt.	CoO.	5Jun43
HATCHER, John Nichols	2dLt.	CoO.	23Oct43

"B" Company

PLANTIER, George Stephen	1stLt.	CO.	10Apr42
BAYER, Philip "P"	1stLt.	Co-X.	29Oct42
DAISLER, Vincent Augustine	1stLt.	CoO.	29Oct42
MC CALL, Ernest Charles, Jr.	1stLt.	CoO.	12Nov42
MC LEOD, Stanley Norman	1stLt.	CoO.	*10Apr42
WHEELER, Warren Starbird	1stLt.	CoO.	12Mar43

"C" Company

WYMAN, Arthur Harvey	Capt.	CO.	8Apr42
GIBSON, Robert Leslie	1stLt.	Co-X.	1Nov42
FLEMING, William McKinley	1stLt.	CoO.	* 8Apr42
KIRBY-SMITH, Ephraim	1stLt.	CoO.	22Jun43
LIVELSPERGER, Charles "K"	1stLt.	CoO.	* 8Apr42
TREMAINE, Hugh Stewart	1stLt.	CoO.	10Nov42
JENNE, Otis Paul, Jr.	2dLt.	CoO.	23Oct43

"D" Company

RODGERS, Robert James	Capt.	CO.	8Apr42
SMITH, Douglas Meeker	Capt.	Co-X.	9Apr42
GILLISPIE, John Lowell	Capt.	CoC.	19May42
COCHRAN, Joseph William III	1stLt.	CoO.	1Nov42
DUPLANTIS, John Dudley	1stLt.	CoO.	7Jan43
BOLDEN, Roger Andrew	1stLt.	CoO.	7Jan43
KAUFMAN, Samuel, Jr.	1stLt.	CoO.	12Mar43
PORTER, James William	1stLt.	CoO.	29Oct42
ROMO, Robert	1stLt.	CoO.	26Jun43

Second Battalion
Hq. Company

MOWOLEY, Odell Maurice	LtCol.	BnComdr.	10Apr42
NICHOLS, Charles Steven, Jr.	Maj.	Bn-X.	12Apr42
SIPPA, Louis Gerald	Capt.	Bn-3.	10Apr42
WATKINS, William Thomas	Capt.	Asst Bn-3; LiaisonO.	10Apr42
JAWALKA, Michael	1stLt.	Bn-2.	10Apr42
KUHN, Walter Frederick, Jr.	1stLt.	LiaisonO.	7Jan43
QUACKENBUSH, Byron Allen	1stLt.	BnComO.	*22Jun42
WHEELER, Harry Eugene	1stLt.	Bn-1; CoHqCo.	10Nov42
IZARD, Earl	2dLt(MT)	Bn-4.	*10Apr42
MURPHY, Ralph Butler	2dLt.	CoO.	5Jun43
SAIDMAN, Aaron Gilbert	Lt(MC)	BnMedO.	24Jul42
STEINBERG, Richard Mitten	Lt(MC)	AsstBnMedO.	20Oct42

"E" Company

HARRIS, Lawrence Paxton	Capt.	CO.	10Apr42
ALLEN, Edgar Lewis	1stLt.	CoO.	* 3Nov42
AMBROSE, Jay Stuart	1stLt.	CoO.	3Nov42
CARROLL, Daniel Anthony	1stLt.	Co-X.	*10Apr42
HUFF, Joseph Winston	1stLt.	CoO.	1Jan43
SULLIVAN, James Watson	1stLt.	CoO.	1Nov42
HALL, Donald Raymond	2dLt.	CoO.	23Oct43

"F" Company

HUGHES, Alfred Herman	Capt.	CO.	10Apr42
FAX, Richard Joseph	1stLt.	Co-X.	* 6Jan42
BEARDSLEE, Paul Clifton, Jr.	1stLt.	CoO.	1Nov42
BRAUN, Ralph Louis	1stLt.	CoO.	2Nov42
FORDHAM, Palmer Burdette	1stLt.	CoO.	*10Apr42
YEWELL, Malcolm Monnette	1stLt.	CoO.	12Mar43
ERMENIC, Joseph	2dLt.	CoO.	23Oct43

"G" Company

ROBINSON, James Merrill	Capt.	CO.	10Apr42
WHEAT, Edward Bernice	1stLt.	Co-X.	10Nov42
KIRBY, Edward Stephan	1stLt.	CoO.	31Oct42
JANICK, Tony	1stLt.	CoO.	7Jan43
WISDOM, Joseph Eugene	1stLt.	CoO.	12Mar43
WOLCZAK, Stanislaus Michael	1stLt.	CoO.	*10Apr42
MOHLER, John Joseph	2dLt.	CoO.	23Jun43

"H" Company

FARRELL, Robert Edward	Capt.	CO.	10Apr42
HOOPES, Warrick George	Capt.	Co-X.	10Apr42
SEXTON, George Edward	Capt.	CoO.	10Apr42
GODFREY, Coulbourn Horne	1stLt.	CoO.	7Jan43
MYERS, Thomas Arthur	1stLt.	CoO.	9Nov42
NOTNAN, Robert Joseph	1stLt.	CoO.	25Jun43
PAIGE, Mitchell	1stLt.	CoO.	*10Apr42
RENO, William Amos	1stLt.	CoO.	*10Apr42
SANDERS, Percy LeRoy	1stLt.	CoO.	*10Apr42

Third Battalion

WILLIAMS, William Richard	LtCol.	BnComdr.	10Apr42
PIPER, William John, Jr.	Maj.	Bn-X.	22Jun42
KING, William Joseph	Capt.	Bn-4.	10Apr42
FASER, Karl Edward	1stLt.	BnComO.	16Jun42
MICKLE, Richard Hall	1stLt.	Mun&LiaisonO.	* 1Nov42
MORTON, Robert Ball	1stLt.	Asst Bn-3; LiaisonO	7Jan43
PRICE, Paxton Stanley	1stLt.	Bn-2; BnGasO.	7Jan43
OLMSTEAD, Wallace Kellogg, Jr.	2dLt.	LiaisonO.	25Jan43
ASHTON, Cyril William	WO.	Asst Bn-1; BnPslO.	*13Apr43
POSIK, John	WO.	Bn-1; CO HqCo.	*10Apr42
STEWART, Frank Ashbrook	Lt(jg)(MC)	BnMedO.	22Jun42
HAGAN, Edward J.	Lt(jg)(MC)	AsstBnMedO.	

"I" Company

CROLL, Gilbert Halsday	Capt.	CO.	13Apr42
BUTTERMORE, John Jay	Capt.	CoO.	15Jul42
BOWERS, Landon Emanuel	Capt.	Co-X.	13Apr42
FERGUSON, Carl Daniel	1stLt.	CoO.	5Apr42
HOYT, William Henry	1stLt.	CoO.	1Nov42
ULRICH, Carl	WO.	CoO.	*13Apr42
BAILEY, William Walter, Jr.	2dLt.	CoO.	

"K" Company

WEBER, John Frederick	Capt.	CO.	13Apr42
SWARLEY, James Vincent	Capt.	Co-X.	13Apr42
HUNTER, Jack Holmes	1stLt.	CoO.	*13Apr42
MARTIN, Oswald Wright, Jr.	1stLt.	CoO.	1Nov42
PIERCE, Harold Clifton, Jr.	1stLt.	CoO.	13Jun42
RICK, Norbert Vincent	1stLt.	CoO.	5Apr42
COLLIS, Harold Jay	2dLt.	CoO.	23Oct43

"L" Company

MORAN, William	Capt.	CO.	13Apr42
CAMPBELL, William Floyd	1stLt.	CoO.	*13Apr42
LEGANZA, Joseph	1stLt.	CoO.	8Jan43
O'LEARY, Thomas Jeremiah	1stLt.	CoO.	10Mar43
BREVI, Carl Anastasio	2dLt.	CoO.	25Jun43
GARDNER, Arthur Bernard, Jr.	2dLt.	CoO.	*13Apr42
KELLEY, Joseph Francis	1stLt.	CoO.	23Oct43

"M" Company

OPIE, Hierome Lindsay	Capt.	CO.	13Apr42
UMBARGER, Floyd McKenna, Jr.	Capt.	Co-x.	13Apr42
HUBBS, Howard Leon	1stLt.	CoO.	*13Apr42
HUGHES, Stanley Smith	1stLt.	CoO.	13Apr42
MC DONNELL, Peter Edward	1stLt.	CoO.	8Jan43
KEATING, Maurice Joseph	1stLt.	CoO.	1Nov42
CUMMINGS, Leonard Otto, Jr.	2dLt.	CoO.	25Jun43
GIDDIS, Joseph Anthony	2dLt.	CoO.	5Jun43
PODEMSKI, James Thomas	2dLt.	CoO.	25Jun43

ELEVENTH MARINES
H&S Battery

PEPPER, Robert Houston	Col.	R-Comdr.	5Apr40
LUCKEY, Robert Burneston	LtCol.	R-X.	22Jun42
ENNIS, Louis Augustus	Maj.	R-3.	20May42
PREGNALL, Daniel Sheppard	Maj.	R-2.	22Jun42
SCHREIER, Robert Leon	Maj.	R-ComO.	22Jun42
DE KOSTER, Dale Keith	Capt.	R-MTransO.	10Jun42
FAIRCLOUGH, James	Capt.	BtryO.	10Jun42
GRIFFIN, David Reese	Capt.	Asst R-3.	20Jun42
HARRIS, Charles Disbrow	Capt.	Temp d.	22Jun42
MANER, Floyd Cecil	Capt.	R-1; R-Adj.	20May42
PARRISH, Gouverneur Hogg	Capt.	RPM.	1Jan42
DALGLISH, Gordon Reid	1stLt.	R-4.	22Jun42
WILLIAMS, Lloyd Orval	1stLt.	R-Mun&OrdO.	22Jun42
BROADUS, Junior Burge	2dLt (Arty)	Asst R-OrdO.	10Apr42
BLAINE, Sidney Elisha	WO.	Asst R-MTransO.	*20May42
MATCHETT, John Wilmarth	WO.	Asst R-ComO.	*22Jun42
PAUL, William Merle	WO.	Asst R-4.	*22Jun42
ANDO, Elmer Geza	WO.	R-PayOffice.	*10Apr42
EGGERS, Harold Berman	WO.	R-PayOffice.	*22Jun42
RICHARDSON, Leland Lester	WO.	R-PayOffice.	*22Jun42
JOHNSON, Thomas Lee	LtComdr(MC)	R-Surg.	12Mar43
FITZGERALD, James Joseph	Lt(ChC)	R-Chap.	22Jun42
NASH, Claude Hamilton, Jr.	Lt(DC)	R-Dent.	28Dec42
FRANZ, James Giffen	Lt(jg)(ChC)	Asst R-Chap.	18Apr43

- 22 -

First Battalion
H&S Battery

FIELDS, Lewis Jefferson	LtCol.	BnComdr.	22Jun42
BOOKHART, Hoyt Ulmer, Jr.	Maj.	Bn-X.	10Apr42
WILSON, Elliott	Maj.	Bn-3.	10Apr42
ABNEY, Louis Dealbary, Jr.	Capt.	Bn-1; CO H&SBtry.	10Nov42
MOYER, Charles Orville	Capt.	KIA 26Dec43.	10Apr42
ALDERSON, Robert Merle	1stLt.	Asst Bn-3; BnGasO.	10Nov42
CATER, Maurice Leroy	1stLt.	BnMTransO.	12May42
DIVINEY, John Carl	1stLt.	KIA 26Dec43.	*10Mar42
DOUVILLE, Charles Gregory	1stLt.	Bn-4.	10Mar42
MARSH, Henry Hardison	1stLt.	Asst Bn-4.	*12Mar42
TOONE, Winfred Basil	WO.	BnOrdO.	25Jun43
ADDISON, Jack Jenkins	Lt(MC)	BnMedO.	3Nov42
PICKELL, William Clell	Lt(jg)(line)	BnNavMunfireObs.	11Oct42

"A" Battery

HIGGINS, James Benton, Jr.	Capt.	CO.	10Apr42
NORRIS, Glen Earl	Capt.	Btry-X.	10Apr42
BRANES, Alfred Fenton	1stLt.	BtryO.	25Jun43
HARDWICK, Winchester Dana	1stLt.	BtryO.	10Apr42
LARKIN, William Francis	1stLt.	BtryO.	25Jun43
SPIEGEL, "S" Arthur	1stLt.	BtryO.	25Apr43

"B" Battery

CHAISSON, John Robert	Capt.	CO.	10Apr42
HALL, John Isom	Capt.	BtryO.	10Apr42
DAYTON, Francis Patrick	1stLt.	Btry-X.	22Jun42
DORSEY, Peter Robert	1stLt.	BtryO.	25Jun43
JACKSON, Kenneth James	1stLt.	BtryO.	18Apr43
KLOPF, Richard Henry, Jr.	1stLt.	BtryO.	25Jun43
MC FALL, Kenneth Warren	1stLt.	BtryO.	10Apr42
SHIFTER, Ernest	WO.	BtryO.	*10Apr42

"C" Battery

CROWLEY, John Donegan	Capt.	CO.	13Apr42
FITZGERALD, William Joseph, Jr.	Capt.	Btry-X.	10Mar42
CHAMPION, Earl Edward	1stLt.	BtryO.	*13Apr42
DUBBS, Dale Robert	1stLt.	BtryO.	25Jun43
GLESENER, Richard Frederick	1stLt.	BtryO.	18Apr43
SACK, Robert Moffitt	WO.	BtryO.	*12Apr42
KRAUSE, Felix John	1stLt.	BtryO.	

Second Battalion
H&S Battery

WOOD, Noah Preston, Jr.	Maj.	BnComdr.	22Jun42
BISHOPP, Fred Thomas	Maj.	Bn-X.	20May42
SWIFT, Archie Dean, Jr.	Maj.	Bn-3.	10Apr42
BLANDFORD, John Russell	Capt.	LiaisonO.	20May42
BOWDOIN, George Edward	Capt.	Temp d.	8Jun43
HARRIS, James Allen	Capt.	Bn-2.	20May42
TRELEAVEN, Lewis Frederick	Capt.	Bn-4.	22Jun42
WHITAKER, Meade,	Capt.	Bn-1; CO H&S Btry.	20May42
SORENSEN, Earl Richard	Capt.	Asst Bn-3.	10Nov42
KUSIAK, John Michael	1stLt.	BnQMO.	*20May42
MC BRIDE, Harry Ferdinand	1stLt.	BnMTransO.	*20May42
FISHER, Clarence Theodore, Jr.	1stLt.	BnComO.	*20May42
NORRISH, Robert Leslie	WO.	Asst Bn-1; BnPslO.	*20May42
PAYSEUR, Odell John	WO.	BnOrdO.	*20May42
CALLAGHAN, Desmond Hays	Lt(MC)	BnMedO.	25Jun43
MUSOLF, Lloyd Daryl	Lt(jg)(line)	Temp d.	11Oct42
PRAY, Charles Albert	Lt(jg)(line)	BnNavGunfireObs.	11Oct42
SPARKS, Glenn Tesney	2dLt.	Awtg assignment	*22Jun42

"D" Battery

COBHERN, William Hunter	Capt.	CO.	1Nov42
PEARCE, James Tribble	1stLt.	Btry-X.	10Nov42
HALL, Martin Bernard	1stLt.	BtryO.	*20May42
MOORE, Charles Ellington	1stLt.	BtryO.	18Apr43

"E" Battery

GOOD, George Lewis	Capt.	CO.	20May42
STAMPFLI, Fritz	1stLt.	Btry-X.	10Nov42
BARKER, Zachariah Allen	1stLt.	BtryO.	25Jun43
MAY, Charles Harold	1stLt.	BtryO.	*20May42
BATSON, George Joseph	2dLt.	BtryO.	20May42

"F" Battery

MOODY, William Deane	Capt.	CO.	20May42
PRESTON, Robert Sumner	Capt.	Btry-X.	10Nov42
CLARK, Ronald Adelbert	1stLt.	BtryO.	*20May42
CRANE, Leonard Robert	1stLt.	BtryO.	18Apr43
ZORTHIAN, Barooyr	1stLt.	BtryO.	10Nov42
GROFF, Andrew Milton	2dLt.	BtryO.	*20May42
MC NABB, Ellis Revere	WO.	BtryO.	*20May42

Third Battalion
H&S Battery

THOMPSON, Forest Carson	LtCol.	BnComdr.	20May42
FOLEY, Ernest Paul	Maj.	Bn-X.	12Mar43
WELLMAN, Henry Marvin	Maj.	Bn-3.	22Jun42
COHEN, Abraham Jacob	Capt.	BnLiaison&GasO.	10Jun42
GILLESPIE, Searle Wilson	Capt.	Asst Bn-3.	22Jun42
PAYNE, Richard William	Capt.	Bn-2.	8Jan43
SPILTOIR, Charles Francis, Jr.	Capt.	Bn-1; CO H&SBtry.	22Jun42
FAUROT, Jay Lyle	1stLt.	BnMTransO.	18Apr43
PETERSON, Alfred Howard	1stLt.	Bn-4.	22Jun42
HIRT, Paul LeRoy	2dLt.	BnComO.	*22Jun42
SMITH, William Theodore	2dLt.	BnPslO.	22Jun42
CLUTZ, Paul Alexander	Lt(MC)	BnSurg.	22Jun42
CALKINS, Wendell Hyman	Lt(line)	BnNavGunfireObs.	11Oct42
BESCH, Robert Woodruff	1stLt.	Awtg. assignment	25Jun43

"G" Battery

TURNER, Ivan Russell	Capt.	CO.	11Nov42
WANDER, William Winthrop	1stLt.	Btry-X.	11Nov42
CLARK, Herbert Howard, Jr.	1stLt.	BtryO.	22Jun42
DE TEMPLE, Eugene Howard	1stLt.	BtryO.	*10Apr42
BUSH, George James	CWO.	BtryO.	22Jun42

"H" Battery

GALYSH, Theodore Richard	Capt.	CO.	10Jun42
O'NEIL, Edward George	1stLt.	Btry-X.	11Nov42
GALBREATH, Robert Ellis	1stLt.	BtryO.	*20May42
LANDEN, John Hains	1stLt.	BtryO.	13Mar43
MALLON, James Robert	1stLt.	BtryO.	*22Jun42
MOBERLY, David Lyle	1stLt.	BtryO.	11Nov42
QUELCH, Kenneth Harold	WO.	BtryO.	*22Jun42

"I" Battery

POUNDS, James Arthur III	Capt.	CO.	11Nov42
ENGLEBERT, Lincoln Edwin	1stLt.	BtryO.	18Apr43
KNOX, Norman Wilfred	1stLt.	BtryO.	18Apr43
MAXWELL, Albert	1stLt.	BtryO.	*22Jun42
GILLIS, Laughlin McNeil	2dLt.	BtryO.	*22Jun42

Fourth Battalion
H&S Battery

HUGHES, Thomas Brandenburg	LtCol.	BnComdr.	22Jun42
HEELY, Dale Horstman	Maj.	Bn-X.	22Jun42
RUSSELL, Joe Brant	Maj.	Bn-3.	22Jun42
MC NEILL, James David	Capt.	BnPslO.	22Jun42
MEHRLUST, Jesse Pfeiffer	Capt.	CO H&SBtry.	22Jun42
SMITH, Marsnall	Capt.	Bn-2; BnGasO.	22Jun42
BRADLOCK, Henry Yost	1stLt.	Bn-4.	22Jun42
BUMP, Clinton Eugene	1stLt.	BnMTransO.	10Apr42
POLIN, Marvin Henry	Capt.	LiaisonO.	10Nov42
RESMANN, Donald Hillary	1stLt.	BnComO.	22Jun42
USHER, Robert Austin	1stLt.	BnReconO.	22Jun42
WATSON, Thomas Alan	1stLt.	Asst Bn-2.	*22Jun42
GENOBLES, William Joseph	2dLt.	BnOrdO.	22Jun42
GALGANO, Rocco Salvatore	Lt(MC)	BnSurg.	22Jun42
SULLIVAN, Peter Francis	Lt(line)	BnNavGunfireObs.	11Oct42
MITCHELL, Randall Lee	2dLt.	Awtg assignment	

"K" Battery

SMITH, Ivan Lester	Capt.	CO.	22Jun42
LODWICK, Seeley Griffiths	1stLt.	BtryO.	10Apr43
MOORDALE, Richard Melvin	1stLt.	BtryO.	22Jun42
ROEBUCK, Albert Murlin	1stLt.	BtryO.	*22Jun42
CARTER, Paul	WO.	BtryO.	* 8Jan43

"L" Battery

MARSOLINI, Robert Anthony	Capt.	CO.	22Jun42
CROTINGER, James Allen	Capt.	Btry-X.	10Mar42
BROWN, Ronald Allison	1stLt.	BtryO.	22Jun42
PETERSON, Gordon Cole	1stLt.	BtryO.	25Jun43
STAPLES, Murray Miner	1stLt.	BtryO.	18Apr43

"M" Battery

HAMMOND, Charles Phillip	Capt.	CO.	10Jun42
WINEY, Ray Keys	Capt.	Btry-X.	22Jun42
NIXON, George Stuart	1stLt.	BtryO.	22Jun42
ROACH, Rochard Earl	1stLt.	BtryO.	*22Jun42
VANCE, Lee Perry	2dLt.	BtryO.	5Jan43
MANGOGNA, Peter	WO.	BtryO.	*22Jun42

Fifth Battalion
H&S Battery

NEES, Charles Martin	LtCol.	BnComdr.	22Jun42
MOFFATT, James Hugh	Maj.	Bn-X.	10Apr42
WOOSTER, Samuel Stuart	Maj.	Bn-3.	10Apr42
HANNAN, William James	Capt.	BtryO.	23Oct43
CODNER, William Francis	1stLt.	BnOrdO.	22Jun42
DUGGIN, Marshall Edward	1stLt.	Bn-1; CO H&SBtry.	*10Apr42
HUNT, Richard Morton	1stLt.	BnAirO.	8Jan43
MATTHEWS, Billy Watson	1stLt.	BnComO.	*20May42
SIMMONS, Mitchell Forest	Capt.	Bn-4.	10Nov42
SMITTCAMP, Earl Stanfield	1stLt.	Ass Bn-2; BnMTransO.	19Apr43
TURNER, Robert Archer	1stLt.	Bn-2.	20May42
WOODS, Dick Hoblit	1stLt.	Asst Bn-3	18Apr43
GEBHART, John Armin	WO.	BnPslO.	*22Jun42
TATE, Walter Lawrence	WO.	AsstOrdO.	*10Apr42
HILLYER, Edwin Albert	Lt(jg)(MC)	BnMedO.	12Mar43

"N" Battery

MILLER, William Marshall	Maj.	CO.	22Jun42
JONES, William Nicholas	Capt.	Btry-X.	22Jun42
FOWLER, Charles William	1stLt	BtryO.	10Mar43
HONEYCUTT, Adolph Jenkins	1stLt.	BtryO.	18Apr43
MC CLEAN, Robert Earl	1stLt.	BtryO.	

"O" Battery

BRADBURY, John Douglas	Capt.	CO.	23Apr42
CARTWRIGHT, Abel Fisk	Capt.	Btry-X.	5Jun43
AADENSEN, Grant "C"	1stLt.	BtryO.	13Apr43
MC BRAYER, Roy "L"	1stLt.	BtryO.	12Mar43
MILLER, William Rosewarne	1stLt.	BtryO.	10Mar42

"P" Battery

APPLETON, Maurice Langhorne, Jr.	Capt.	CO.	22Jun42
SMITH, Richard Worthington	Capt.	Btry-X.	10Nov42
DOAK, Thomas Edgar	1stLt.	BtryO.	18Apr43
SCHAILL, Paul Moore, Jr.	1stLt.	BtryO.	10Nov42
CAMPBELL, Frank Wilson, Jr.	1stLt.	BtryO.	

SEVENTEENTH MARINES (ENGINEER)
H&S Company

Name	Rank	Duty	Date
ROSECRANS, Harold Ellett	Col(EDO)	R-Comdr; DivEngrO.	20May42
MC GUINNESS, John Peter	Maj (EDO)	R-X; R-3.	10May42
STILES, William Alfred	Maj(EDO)	R-4.	22Jun42
CLARKE, Robert Smith, Jr.	Capt(EDO)	CO H&SCo.	9Jun42
IHLI, Leo Alvin	Capt(EDO)	Asst R-3;AsstDivEngr	023Oct43
KENT, William Irwin	Capt.	R-1; R-Adj.	22Jun42
LANGE, Albert Nicholas	Capt(EDO)	R-2.	22Jun42
BUKOWY, John Joseph	1stLt(EDO)	R-MTrans).	15May42
KILLSGAARD, Thor "E"	1stLt	CoO.	23Jun43
MAC LELLAN, Lewis Fred	1stLt	R-ComO	22Jun42
OWENS, William Harrison, Jr.	1stLt(EDO)	ChemO.	7Jan43
ROONEY, Francis James	1stLt(EDO)	ConstrO.	15May42
SCHMITZ, John Alfred	1stLt(EDO)	AsstEngrO	7Jan43
ADAMS, Paul	WO.	Asst R-1; PslO	*22Jun42
GIBSON, George Gordon	WO.	Asst R-4.	*12May42
HOFFECKER, Fred	WO(EDO)	ConstrSect	*20May42
LEADON, Robert Aloysius	WO.	RPM.	*22Jun42
NEAL, Robert Lee, Jr.	WO.	R-PayOffice	*22Jun42
KITTS, Albert Warren	Lt(MC)	R-Surg	22Jun42
TURNEY, William Bisdee	Lt(MC)	Asst R-Surg.	
GLASSER, Arthus Frederick	Lt(jg)(ChC)	R-Chap.	15Feb43
REILLY, John Victor	Lt(jg)(DC)	R-Dent.	11Mar43

First Battalion
Hq. Company

Name	Rank	Duty	Date
CROCKETT, Henry Humphreys	Maj(EDO)	BnComdr.	16May42
IGLEHEART, Austin Smith, Jr.	Maj(EDO)	Bn-X.	22Jun42
COOPER, Francis Loren	Capt(EDO)	BnAdj; CO HqCo.	22Jun42
HUTTON, Albert Atkinson	Capt(EDO)	Asst Bn-3.	22Jun42
ROSE, Murray Fontaine	Capt(EDO)	Bn-2.	8Jun42
SCHULDER, Sidney	Capt(EDO)	Bn-3.	22Jun42
MC LELLAN, Daniel Joseph	1stLt(EDO)	Bn-4.	17Jan43
SCOTT, Earl Redondo	1stLt(EDO)	BnGasO.	4Jan43
FRANCE, Elmer	WO.	BnComO.	*22Jun42
WALSH, Maurice Robert	Lt(MC)	BnMedO.	1Aug42

"A" Company

Name	Rank	Duty	Date
SCHOENFELDER, Eugene Thomas	Capt(EDO)	CO.	14May42
WITHERELL, Josiah Chester	Capt(EP)	Co-X.	1Jul43
FARRELL, Cliffoed Henry	1stLt(EDO)	CoO.	22Jun42
SNYDER, Robert Clarence	1stLt(EDO)	CoO.	17Apr43
VAN BUREN, Werner Joseph	1stLt(EDO)	CoO.	5Apr42
WHITE, George Robert	1stLt	CoO.	20Jun43

"B" Company

Name	Rank	Duty	Date
ALEXANDER, Guy Elkanah	Capt(EDO)	CO.	22Jun42
SHAW, Marshall Leoby	1stLt(EDO)	Co-X.	16May42
NEWTON, Edward Delaplaine	1stLt(EDO)	CoO.	11Mar43
RATHMELL, John Nicely	1stLt	CoO.	11Mar43
SIVEC, John Edward	1stLt(EDO)	CoO.	*22Jun42

"C" Company

JOYNER, Jim McMurray	Capt(EDO)	CO.	17May42
ALDWORTH, John Gray	1stLt.	Co-X.	23Oct43
GINGHER, Harold Raymond	1stLt(EP)	CoO.	26Jun43
MC KEE, James Gregory	1stLt(EP)	CoO.	23Jun43
TURNBULL, Samuel Casement	1stLt(EDO)	CoO.	2Dec42
SHIRLEY, Charles Willis	2dLt.	CoO.	1Sep42

Second Battalion
Hq. Company

BALLANCE, Robert Green	LtCol(EDO)	BnComdr.	20Jun42
SMITH, Levi Walter, Jr.	Maj(EDO)	Bn-X.	10Jun42
MORGENTHAL, Nathaniel	Capt.	Bn-3.	22Jun42
SIVERTSEN, Warren Soltau	Capt(EDO)	Bn-2.	22Jun42
BARKER, Lloyd Francis	1stLt.	MtransO.	22Jun42
DENLEY, Robert Hartwell	1stLt.	Bn-1; CO HqCo.	19Feb43
FULLER, Leslie	1stLt.	BnComO.	*10Jun42
PIEL, Russell	1stLt.	Bn-4.	10May42
SCHROEDER, Edward Joseph	WO.	BnPslO.	*22Jun42
FINTON, Max Arthur	Lt(MC)	BnMedO.	23Sep42
HAUGRUD, Earl Marion	Lt(MC)	BnSurg.	11May43
NEBEKER, Don Paul	Lt(MC)	AsstBnSurg.	25Jun43

"D" Company

WALTON, Franklin Paul	Capt.	CO.	16May42
HANSEN, Teddy Lamar	Capt(EDO)	Co-X.	22Jun42
HEUSSNER, John Henry	1stLt.	CoO.	19Feb43
KENNEDY, John Malcolm	1stLt.	CoO.	12Mar43
MALONE, James Lawrence, Jr.	1stLt.	CoO.	22Jun42
MC HENRY, John Joseph	1stLt.	CoO.	8Jan43
SLOWAKIEWICZ, Stanley William	1stLt.	CoO.	8Jan43
MC CARTER, Lawrence Aaron	WO(EDO)	CoO.	*22Jun42

"E" Company

HEEPE, William Jacob	Capt.	CO.	22Jun42
SMITH, Harry Beasley	Capt.	Co-X.	22Jun42
PALMER, Olin Haywood, Jr.	Capt.	CoO.	22Jun42
BUSS, John Walter	1stLt.	CoO.	25Jun43
DRAPER, Frederick Farwell	Capt(EP)	CoO.	1Jul43
HURDLE, Earl Anderson, Jr.	1stLt.	CoO.	22Jun42
MILNER, James	WO.	CoO.	*22Jun42

"F" Company

MUELLER, John Leo, Jr.	Capt.	CO.	22Jun42
HILL, William Bethel, Jr.	Capt.	Co-X.	10Jun42
BUTLER, John Jarvis IV	Capt.	CoO.	22Jun42
JUSTICE, Joseph Bruce	1stLt.	CoO.	*22Jun42
MERRILL, Donald Candee	1stLt.	CoO.	8Jan43
RICH, Stanley Haven	1stLt.	CoO.	22Jun42
TURNER, Frank William	1stLt	CoO.	*22Jun42
WALTERS, Roy Lee	Capt.	CoO.	22Jun42

- 29 -

Third Battalion
Hq. Company

WOODS, Thomas Alfred	Comdr(CEC)BnComdr.	18Jun43
REDD, James Terrel	LtComdr(CEC)Bn-X.	19Sep42
HEATLEY, William	LtComdr(MC) SrMedO.	19Sep42
HERPEL, Henry James	Lt(DC) BnDentO.	19Sep42
MEEHAN, Daniel Francis	Lt(ChC) BnChap.	2Dec42
SCALES, Hunter Ledbetter	Lt(MC) AsstMedO.	24Sep42
WICKES, William Warren	Lt(CEC) Bn-3.	19Sep42
EBERLE, William Dey	Lt(jg)(CEC)CO HqCo.	20Jan43
MAIN, William Henry	Lt(jg)(SC)BnSupO.	19Sep42
HARDEN, Kenneth Eugene	Ens(SC) BnDO.	
MURRAY, John Richard	Ens(SC) BnCommissaryO.	31Jan43
PETERSON, James Edward	Ens(CEC) BnPslO.	9Oct43
POU, James Francis	Ens(CEC) BnMTransO.	25Jun43

"G" Company

ECKARDT, Jack Archer	Lt(CEC) CO.	19Sep42
CANTY, Godfrey Lawrence	Lt(CEC) CoO.	12Mar43
ROSEBRAUGH, Vernon Hart	Lt(jg)(CEC)CoO.	19Sep42
KYRIACOPULOS, John Charles	Ens(CEC) CoO.	9Oct43
FINK, Alvin Henry	Carp(CEC) CoO.	

"H" Company

FARRELL, Charles Breyer	Lt(CEC) CO.	19Sep42
FAHEY, Kenneth Carlton	Lt(jg)(CEC)CoO.	
KIRBY, Donald Lee	Lt(jg)(CEC)CoO.	19Sep42
SCHNURR, Francis Maurice	Ens,(CEC) CoO.	19Sep42
HANSEN, Stanley Severin	Carp(CEC)CoO.	24Sep42
HAYES, Vernon Marshall	Carp.(CEC) CoO.	9Oct43

"I" Company

CRUBEN, Ray Nicolas	Lt(CEC) CO.	19Sep42
CREIM, Conrad	Lt(CEC) Co-X.	19Sep42
KINNEY, John Erwin	Lt(jg)(CEC)CoO.	19Sep42
TUNISON, James Dexter	Ens(CEC) CoO.	9Oct43
DATH, Gerard Henry	ChCarp(CEC)CoO.	20Oct42
VAN HOUTEN, Norval Judson	Carp(CEC) CoO.	9Oct43

TWELFTH DEFENSE BATTALION
H&S Battery

HARRISON, William Hartwell	Col.	BnComdr.	20Jan43
HOLMES, Merlyn Donald	LtCol.	Bn-X.	20Jan43
CHARLESWORTH, Stuart MacRea	Maj.	BnLoad&EngrO.	20Jan43
MC GLAEHAN, Robert Charles	Maj.	Bn-3.	20Jan43
CHASE, Gordon Elms	Capt.	BnCom&MessO.	20Jan43
GLICK, Jacob Ezra	Capt.	CO H&SBtry; RadarO.	20Jan43
LOW, Stanley Dana	Capt.	Asst Bn-3.	20Jan43

H&S Battery (Cont'd)

PARKE, Harry Morris	1stLt.	Bn-4, AAQM.	20Jan43
STARK, Porter William	1stLt.	BnMTransO.	20Jan43
WEBER, Edward Graf	1stLt.	BnAdj.	20Jan43
WEIST, Joseph Oliver	1stLt.	BnOrdO.	16Jul43
HILL, Ivan Cecil	WO.	BnPM	13Oct42
SLACK, LaRue Charles	WO.	AsstBnComO.	20Jan43
PARKER, John T. Jr.	LtComdr(ChC)BnChap.		7Dec42
BARR, John F.	LtComdr(MC)BnSurg.		28Mar43
DAVEY, William P.	Lt(jg)(MC)AsstBnSurg.		20Jan43
SMALLEY, Marls L.	Lt(jg)(DC)BnDentO.		20Jan43

Anti-Aircraft Group

NOYES, Harry Floyd, Jr.	Maj.	CO.	20Jan43
LYMAN, Andrew Irvine	Maj.	Grp-X.	20Jan43
BARTLEY, Whitman Strong	Capt.	CO "D"Btry.	20Jan43
HICKS, Alton Lucian	Capt.	RadarO.	20Jan43
JOHNSON, Paul William	Capt.	CO "E"Btry.	20Jan43
MC UMBER, Henry Harrison, Jr.	Capt.	RangeO.	20Jan43
FLATHMANN, Eugene Rumph	1stLt.	"G" BtryO.	20Jan43
MC GREW, Cassius LeRoy	1stLt.	"F" BtryO.	20Jan43
PARISOT, John Eugene	1stLt.	CO "G"Btry.	20Jan43
WILLIAMS, Grover Cleveland, Jr.	1stLt.	CO "F"Btry.	20Jan43
WRIGHT, Richard Albert	1stLt.	"D" BtryO.	20Jan43
RAUEN, John Hubert, Jr.	2dLt.	"E" BtryO.	16Jul43
THEROS, Arthur George	2dLt.	"F" BtryO.	16Jul43
SMALL, Chase	1stLt.	GrpO.	
SHAW, John Bundy	1stLt.	GrpO.	
MARTIN, Dale William	WO.	GrpO.	

Seacoast-Artillery Group

REINBERG, Louis Cloney	LtCol.	CO.	20Jan43
BENSON, Francis William	Maj.	Grp-X.	20Jan43
WALTON, Samuel Barton, Jr.	Capt.	CO "A"Btry.	20Jan43
GEISER, Gilbert John	1stLt.	"A" BtryO.	20Jan43
KIPP, Harry Ernest	1stLt.	CO "B"Btry.	20Jan43
LEONARD, Albert Edwin	1stLt.	"A" BtryO.	18Apr43
RANDALL, Thomas Langworthy	1stLt.	"B" BtryO.	20Jan43
CONDO, Charles	CWO.	GrpMain&MunO.	20Jan43
PRICE, Paul Higdon	WO(Gen)	"B" BtryO.	20Jan43
SCHWALBE, Reginald Douglas	WO.	GrpO.	
SCHUMACHER, Charles Matthew	2dLt.	GrpO.	
LULL, Howard William	2dLt.	GrpO.	

Special Weapons Company

LAW, Edwin Augustus	LtCol.	CO.	20Jan43
JACYNO, Joseph Roche	Maj.	Grp-X.	20Jan43
CURTIS, Allen, Jr.	Capt.	CO "I"Btry	20Jan43
MUNDAY, Jack Rupert	Capt.	"H"BtryO.	20Jan43
WRIGHT, Raymond Duane	Capt.	CO "H"Btry.	20Jan43
COFFEY, Albert Raymond	1stLt.	"I"BtryO.	20Jan43
MOORE, Clarence Carlisle, Jr.	1stLt.	"H"BtryO.	20Jan43

Special Weapons Group (Cont'd)

POWERS, Edward Theodore	1stLt.	"H"BtryO.	20Jan43
SIEVERS, Richard Harris	1stLt.	"I"BtryO.	20Jan43
TOUSSAINT, Roger Sidney	1stLt.	"I"BtryO.	20Jan43
STAGG, Hannon William	WO.	GrpMaintO.	20Jan43
ALLEN, John Otho	2dLt.	GrpO.	
GEIST, Stanley	2dLt.	GrpO.	

ORDERED IN AND ADDITIONS:

BOCK, Martin Robert, Jr.	2dLt.	f/arty/d.	
BOLAND, Robert H.	1stLt.	Ord in f/d/w 11thMar.	
BROWN, Lawrence C.	2dLt.	Ord in f/ord/d.	
CASKIE, Marion Maxwell, Jr.	2dLt.	Ord in f/arty/d.	
FORREST, George J.	2dLt.	Ord in f/ord/d.	
FOSTER, Ramsey M.	WO(A&I)	Ord in.	
GOFF, Joseph Bayard	2dLt.	Ord in f/arty/d.	
HILLIARD, Robert Courtney	2dLt.	Ord in f/arty/d.	
HUGHES, William Henry	2dLt.	Ord in f/arth/d.	
LEASE, Richard J.	2dLt.	Ord in f/ord/d.	
MOZLEY, Warren Keith	2dLt.	Ord in f/arty/d.	
NUGENT, Robert L.	2dLt.(VB-L)JapIntp. (Ord in).		
MUNRO, Burton S.	LtComdr(MC)CoO. ("B"1stMedBn.)		
SKETOE, Clayton David	WO(PD)	OIC DivPO; AsstDivMailO. (DivHqBn)	#22Jun42
SWANSON, Gordon Ira	2dLt.	Ord in f/arty/d.	
WALKER, Charles Eugene	1stLt.	Ord in f/arty/d.	
ZIMMERMAN, Arthus Alvin	2dLt.	Ord in f/arty/d.	

* Was an enlisted man upon departure from the USA.

CPSIA information can be obtained
at www.ICGtesting.com
Printed in the USA
LVHW081016190922
728733LV00019B/255